Troubleshooting Local Area Networks

S Harris
S Nugus
D Morgan

MANCHESTER • OXFORD

British Library Cataloguing in Publication Data

Harris, S.
  Troubleshooting Local Area Networks
  I. Title II. Nugus, S III. Morgan, D
  004.68
 	
ISBN 1-85554-168-8

© TechTrans Limited, 1992

All rights reserved. No part of this publication may be reproduced, stored in a retrieval system, or transmitted, in any form or by any means, without the prior permission of NCC Blackwell Limited

First published in 1992 by:

NCC Blackwell Limited, 108 Cowley Road, Ocford OX4 1JF, England.

Editorial Office: The National Computing Centre Limited, Oxford House, Oxford Road, Manchester M1 7ED, England.

Typeset in 10pt Palatino by TechTrans Ltd, Kidmore End, Reading, RG4 9AY; and printed by Hobbs the Printers Ltd, Southampton, SO9 2UZ.

ISBN 1-85554-168-8

Contents

Introduction		7
1	**Local Area Network Technology**	**9**
	What comprises a network?	9
	LAN developments	9
	A definition of a LAN	10
	Network hardware	11
	Network topologies	11
	Transmission media	16
	Network standards	19
	Standards setting organisations	20
	File server configuration	24
	Network workstations	28
	LAN operating environments	32
	Networked applications	34
	Network management	37
	Summary	39
2	**The Nature of Network Problems**	**41**
	Why is network troubleshooting different?	41
	A categorisation of network problems	41
	Ten situations of network problems	47
	Causes and effects	53
	Summary	56
3	**The Network Access Procedure**	**57**
	Introduction	57
	Foundations	57
	Network drive mappings	58
	Network trustee rights	61
	A typical network access procedure	62
	The CONFIG.SYS file	63
	The AUTOEXEC.BAT file	65
	The SHELL.CFG file	66
	The system login script	68
	The PRE_HELP.BAT file	72
	The HELP.BAT file	73
	System response during the login process	74
	Summary	75

4 CONTENTS

4	**The Application Access Procedure**	**77**
	Introduction	77
	The menu utility	77
	Designing a menu system	80
	A sample extract from a MAIN.MNU menu file	82
	Batch-file processing	85
	The menu system support batch files	90
	The printer control support batch files	93
	Appearance of the system during execution	95
	Summary	96
5	**Troubleshooting Software Related Problems**	**97**
	General guidelines	97
	Conflicts	97
	Resolving software problems	101
	Product specific problems	102
	Summary	104
6	**LAN Management Software**	**105**
	Why is LAN management software necessary?	105
	Network utilities	105
	Network monitoring/analysis systems	106
	Network fault diagnosis systems	107
	User assistance systems	108
	Summary	109
7	**Troubleshooting Component Faults**	**111**
	Introduction	111
	A structured approach	111
	Routine checks	115
	Problem reports and fault logs	116
	Hand control to the troubleshooter	119
	Heat and moisture	122
	Diagnose a particular peripheral or unit	122
	The power supply	122
	Disk drives	124
	System board	131
	Display unit	134
	Keyboard	136
	Transmission media problems	136
	Network technologies	141
	Arcnet	141
	Ethernet	146
	Token-ring	151
	Technology independent systems	154
	Summary	156
8	**Optimising Performance**	**159**
	Optimising system response times	159
	Performance limitations	159

	Balancing requirements	159
	Identifying the bottleneck	160
	Performance variations	160
	Upgrading components	161
	Workstation memory	163
	Why optimise?	169
	Summary	169
9	**Security Issues**	**171**
	Why is network security important?	171
	NetWare security	171
	The login process	172
	File and directory access	174
	Physical security	176
	Transaction tracking	177
	Intruder tracking	178
	The security utility program	178
	Biometrics	178
	Summary	179
10	**Data Protection**	**181**
	Preventing disaster	181
	SFT level I	181
	SFT level II	182
	SFT level III	183
	Viruses and inoculation	185
	Disaster recovery	188
	Backups	190
	Power	193
	Testing the disaster plan	195
	Summary	195
11	**Measuring User Satisfaction**	**197**
	A holistic approach to measurement	197
	User information satisfaction	197
	Using a questionnaire to measure the success of an office automation network	198
	Repeat surveys	217
	Summary	217
12	**Conclusion**	**219**
	Future developments	219
Appendices		
	Glossary	221
	Bibliography and reading list	237
Index		**239**

Introduction

One of the latest issues in personal computing is how PC users and supervisors can better control the personal computer environment in which they work. It is no longer satisfactory to depend solely on engineers to diagnose and fix problems, as maintenance contracts can be costly and the downtime incurred whilst waiting for repairs cannot be tolerated. As PC configurations become more complex, so the necessity for PC users to understand more about how their system functions increases.

This is especially true when dealing with computer networks. Whereas the failure of a standalone system may affect one or two people, problems that affect the operation of a network will be felt by many users and so the cost to the organisation can be enormous. The need for individuals to master their computers has come about because general attitudes to computers have changed as they have affected a greater and greater part of working life. Only a few years ago the inside of a personal computer was considered to be completely off limits. Anyone who opened the systems box on his/her own was considered crazy or stupid, or perhaps both. After all, it was full of printed circuit boards, semi-conductors, microprocessors and other highly technical, if not downright mysterious and intimidating things. Thus when anything went wrong you had to have an expert come and see it. The first PC networks that were installed were considered in much the same way; any problems were deemed to be beyond the scope of the network supervisor and were referred to the vendor or consultancy that provided the system.

This arrangement can work well, especially for the experts, who are often called out to fix quite trivial problems and paid significant fees. In fact many of the so called experts are not all that expert. The high demand for people in the spectacularly fast growing personal computer industry has meant that frequently insufficient training is given to technical support people; if a person fixing your machine has 3 or 4 years experience then you are very lucky. Of course, the reality is that you don't need to have highly skilled or experienced people fix a personal computer. In fact you yourself, with a bit of preparation, ie reading a book, buying a few tools and a bit of patience can actually do quite a lot. It is also useful to talk to other users and to your supplier. If you do call an engineer make sure that you watch what he/she is doing and ask as many questions as you can.

When personal computers cease to function correctly it is invariably due to one or more of the following three types of problems:
- The user does not know how to operate the system and thus is getting a different result to what he/she is expecting. This leads to a fault which is often referred to as finger trouble.
- The software and the hardware have not been correctly configured, or there is a conflict between the two and thus there is a mismatch which has to be resolved.

– A component has failed. As personal computers are actually very reliable this is perhaps the least probable cause of a problem. Nonetheless component failure does occur and must be rectified.

This categorisation applies equally well to standalone PC systems and computer networks, although the steps that will be required to fix such problems will often differ greatly. The purpose of *Troubleshooting Local Area Networks* is to examine and investigate the causes and effects of these problems, leading to a discussion of the techniques and methods required for remedial action. However, before an in-depth investigation of such situations can be carried out, it is necessary to provide some background information and introduce the concepts, ideas and terminology that will be encountered. The interactions between the hardware and software components of the system will be examined, as these play a major role in determining the reliability and performance of any system.

The book is not intended to train you to be a network engineer, but rather to help you familiarise yourself with computer networks and to learn how to control and maintain the network in the most effective way. Various techniques for problem diagnosis and isolation are investigated, and a number of step by step guides for remedial action will be provided. If, as in many cases, an experienced engineer is required to fix a fault, it is hoped that after reading this book users will be able to properly brief the experts in order that the correct repair be made as speedily as possible.

In addition to these specific areas, the book will look at the underlying factors that determine the reliability, performance and effectiveness of the network. In this sense, we have adopted a somewhat informal definition of a network, in that a network can be considered to be the 'glue' that ties a number of different computers together. At a hardware level there is little to differentiate networked PCs from standalone PCs. However at the operating system or software level all the rules change. It is our belief that most of the problems encountered on networks are due to the improper configuration of either the network operating system itself or of the improper configuration of applications used on the network. Thus you will find the focus of this book directed more towards issues concerning the Network's operating system than at the network hardware. This does not mean that we will not be addressing specific hardware issues, indeed in addition to a discussion of the hardware concepts we will be answering a number of commonly-asked hardware and software questions throughout this book.

Finally, before embarking on the journey to becoming a troubleshooter a word of caution is appropriate. Network troubleshooting is recommended to users because it will reduce the inconvenience caused by minor faults or incorrect configurations, and speed up rectification of such problems. Doing your own troubleshooting will also reduce corporate bills for maintenance, and minimise the losses due to network downtime. However, there is a definite risk associated with troubleshooting. This risk is not only one of damaging the equipment or the data used on the network, but also of possible harm to yourself, primarily due to electric shock. Therefore it is essential that care is taken before commencing any operations that may expose the troubleshooter to any risk. Where appropriate, reminders have been placed in this book to prompt the reader to ensure that suitable safety precautions have been taken.

In short the troubleshooter must always place his/her safety first. The second concern is to ensure the equipment is not damaged, and finally the speedy repair and installation of the system.

1 Local Area Network Technology

1.1 WHAT COMPRISES A NETWORK?

Gone are the days when networks consisted of cheap cabling systems used to share a printer. Here are the days when networks consist of expensive cabling systems used to share a printer.

Joke or reality? – *Networks are generally underutilised. Grossly underutilised.*

Whether this situation exists because of the confusing array of options available on the market, or simply because of a lack of faith in the technology to handle anything more complex than printer sharing is difficult to tell. Whichever way it falls one thing is for sure, network managers need to be aware of the various options available to them and how those options relate to each other.

This chapter surveys the topologies and the transmission media that are appropriate for use within a Local Area Network (LAN). Together these factors influence the type of data that may be transmitted across a network, the efficiency of that transmission, and even the kinds of applications that can be supported by that network. The advantages and disadvantages of the respective technologies are also discussed where applicable.

The chapter continues with a discussion of the different file server and workstation configurations that may be encountered, together with the advantages and disadvantages of each.

1.2 LAN DEVELOPMENTS

Before looking at specific technologies it is useful to take a brief look at the trends that have brought about the current state of the network industry.

With the rapid advance of technology over the past decade there has been a sharp decline in the cost of processing power. Most of the machines now sitting on corporate desks have at least the equivalent power and ability of the minicomputers of just a few short years ago. The distribution of this computing power has had the effect of capacitating the individuals who have tired of the slow response times, long waitlists, and bureaucracies of the centralised time-sharing systems. However as the numbers of personal computers have risen, so has the need to obviate one of their most restricting limitations, their inability to communicate with each other effectively.

The stumbling block to this progression has been primarily one of cost. It is only in recent years that the costs associated with linking personal computers have fallen below the value of the real benefits deriving from that linkage. These lowered costs initially allowed for the sharing of expensive peripheral devices, such as laser printers, among two or more users. Lately however, application developers have begun writing programs that take advantage of the ability of networks to allow groups of people to work together more effectively and efficiently. Documents and other data files can be stored in a central location for use by whoever may require them, indeed project groups are even able to simultaneously work with and update information stored on the network.

The progression towards the effective sharing of on-line mass storage devices was pioneered by a relatively unknown company by the name of Novell, although it was only really with the introduction by Intel of the 80286 microprocessor and by Microsoft of version 3 of MS-DOS for personal computers that the industry really started to take off. This version of DOS allowed for the first time, common methods via which to access and share files at the operating system level.

In general LAN technology has matured markedly over the past few years and is now stable enough for organisations to use for "mission critical" work, although it should be said that the industry still has many leading and bleeding edge components to it. Unfortunately the current situation is still far from the ideal of being able to tie any computer to any other computer in a manner transparent to the user. Evidence of the industries shortcomings abounded at the 1990 NetWorld conference in Dallas. ShowNet was designed to connect vendors, kiosks, and even show hotels together. It was to bring show and product information to the users and conference attendees. Mostly, it didn't work. According to Database Advisor,

> ...given the number of network Special Forces attending, that ShowNet couldn't be fixed prior to or even on the first day of the show is an embarrassment to the industry, no matter who is responsible.

1.3 A DEFINITION OF A LAN

What exactly is meant by the term 'Local Area Network' ? A useful definition of the concept is provided by the *Handbook of Computer Communications Standards* (1990):

> A Local (Area) Network is a communications network that provides interconnection of a variety of data communicating devices within a geographically small area.

There are three significant elements to this definition:

- The first is that a local area network is primarily a communications network. It is responsible for the movement of data from one location to another. The issues of protocol which enable various devices to talk to each other (and to the network) are of obvious importance, although they are beyond the scope of this book.
- The second point about this definition is that the phrase 'data communication devices' is to be interpreted in the broadest possible sense. Thus many different types of devices can be incorporated within the LAN definition. Examples include:
    - Computers
    - Terminals

- Peripheral devices
- Sensors (temperature, humidity, security sensors)
- Telephones
- Television transmitter and receivers
- Facsimile.

Of course at this stage not all networks are capable of handling all of these devices. However as the move towards 'multi-media' computing continues, the requirement for attaching these and many other devices in an integrated manner will become more and more of an issue.

A good example of the way in which varied devices can and will be used in future networking systems is illustrated by LANtastic's Voice Adapter. This device makes it possible to record and play back voice at the workstation and send it over the LAN. This form of voice mail is the basic application, and the system enhances this feature by allowing real-time voice conversations over the LAN, effectively allowing it to be used as an intercom.

– The third significant element of this definition is that a local network covers a small geographic area. This point emphasises that a local area network is exactly that; *local*. Most LANs are contained within a single department or building, although it is possible to have a LAN stretching across several buildings or across a campus. Borderline cases exist where the LAN stretches more than 20 or 30 kilometres. The major reason for including a reference to size in the definition is that different technologies are required for linking computers over greater distances.

1.4 NETWORK HARDWARE

There are many different hardware concepts and technologies that are unique to the issues of networks and networking. These areas include the following:

– Topologies
– Transmission Media
– Standards
– File Server Configurations
– Workstation Configurations.

There are a number of other hardware devices that are specific to each of the major LAN technologies, including active and passive hubs, routers, repeaters, etc. These are covered in greater detail in Chapter 6, in conjunction with other technology-specific hardware issues.

1.5 NETWORK TOPOLOGIES

Simply stated, a network topology refers to the way in which the various end-points, nodes, or workstations on a network, are interconnected. In other words the network architecture. Of the many different approaches that have been used over the past years, only three major structures have come into widespread use. The common structures are *star*, *ring* and *tree*.

12 NETWORK TOPOLOGIES

The following diagrams and explanations highlight the essential formats and distinctions of the various topologies mentioned above.

1.5.1 THE STAR TOPOLOGY

In a star topology each workstation is attached to a central 'switch-box', as shown in Figure 1.1. A workstation will send a communication request to the switch-box asking to be connected to another workstation. A circuit will be set up within the switch-box connecting the two workstations as if they were connected directly to each other.

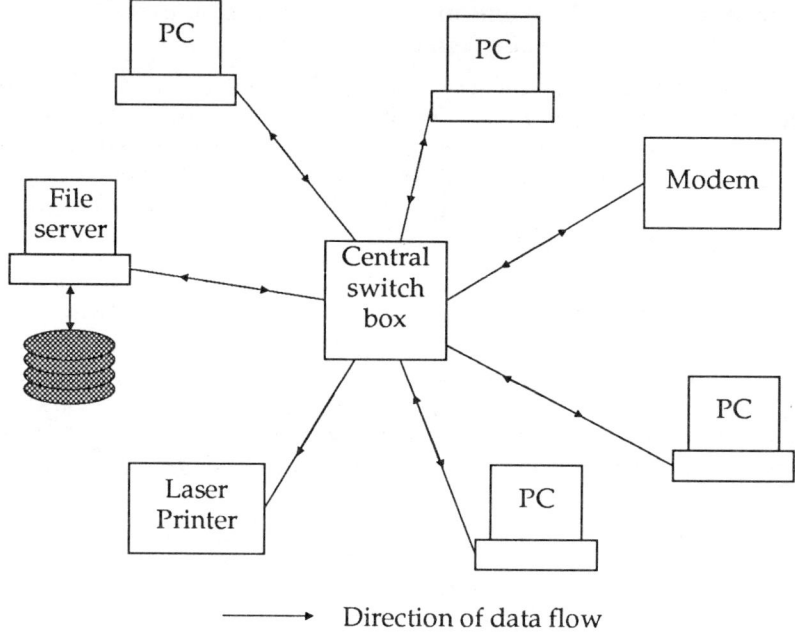

Figure 1.1 The Star topology

The central switch-box is consequently a complex device that bears the burden of the communications link, whereas the communications processing burden on the workstations is minimal.

The star topology is not ideally suited to local area networks of the kind discussed in this book. An example of a star topology would be the PBX digital telephone exchange used within many organisations. Having said that, it is important to bear in mind that certain elements of the network will in fact behave in a manner very similar to that described above. A prime example of this is the active hub in an ARCnet network, a device that allows a star-type configuration to be connected to the network.

1.5.2 THE RING TOPOLOGY

A ring topology consists of a closed loop made up of a set of connected repeaters. The repeater thus has both an input and output connection through which data is transmitted in one direction only, meaning that the data circulates around the ring.

Each station attaches to the network at a repeater, transmitting data in predefined blocks. Each block contains data as well as some control information (such as the address of the destination workstation). Large amounts of data are broken up into a series of smaller blocks prior to transmission. The data blocks will circulate around the ring and its contents will be copied into a buffer on the destination workstation until the data block is finally removed by the original source workstation. The logic controlling data insertion, data reception and data removal of these data blocks is contained within the workstations. The ring topology is shown in Figure 1.2.

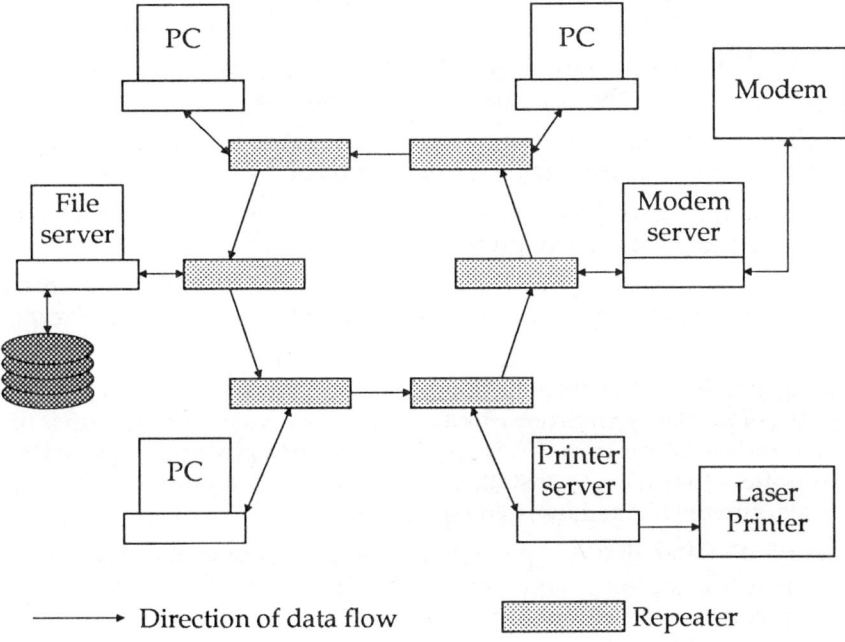

Figure 1.2 The Ring topology

In a ring topology the network devices are relatively simple (unlike the star topology), however the workstations must provide framing of the data blocks and access control. This tends to mean that there is a performance overhead associated with such configurations, as the design of the hardware/software systems that take care of this task must be sufficiently flexible to work with a wide variety of computing devices.

As the major alternative to the tree topology for local area networks, the ring topology has enjoyed considerable popularity in Europe and has recently gained acceptance in the USA primarily thanks to the release of a number of products from IBM (especially the Token-Ring network products)

When compared directly with the other topologies, its advantages include:
- Greater distances can be covered with less degeneration of the signal at high speeds.
- The electronics and maintenance are simpler than for multi-point lines.

- Fault isolation and recovery are simpler than with bus/tree.
- Duplicate workstation addresses can be more easily detected and catered for in the ring topology than for the bus/tree topology.

Its disadvantages are:
- Cable vulnerability. If there is a break at any point in the ring the entire network can be disabled.
- Repeater failure. As with the cable, failure can break the ring and disable the network.
- Locating the point of failure requires access to all points on the ring, and unusually large pockets for all the keys that need to be carried.
- Installation of new workstations on the ring requires breaking the ring to install a new repeater and subsequently the disruption of the network.
- The size of the network is limited by practicalities of maintaining a large number of repeaters given the above problems.
- Recovery from transient errors is difficult given that no particular workstation is assigned as a controller, thus no workstation may wish to assume responsibility for the error.
- Timing problems. Synchronisation of the repeaters is necessary, but due to a number of primarily environmental problems, such synchronisation is often inaccurate and problems arise. These problems place a physical limit on the number of repeaters that may be installed on a ring. For example, the IBM limit of 72 repeaters on unshielded, twisted pair cable.

It is important to note that it is possible to alleviate many of the above problems by employing a hybrid star-ring topology. However the concepts remain valid to this particular topology wherever it is employed.

1.5.3 THE TREE TOPOLOGY

In a tree topology the communications network consists entirely of the transmission media. There are no switches or repeaters. The workstations attach (via appropriate hardware) directly to the cabling system. A transmission from a workstation will propagate the entire network, and can be received by all other workstations attached to the cabling system. A typical tree topology is shown in Figure 1.3.

Obviously only one workstation can transmit at a time, and thus some form of access control is required. As with the ring topology this logic is contained within the workstation, and a similar process of breaking the data down into blocks is utilised.

The network in this case is simply a passive transmission medium with no control logic of its own.

1.5.4 THE BUS TOPOLOGY

The often-mentioned bus topology is actually a special case of the tree topology. In it there is usually just a single trunk, rather than multiple branches. This topology is the most widely used and enjoys considerable popularity in the USA. It is typified by Ethernet installations. A typical bus topology is shown in Figure 1.4.

LOCAL AREA NETWORK TECHNOLOGY 15

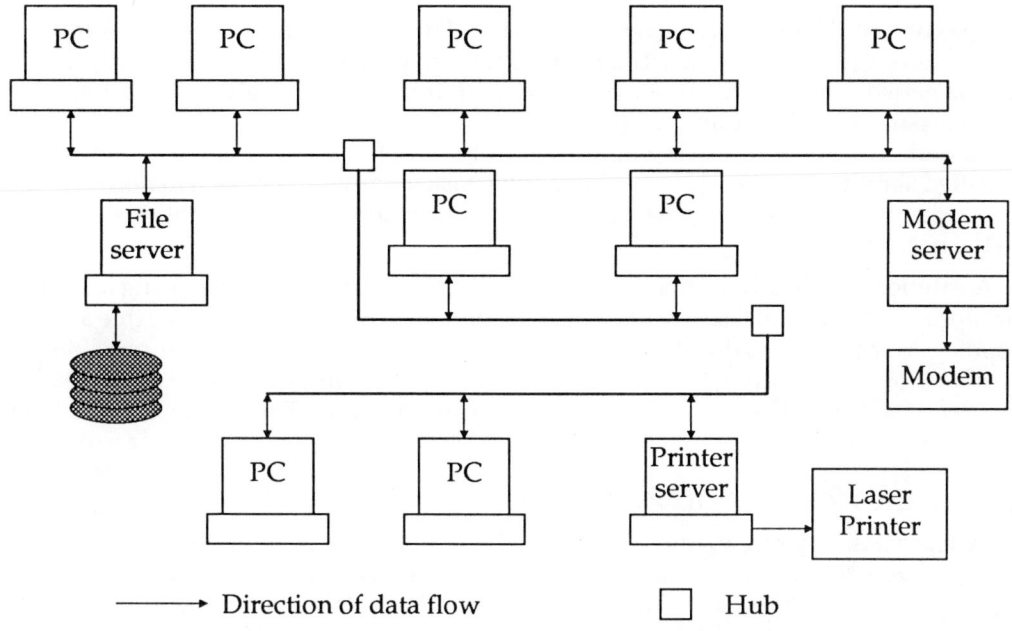

Figure 1.3 The Tree topology

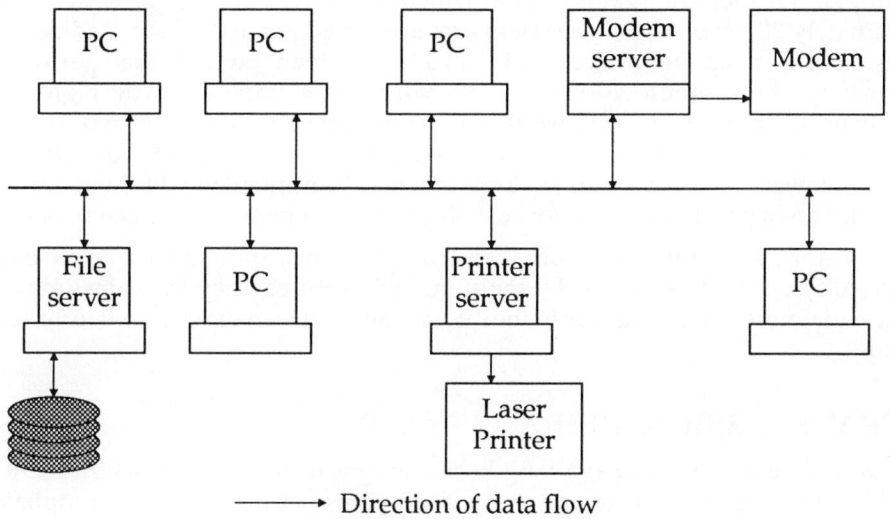

Figure 1.4 The Bus topology

Unlike the ring topology, the tree and bus topologies are not 'peer-to-peer' in nature and the process of determining which workstation can transmit is often performed by a controlling workstation. This method has however been relegated recently in favour of a newly-developed variety of medium access protocols.

A second problem is that of signal balancing. This means that a device must transmit a signal strong enough to reach its destination, yet not so strong that other nearby devices on the network are saturated or even destroyed. Interference is not really an issue on a simple point-to-point connection, however the interference created by devices on a 200-hundred station network would require that 39000 signal-strength constraints be satisfied simultaneously. This is an impossible task for anything but small networks and subsequently network performance can deteriorate markedly as more stations are added to the network.

A solution is to break the network up into a series of small segments using amplifiers or repeaters between the segments. This is essentially a hybrid between the tree and ring topologies, however it does in its own way create new problems. The possibility of workstations transmitting blocks of data simultaneously on different segments leads to the need for mechanisms of collision detection and recovery. Performance degradation again results.

1.5.5 PRACTICAL TOPOLOGIES

In practice it is very rare to find a LAN based purely on one of the above topologies. It is much more common to find LANs implemented as hybrids between two of the previously defined architectures. Thus star-ring, tree-ring or tree-star topologies are becoming increasingly more popular as they alleviate some of the problems inherent in the original architectures.

Hybrid LANs also allow a greater amount of flexibility in the design of the network. For example, consider an organisation in which there are a number of network users. Approximately 20 percent of these users account for 80 percent of the loading on the network. If all workstations are connected to a bus or tree type LAN then performance problems may occur, as the low-loading users will have to compete with the high-loading users whenever they wish to transmit data. However, by creating a hybrid LAN, a high-performance star or ring may be allocated for the express use of the high-loading users, and a lower-cost, lower-performance tree may be implemented for the remainder of the staff. Thus a practical balance of cost, flexibility and performance can be achieved.

Hybrid LANs do of course produce their own problems, and whilst they are conceptually no different to those posed by the pure architectures, they are sometimes more difficult to diagnose and isolate due to the interactions between the different technologies involved.

1.6 TRANSMISSION MEDIA

Transmission media choices have long been thought to be the sole determinant of a network's capability and functionality, and many firms place far too much emphasis on the selection of cable types during the design and configuration phases of their network implementation, often at the expense of other more important factors. As has been explained above, this notion is incorrect, and there are in fact many other factors that determine the network's performance.

However, the choice of transmission media is still an important one, as it defines the cost and ease of installation of the network, as well as the likely problems that may be encountered once the network is up and running.

The choice of transmission media is seldom determined by the organisation's decision to adopt a specific topology. The two major topologies, ie star-ring and tree-ring are both able to support all of the main categories of cable type, notably coaxial, twisted-pair, and optical fibre. Each type of cable differs significantly, having its own advantages and disadvantages when compared to the others.

1.6.1 COAXIAL CABLE

The most versatile transmission medium available for networks, coaxial cable is still the most popular cable type in most organisations. Typified by television antenna cable it consists of two conductors. A hollow outer conductor surrounds a solid, narrow inner conductor, the two being separated by a solid insulating material. A shielded jacket surrounds both. The diameter of coaxial cable varies from 5mm to approximately 25mm although coaxial cable of 300mm or greater is available for other applications. Figure 1.5 shows the construction of coaxial cable.

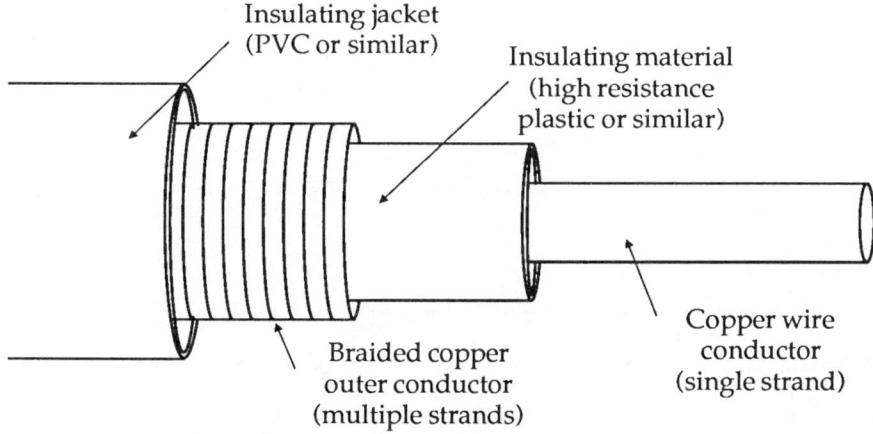

Figure 1.5   Construction of coaxial cable

There are two types of coaxial cable:
- Baseband
- Broadband.

Baseband coaxial cable can be used in almost any topology, and is often known by its technical specification of 50-ohm. The term baseband implies that the cable can carry only one signal at a time. This allows high-speed, inexpensive digital transmission methods to be used by the LAN devices, and for this reason it is the most popular type. Typically a baseband LAN can support about 100 devices.

Broadband coaxial cable is sometimes called 75-ohm coaxial. The term broadband means that a single cable is capable of carrying several signals, with each one being distinctly separate from the others. In this sense, it may be considered analogous to cable TV systems, in which a single cable carries several different TV channels. Due to the increased complexity of the signal, broadband LANs require sophisticated, more expensive devices, and therefore they are less popular. However, a typical broadband LAN can

18 CABLING

support thousands of devices, although high-performance versions of the broadband coaxial may limit this somewhat.

Interference is still an issue with both forms of coaxial cable, but whilst dependent on application, it is not as much of a problem as it is with twisted pair. Coaxial cable costs generally fall in between those of twisted pair and optical fibre cable.

1.6.2 TWISTED PAIR CABLE

Extremely common throughout the world, twisted pair is used extensively within a building to connect telephones. It consists of two spirally-bound, insulated wires that together act as a single communication link. This construction can be seen in Figure 1.6.

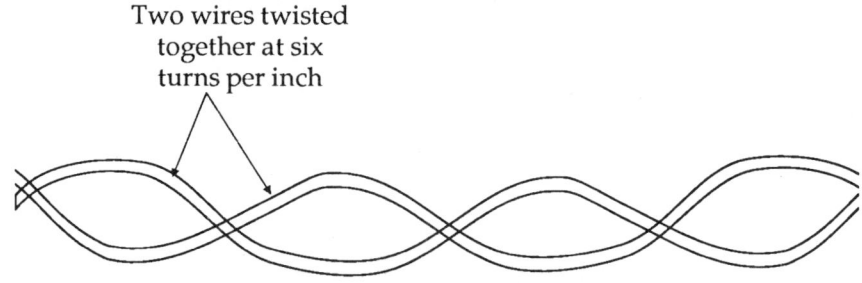

Figure 1.6 Construction of twisted pair cable

Twisted pair is a less expensive, but is also a lower performance alternative to coaxial cable and is able to support fewer stations. Relative to the other media it is more susceptible to interference and data transmission is easily disrupted by adjacent power cords or even other twisted pair cables. Shielding the wire, and/or twisting the cable can reduce the interference somewhat, but coaxial cable remains superior.

The prime advantage of twisted pair has been one of cost. Many buildings already have twisted pair cable in ductings as excess from telephone installations. Due primarily to their widespread use, the cost of this cable is negligible, however the overall installation cost tends to be inflated due to increased labour charges.

1.6.3 OPTICAL FIBRE CABLE

Still a new and rapidly improving technology it is difficult to be precise about the limitations and applicability of optical fibre cable. Yet this medium already presents some exciting possibilities for the future of networking.

It consists of a thin strand of glass and plastic fibre capable of conducting a ray of light. Each fibre core is surrounded by its own cladding (a glass or plastic coating with different optical properties to the core), and is enclosed, either on its own or together with a group of other fibres, within an outer protective jacket, as can be seen in Figure 1.7.

One or more rays of light can be transmitted, usually by an injection laser diode (ILD) or light-emitting diode (LED), along the length of this cable at extremely high speeds and

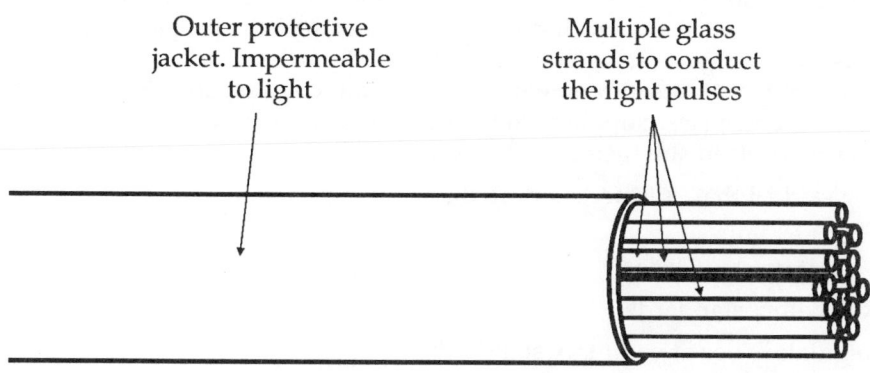

Figure 1.7   Construction of fibre optic cable

with negligible degradation due to interference. Present technology supports transmission over distances of between 6km and 8km without repeaters. Optical fibre offers excellent security as no electrical emissions are generated. Furthermore, due to the fact that optical fibre cable can carry several signals, it is a broadband medium and is therefore capable of transmitting several independent signals to many thousands of devices.

The cost of an optical fibre installation is considerably higher than that of coaxial cable. This is not primarily due to the cost of the cable itself, which retails for approximately two to three times as much as coaxial, but rather the other network devices such as transceivers, network interface cards, repeaters etc. These devices have to handle the conversion of electrical signals to light at extremely high speeds, and therefore tend to use state of the art technology. This of course entails state of the art costs.

1.7 NETWORK STANDARDS

The computer industry was, and still is, dominated by suppliers who wish to monopolise their customers. As a result networks have suffered from a lack of industry-wide standards. The major suppliers have insisted on pursuing a policy of developing their own proprietary 'standards', which of course are supported by no-one but themselves.

Apart from the confusion among customers, this narrow-minded approach has led to unrealistically high prices for connectivity products. Mass production methods are not employed as they would if a single standard was adhered to, and many of the suppliers are embroiled in a mud-slinging match of major proportions as they debate (and market) the relative strengths of their own products and the weaknesses of their competitor's products.

This situation looks set to alter over the next few years. Manufacturers are beginning to supply products that conform to one or other of the major standards that have been proposed by bodies such as the Institute of Electrical and Electronic Engineers (IEEE) and the International Standards Organisation (ISO). The principal advantage of such standardisation is that products from different suppliers will be able to communicate with each other, thus giving the customer added flexibility in selecting a system.

20 NETWORK STANDARDS

Unfortunately standards tend to freeze technology. A set of standards can take years to draw up and finalise, by which stage they can result in the promotion and adoption of obsolete technology. Although this is most certainly an issue, too much has been made of it by the large manufacturers, who are often directly responsible for delaying the process in the first place. Suppliers in the computer industry tend to hijack the standardisation attempts to suit their own purposes.

Having said all that, it is necessary to distinguish between three forms of standards. They are:-
- Voluntary standards
- Regulatory standards
- Regulatory use of voluntary standards.

1.7.1 VOLUNTARY STANDARDS

Voluntary standards are drawn up by standards-making organisations such as the Institute of Electrical and Electronic Engineers (IEEE), the International Standards Organisation (ISO) and the American National Standards Institute (ANSI).

They are voluntary in as much as their existence does not compel their use. Manufacturers will utilise them if they perceive benefit, however there are no legal implications involved in a manufacturer choosing to go his own way if he believes that he holds a competitive advantage due to his own research and development. These standards are generally drawn up by representatives from interested parties whether they be government or industry members.

1.7.2 REGULATORY STANDARDS

Regulatory standards are drawn up by government agencies with the intention of meeting some defence, economic or other public objective. They are enforced by law and must be met by manufacturers providing services within the context of those regulations.

1.7.3 REGULATIONS ENFORCING PREVIOUSLY VOLUNTARY STANDARDS

Relatively new on the scene is the introduction of regulations enforcing previously voluntary standards. A typical example of this is the introduction of legislation requiring that any networking products purchased in Europe by governmental departments after 1992 must conform to the OSI networking model and related standards. The consequences of this action will obviously be felt far beyond the bounds of governmental departments. Manufacturers who wish to be able to bid for public tenders are going to have to develop conforming products, which will inevitably flow over into general industry.

1.8 STANDARDS SETTING ORGANISATIONS

Primarily, the two organisations concerned with developing standards for the networking environment are the International Standards Organisation (ISO), and the Institute of Electrical and Electronic Engineers (IEEE). Both of these bodies are funded by government and industry, drawing their membership from industry, academia, user groups and government departments. They have both been established for many years, and have produced standards for many different aspects of the electronics, communications and computer environments.

1.8.1 THE ISO

In terms of networking, the OSI (open systems interconnection) reference model proposed by the ISO is one of the most popular. In actual fact the OSI model is not a set of specific standards at all, but rather an acknowledgement of the necessity for specific industry standards. It encourages the development of specific network standards on seven different levels. Figure 1.8 shows these levels diagrammatically.

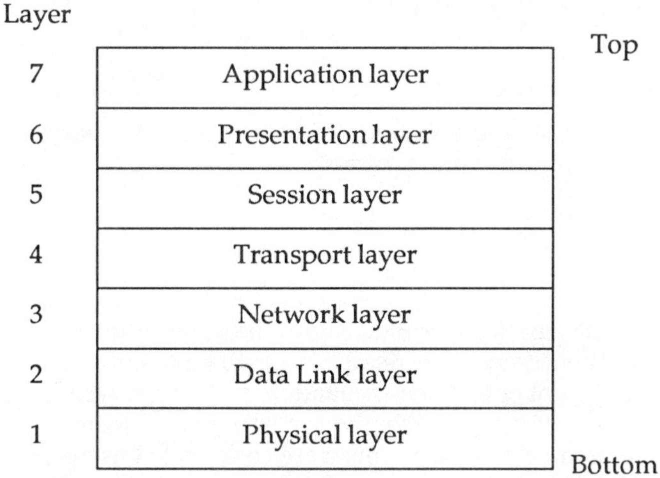

Layer		
7	Application layer	Top
6	Presentation layer	
5	Session layer	
4	Transport layer	
3	Network layer	
2	Data Link layer	
1	Physical layer	Bottom

Figure 1.8 The ISO/OSI seven layer model

The OSI model states that there are really seven different layers to the interconnection problem. It states that standards need to be developed individually for each of these layers and it specifies the constraints and scope for each layer and the manner in which that layer is to communicate with other layers. The OSI model additionally requires that the standards developed for each layer make no assumption about any pre or superseding layer's standards. This implies that users should (in theory) be able to mix-and-match products from different suppliers (manufactured according to a relevant set of standards for that layer) at each of the different layers and remain confident that the final network operates according to specification.

However, one problem that has plagued the OSI model is that until very recently there was little support for it in its original form. Those manufacturers that adopted it for the design of their systems tended to subtly modify it, either to allow extra features in their products to be used or to enhance the interaction of different layers, etc. Fortunately this situation is set to change as there is now substantial governmental support for OSI. Therefore most manufacturers will soon be producing 100 percent OSI-compliant products.

1.8.2 THE IEEE

The IEEE have approached the issue of standardisation from a slightly different viewpoint. They proposed the original standards which were adopted by the major manufacturers for Ethernet, Token Ring, ARCnet, etc. However, rather than attempt to develop an all encompassing set of standards that could be applied to any network, the IEEE produced standards that more accurately defined practical hardware and software standards. Thus whilst the IEEE standards are not as flexible as the proposed ISO model, they work in practice and are adhered to by the majority of system manufacturers.

IEEE standards are numbered according to the committee that sat to draft the specifications. Therefore the IEEE standards relating to Ethernet are known as the IEEE 802.2 and 802.3 specifications, whilst those relating to Token Ring are referred to as the 802.5 specifications.

1.8.3 INDUSTRY STANDARDS

In this section the discussion of standards will be limited to a clarification of the three most widely used network structures, namely:

– Ethernet
– Token Ring
– ARCnet.

These standards each specify a unique communication protocol and messaging system, and subsequently encompass the related issues of topology and transmission media. Although there are a number of other contenders that might well be mentioned, these three have been chosen because together they constitute 90 percent of installed local area networks. Of the remaining 10 percent, most are constructed using obsolete technology that will not, in all likelihood, be supported for very much longer.

The precise technical specifications relating to the hardware required for each of these technologies are discussed in Chapter 6, as they are most relevant when considering the issues of hardware troubleshooting.

1.8.3.1 Ethernet

Perhaps the most widely known type of local area network, Ethernet was developed in an experimental fashion by Xerox Corporation in the mid-70s.

Xerox announced its intention to develop Ethernet as an industry standard for local area networks and its attempt to achieve these objectives was suitably aided by the enlisting of support from both Intel and Digital Equipment Corporation.

The three participated together and in 1980, the same year as IBM released its first personal computer, they announced version 1 of the Ethernet specification. A slightly modified and improved specification was released as version 2 in 1982.

Based on the IEEE's 802.2 and 802.3 specifications, Ethernet is essentially a protocol for use on a bus topology. It defines a variety of physical transmission media and data transfer rate options.

1.8.3.2 ARCnet

ARCnet is currently not as common as Ethernet or Token Ring but is becoming more and more popular. Its world wide use accounts for around 20 percent of the installed networks, although in some parts of the globe its share increases to around 70 percent.

LOCAL AREA NETWORK TECHNOLOGY

In some ways ARCnet is unique. First, there are no formal specifications upon which it is manufactured, although it is very closely aligned with the IEEE's 802.4 token-bus standard which was specifically designed for military and industrial use. Despite this lack of formal standardisation it has become a *de facto* industry standard.

In design it is significantly more complex than either the Ethernet or the Token Ring standards and draws heavily on the advantages of both.

It is extremely flexible in application and may be installed in whatever topology suits the task (specific hardware exists for the various options). In operation it treats a physical tree topology as a logical ring. A token passing mechanism, similar to that employed in Token Ring, is employed to determine access to the network.

ARCnet has built into it the logic to automatically insert and remove workstations as is required, thus ensuring that maintenance and expansion problems are minimised.

The network is not generally high-performance in nature as a result of the peer-to-peer treatment of the attached workstations, yet a prioritisation scheme can be employed which gives active workstations more frequent opportunities to be serviced.

One of the advantages of not being a formalised standard is that manufacturers are able to modify ARCnet with relative freedom as technology advances and as market-driven demands come to the fore. In practical terms changes are not effected overnight as the need to remain compatible with products from other suppliers remains important.

Unfortunately ARCnet has the disadvantage of not conforming to the specifications of the OSI reference model as it actually spans several layers, not falling neatly into any single one. Thus it seems likely that ARCnet may lose out somewhat to the other technologies when a greater degree of standardisation has been achieved. However, it should be remembered that a truly practical implementation of the OSI reference model is yet to be achieved. The non-conformance of ARCnet to the model does not imply that either of the other two standards are any more successful on a practical level. What it does mean is that the architectural design of the current implementation of ARCnet makes it impossible for it to comply with the model's guidelines. Changes to that design, which are possible due to ARCnet's flexible nature, will negate the problem.

1.8.3.3 Token Ring

Token Ring is probably the oldest ring control technique, originally proposed in 1969, and has become the most popular ring access technique in the United States, Europe, and the majority of the rest of the world.

It is based directly on the IEEE's 802.5 Token Ring specification and enjoys close conformity to the OSI reference model. The widespread notoriety of Token Ring does of course owe a great deal to the considerable marketing machine of IBM, its main proponent.

In reality Token Ring has not been as successful as one might initially think. It is only recently that workable products have emerged from the development labs, and a fair degree of consumer resistance seems to be affecting its adoption.

Token Ring is characterised by monopolistic manufacturers, the most obvious of whom is IBM. However, at a lower level even more of a monopoly exists as only one manufacturer is currently producing the key component for Token Ring adapter cards; Texas Instruments.

It is not foreseen that this situation will last too much longer, primarily because a fundamental design flaw in the TI chip has prompted much legal and other activity on this issue. The outcome of this was that the IBM and TI monopolies were broken, which means that *any* manufacturer may now produce Token Ring products.

Overall, Token Ring is a significant product ideally suited to commercial and light industrial environments, exactly the same environments that Ethernet was designed for. Thus they are often seen to be competing directly with one another. Interestingly enough IBM unofficially ships significantly more Ethernet networks to its customers than it does Token Ring networks.

With a view to the future, Token Ring has, as part of its fundamental architecture, a significant advantage over either Ethernet or ARCnet with regards potential network management facilities. It is possible to program the network operating system in such a way that any communication problems are automatically detected and reported to either the system manager or the network itself for further action.

1.8.4 OTHER STANDARDISATION ISSUES

The above discussions of the standards relating to the major technologies tend to control the overall appearance and operation of the network. However, they have little effect upon the precise hardware components that make up the network. Thus file servers, workstations, printers, plotters, facsimile machines, etc. tend to be very similar between different technologies; the only component that differs greatly between them is the interface card that connects the device to the network.

Therefore there is little standardisation in terms of what can be connected to the LAN. This is in fact a positive attribute of the system, as it provides a great deal of flexibility in the overall configuration of the network. Thus as long as an appropriate interface card can be acquired, any device, irrespective of manufacturer or design, can be connected to the LAN.

The following sections look in more detail at the two most common, and most important LAN devices; file servers and workstations.

1.9 FILE SERVER CONFIGURATION

A network file server is much like any other personal computer, and it has associated with it much the same problems. Power supplies may go up in smoke, hard disks lose their drive, and the various components fight for equal representation via the limited interrupts.

The techniques and methods for dealing with problems of this ilk are covered in other textbooks, and will not be addressed in detail here. However, there are a number of components of the file server that are relevant in terms of network problems. Not only will their failure cause the network to fail, but the overall performance of the network is ultimately dependent upon the performance of these particular devices. They are:

- The microprocessor
- The RAM
- The hard disk drives
- The network interface card.

1.9.1 MICROPROCESSOR

It is not realistic to expect an 8086 or 8088 based PC to be able to run an entire network, so in practical terms the file server should be a minimum of an 80286 based AT, preferably running at 12MHz or more. Ideally it should be either an 80386 or 80486 system, running at 25MHz or greater. This will allow the network to use the high-power optimised network operating systems, such as Netware 386, which have been designed to make maximum use of the facilities offered by the more advanced processors. The Intel i586 is due for release in 1992. Systems based around this processor will obviously be the most powerful yet, and therefore inherently suitable for file server applications.

Tight budgets are usually second only to end-users as the bane of a network manager/administrator's life, and in a situation where a high specification machine is beyond the available resources, then settling for a 80286 presents no major problems. In fact in the majority of situations the performance offered by such a machine is usually excellent. However, bearing in mind the lowered cost of 80386s and in particular the 80386SX machines, it does become difficult to justify not investing in one of these machines rather than a 80286 as the file server, as future software developments may well require high power computers to execute efficiently.

If it is possible that an upgrade to a product such as Netware 386 may be contemplated, then it is unwise to consider the purchase of an 80386SX machine. Whilst existing network products will run correctly on SX machines, the 16-bit data path inherent in the design of SX type motherboards will result in considerable performance degradation, and may not be acceptable for future upgrades.

Irrespective of which microprocessor is chosen, one thing is certain; network operating systems in general are a lot less tolerant of subtle incompatibilities than either DOS or OS/2. It is therefore essential to exercise extreme caution when purchasing 'compatible' machines. The only 100 percent IBM compatible machine, is in fact an IBM machine (and even some of these are a bit questionable). For this reason the major network operating system vendors offer certification programs from which information can be obtained regarding the compatibility of the machine in question. This sort of information is available at very little cost and is well worth the added effort of obtaining it.

1.9.2 RAM REQUIREMENTS

Networking products, much like any other software, require adequate memory for their efficient operation. Unfortunately many firms tend to try and cut costs in this area and get away with the minimum requirements specified by the product developers. This is senseless, and in the long term will lead to problems with network reliability and performance, especially when the system is under heavy load.

All serious network operating systems require memory relative to the size and complexity of the network. Increased numbers of users, installation of an additional hard disk drive or network interface card, or even just increased usage of the network. All of these actions require additional memory resources. Thus providing insufficient memory for the file server will not only significantly curtail the growth potential of the network, but can result in degraded performance and loss of functionality.

One of the problems faced by network managers when configuring a file server is "How much is enough?" Some of the issues that must be kept in mind when answering this question include the following:

26 RAM REQUIREMENTS

1.9.2.1 Operating system kernel

The kernel of the operating system is the software that controls access to data, applications programs and network resources, and also maintains control over network communications. The memory required for this purpose is usually a fixed amount and is often similar to the requirements for any normal piece of software that may be run under the same environment. In other words, for a Novell network the requirement is usually about 500KB, much the same as most DOS-based programs would require. A network operating system based on OS/2 however, would require a significantly larger amount of memory resource.

1.9.2.2 Network drivers

For each network interface card that is installed in the server, a certain amount of memory will be required. This holds the software that controls how the machine communicates with the card, in particular how the data should be packaged so that it is ready for transmission on the network. Installing multiple cards requires not only additional memory for the extra drivers, but also an area of memory for communication between the cards themselves.

1.9.2.3 Number of attached workstations

This will affect issues relating to *file locking, file control blocks*, and *communication buffers* on the file server. Essentially, as more users utilise the network, the system requires more memory to maintain overall control.

1.9.2.4 Hard disk drive capacity

This is the only area where the memory requirements are at all optional, and is also where marked performance increases can be achieved by simply adding memory to the file server. The file server has the ability to very effectively cache the attached hard disk drive and its directory listings. With multiple users accessing the same hard disk drive, and all demanding lightning responses, it is essential that ample memory be given to the file server in order to support its attached drives.

1.9.2.5 Typical RAM requirements for a file server

By way of example Figure 1.9 shows the RAM requirements for a file server using NetWare 286 in an academic environment, derived from the guidelines provided in the Novell NetWare manuals. An analysis of these figures can prove valuable to the understanding of the memory requirements of such a network.

1.9.3 HARD DISK DRIVES

The memory requirement implications for hard drives have already been discussed. However the choice of a particular hard disk drive is of prime importance when setting up or redesigning a network.

By implication a file server requires a large, fast hard disk drive that is able to store all the files that either the system manager or the users might require in addition to the network operating system itself. By implication it must also be reliable and able to work under conditions of heavy use for extended periods of time. To purchase a 'bargain-basement' hard disk drive for use in the file server is an invitation to disaster.

Usage	Itemised	Total
Operating System, Stack Space, and Miscellaneous Buffers.		475
LAN Drivers.		32
1 * Arcnet card	16	
1 * Ethernet Card	16	
File Allocation Tables.		600
600 Mb Hard Disk	600	
File Locking.		1015
75 Workstations	75*0.2	
1000 Open Files Maximum	1000*1	
File Control Blocks.		550
1000 Open Files Maximum	1000*0.55	
Communication Buffers.		125
75 Workstations	75	
Internetwork traffic	50	
Cache Memory.		2400
600 Mb Hard Disk	600*4	
Directory Caching.		1216
Novell Allowed Directory Entries Entries. The default is 512 minimum, plus 128 for every 2 Mb of disk space. Thus for a 600 Mb hard disk drive the default is 38912.	38912/32	
TOTAL RAM REQUIREMENTS (IN KB)		**6413**

Figure 1.9　RAM requirements for a NetWare 286 file server

Just as important is the choice of controller for the hard disk drive. If there is even the slightest possibility of growth, then it is essential to ensure that the chosen controllers are able to support disk mirroring and duplexing features.

A good idea is to look through the machine configurations that have achieved compatibility certification by one or more of the major vendors. It is often the case that the same manufacturer's hard disk drives are being used in many of the approved configurations. These drives are well worth the extra cost that may be involved.

1.9.4 NETWORK INTERFACE CARD (NIC)

The server-NIC combination is often the most decisive factor in the determination of network performance. Placing an 8-bit card into the file server will guarantee 8-bit performance on the network irrespective of the workstation capabilities. On the other hand, placing a 32-bit EISA or MCA card into the file server will provide blindingly fast performance to even the lowliest 8088 based workstation, despite the fact that it is fitted with only an 8-bit NIC.

Thus when funding eventually allows the network manager to purchase an 80486 file server running at 50MHz or more, one thing must be borne in mind: If the machine only has an ISA 16-bit bus architecture, it can never be utilised to its full potential as a file server as the 32-bit NICs cannot be used. At most it will offer only marginally better performance than an 80386 33MHz machine using the same 16-bit NIC.

When shopping for a network interface card one of the prime features that it should offer is a buffer of a reasonable size. This is especially relevant on Ethernet installations. This is because the file server will be receiving transmissions from multiple stations, and when things get busy transmissions can often get missed due to an inadequate buffer size on the NIC.

A final recommendation is that the NIC purchased for the file server comes equipped with plenty of possible interrupt options. If the server is expanded, it may become necessary to place additional NICs into the file server (either to support multiple topologies, or to split the burden on the current cabling system). In this case the shortcomings of only being able to choose from the normal four or five possible interrupt options will become very obvious, as it may in fact be impossible to install the desired selection of cards into the file server due to these interrupt conflicts.

1.10 NETWORK WORKSTATIONS

Network workstations are usually much the same as normal personal computer systems, just as file servers are the same as personal computer systems. Indeed, exactly the same factors apply to the task of troubleshooting a workstation as apply to any faultfinding process. However, as explained earlier, it is not the aim of this book to describe these fundamental troubleshooting procedures, as they are covered in great detail in other textbooks. Therefore when the power supply blows, the monitor stops working and the floppy disk will no longer read, it will be necessary to employ the tools and techniques described elsewhere to achieve a satisfactory remedy.

If however the problem is related to performance in some way, especially network performance, then there is more that can be done to provide a solution. The problems facing the use of networked workstations are extremely varied, thus there are often no simple solutions, and the diagnosis of such problems can be a time consuming affair.

Before considering the problems that can be faced, it is a good idea to consider the components that may be brought together to form a workstation, and in particular those components that may in some way affect performance. As with the server, these fall into four categories:

 - Microprocessor
 - Network Interface card
 - Disks
 - Memory.

Most workstations will include all four of these components, although diskless workstations are becoming more and more popular in support of the ever increasing effort to reduce costs and tighten up on security. In addition to these components the workstation will also have to include the other standard PC components, including the following:

 - A monitor and its associated card

- A power supply
- A mouse and its associated card
- Keyboard
- All other motherboard circuitry, including ROMs.

However, whilst all of these factors will affect operation of the system, and may even affect the way in which the system behaves, they will not fundamentally affect the performance, especially the speed with which applications can be loaded and executed. It is the original four components which exert greatest influence in terms of speed and ability, and therefore it is these components that require more detailed examination.

1.10.1 MICROPROCESSOR

As with standard PCs, the microprocessor is the component which is thought to determine overall performance of the system. Whilst this is not strictly accurate, it is true to say that it does exert perhaps the greatest influence on the speed with which an application will execute once it has been loaded. For many users, this is the thing that they are worried about most. This is especially noticeable when users of a network restrict themselves to using a select few applications, and very rarely exit from one program to run another.

The microprocessor that is used in a workstation is the same as that used in any other PC. It is most often one of the following Intel processors (in ascending order of performance):

- 8088
- 8086
- 80286
- 80386sx
- 80386
- 80486sx
- 80486
- 80586

Obviously those users requiring high-powered applications will need to have a workstation with at least an 80286 processor, whilst the use of an 80386 or 80486 will significantly enhance the operation of the system.

Thus, whilst the choice of processor is important when considering machine-intensive applications, such as CAD, DTP, financial and statistical analysis etc., it has relatively little effect on disk-intensive applications such as database etc. It is the other factors that are most important in these situations.

It should be remembered that some supposedly processor-intensive applications are in fact much more dependent upon the disk than is first realised. The reason for this is that many sophisticated applications use special programming modules known as overlays, which reside on disk until they are required. They are then loaded into the system, executed, and then discarded again. Thus such applications will often need to make frequent disk accesses in order to perform efficiently.

1.10.2 NETWORK INTERFACE CARD

As explained above, the choice of microprocessor does not directly affect the speed with which an application can be loaded. This is controlled by a number of factors, including the following:
- The architecture of the workstation
- The network interface card in the workstation
- The network interface card in the file server
- The loading on the network.

The architecture of the workstation determines which network interface cards can be used. If a 16-bit or 32-bit card can be used, and it is supported by the network, data transfer will obviously be much quicker as twice or four times as much data can be handled at a time. The architecture is to all intents and purposes determined by the processor; 8088 and 8086 systems are 8-bit, systems with an 80286 or 80386SX are 16-bit, whilst those sporting an 80386, 80486 or 80586 are 32-bit systems.

This fact must be kept in mind when the choice of network card is made. For example, it is impossible to fit a 16-bit card into an 8-bit machine, although a 16-bit machine can use either an 8 or 16-bit card. The card must obviously be compatible with the other network hardware and software etc.

However, there is a less obvious problem which is not encountered with high-powered networks, but often occurs in smaller, less powerful systems. The problem relates to the network interface card that is situated in the file server. If any network workstation has a 16-bit card, then it is essential that the file server also has at least a 16-bit card. The reason for this is that if fitted with an 8-bit interface card, the file server will be unable to successfully interpret data it receives from the 16-bit workstation card. What it will actually do is receive the first eight bits transmitted and then generate an error. The workstation automatically retries, and sends the remaining eight bits of data. Thus the whole procedure is considerably slower due to the extraneous error signals that are being transmitted. Therefore, a performance loss will be experienced if the network card in a workstation is upgraded from an 8- to 16-bit card without also changing the file server.

The problem does not manifest itself when a workstation only has an 8-bit card and the file server has a higher capacity one, as the system automatically compensates for variations in technology that are of a lesser specification to the server.

The network loading is also a very relevant factor when considering performance issues. If there are many users on the network, and it is functioning at close to its limit, then performance will be noticeably slower due to the many disk read/write requests that are being received. The only way to alleviate this problem is to upgrade the system with extra file servers, higher performance interface cards, increased disk caching capacity in the file server etc.

Network loading is also a problem when there are several users all attempting to access the same application or data. Performance in such situations can be very poor, due to the fact that the server is receiving many requests to read the same areas of disk over and over. Even with caching this can take quite a time. This typically occurs in education and training establishments, where there may be 40 users in a laboratory, each with their own PC trying to access the same application as the speaker goes through a demonstration.

1.10.3 DISKS

The type and size of disk attached to a workstation is not a real problem, as most application and data storage is handled by the server. However, there may be circumstances in which the provision of a local hard drive is required, for example where a user wishes to run a program that is not available in a network form. In this case it will be necessary to install an appropriate device. A 20MB drive is often sufficient, and has the added advantage of being relatively inexpensive and easy to interface.

It is advisable to discourage users from storing their data on the local drives, as it will soon be found that they will become cluttered with odd files and thus will soon be filled. One way of achieving this is to have a batch file erase any data files that are created on the drive when the user logs out. Thus the user has the choice of copying the files to the network drives or a floppy, or they will be lost.

In terms of floppy disks the choice is arbitrary. The most common size of floppy is currently 5.25 inch, with the standard capacity being 360K. However, the smaller 3.5 inch disks offer a greater storage capacity and have the advantage of being more robust. Additionally the hardware for these devices is slightly more standardised and so less problems will be encountered when using a number of different drives. Whatever choice is made it is very important to standardise throughout the organisation. Therefore, if 5.25 inch disks are chosen, there should be one on every machine. 3.5 inch drives can be provided in addition, but no workstation should be supplied with this as its only drive. Failure to follow these guidelines will introduce problems with users being unable to transfer data to the network from certain machines simply due to disk incompatibilities.

In some high security establishments, hard disk only systems may be installed. These make transferring data onto the computer more difficult, although it does mean that especially stringent backup procedures must be adopted to ensure users' data is not stored only on the local hard disk.

1.10.3.1 Diskless workstations

A trend that is gaining more and more popularity is the use of diskless workstations. These are often entry level machines, based around the 8086 or possibly 80286 processors, but contain neither hard nor floppy disk drives. These workstations offer obvious savings, especially when an entire organisation is to be equipped. They also offer security advantages, as it is impossible for an intruder to copy software or data from the file server onto other media. Thus the chances of disclosing large volumes of data, or of software being pirated, are greatly reduced. However, the intruder will still be able to view the data on the screen, and quite likely obtain a hard copy through a printer.

1.10.3.2 Booting diskless workstations

When a workstation is first switched on, the way in which it boots up is controlled most often by the network card that is installed. Most cards are fitted with an EPROM that contains all of the necessary code to boot the machine, and load the relevant command processor, configuration and batch files from the network. The code will usually offer the user the choice of booting from either a local hard or floppy drive, or through the EPROM routine.

The use of these EPROM based routines is essential for diskless workstations, as without an appropriate device there is no way to get the computer up and running. Thus it is essential to ensure that the chosen network card does in fact offer this form of startup routine.

1.10.4 MEMORY

The memory of the workstation is the same as the memory of any other PC. However, due to the presence of the network, much more of this memory is used by the operating system, network drivers and configuration information than would be consumed on a standalone system. Consequently there is less memory available for the applications and data storage. This means that even standalone applications that are loaded from a local drive may not run if the workstation is connected to the network, and those that do run may suffer from limitations on the amount of data that may be processed and stored.

1.10.5 WORKSTATION COMPATIBILITY PROBLEMS

The use of the network does not greatly affect the way in which the workstation actually runs an application once it has been loaded. Therefore compatibility is still a problem.

Many network vendors, such as Novell, can supply a list of all PCs that are compatible with their products. Choosing a PC from this list will minimise the problems encountered in using the system with a network. Similarly, many software developers have also produced lists detailing which PCs are compatible with their applications etc. Thus to strike a balance, and ensure that no problems will be encountered either with the network or the application, it will be necessary to select a PC which is on both lists, and hence is compatible both with the network and the application.

Alternatively, consider purchasing true IBM systems, as these are the only true 100 percent compatible machines available. However, even some of IBM's more recent offerings seem a little reluctant to run some specialised programs, and hence could be said to be less than 100 percent compatible.

1.11 LAN OPERATING ENVIRONMENTS

Each workstation needs to have an operating system that enables the software supplied by the network to be executed. There are many different operating systems available, although many LAN operating systems support only a limited subset. The following sections outline some of the more popular network operating systems and environments that are encountered:

1.11.1 DOS

DOS is the most common operating environment used for PCs, whether they are connected to a LAN or not. It is also one of the more restrictive, as it has not been significantly updated since it was first introduced for the first primitive IBM PCs. From this point of view, it is likely that the majority of problems experienced on a LAN that relate to DOS are due to the limitations that it imposes. For example, even with DOS 5, quite convoluted techniques and procedures have to be followed if the user wants to use more than 640K of RAM, even though their system may have up to 32MB installed.

The key reason that DOS has remained so popular is that there is so much software available for it. Furthermore, it is likely that users will already be familiar with this software, and will be unwilling to change to anything else.

The most recent release of DOS, version 5, is a great improvement over earlier versions. However, this is seen by many to be an interim step, and it is hoped that the next release will contain all of the features and facilities that users have been requesting for years, but with few of the restrictions that are currently applied.

1.11.2 OS/2

OS/2 is a very powerful operating system, and makes much better use of personal computer facilities than DOS. For example, OS/2 directly supports the use of the full 32MB of on-board RAM that can be fitted to 80386 systems. This means that the number of possible applications for OS/2 is much greater, as there are fewer constraints on program size and sophistications.

Having said this, it is important to realise that OS/2 is in itself very power hungry. It generally requires a minimum of 8MB of memory to run in a satisfactory manner, whilst at least 16MB is required if any serious development work is to be done using spreadsheets etc.

Another problem with OS/2 is that there are relatively few applications available for it, although this situation is constantly improving.

1.11.3 MACINTOSH

One of the fundamental principles behind the design of Novell NetWare is that it should allow as varied an array of components to be connected through the network as possible. Thus whilst everyone knows that it supports all levels of PC from 8088 to 80586, it is sometimes not appreciated that other systems, such as the Apple Macintosh can also be incorporated.

In many organisations there are users who have been using such systems successfully for a number of years, but in the event of the installation of a network they are forced to change to using PCs. This needn't be so, as most networks support these technologies.

One of the greatest advantages to the Macintosh is its functionality in terms of DTP applications. It is generally agreed that the Macintosh is the best non-specialised machine for this purpose, and there are many different DTP products that take advantage of its excellent features.

1.11.4 WINDOWS

Windows is an operating environment, rather than an operating system. As such it is used in addition to DOS, to make it easier for users to make the most of the features of their system and applications programs.

Until recently the task of running Windows with a network was far from trivial. However special device drivers have been made available which significantly simplify the process.

1.11.5 GEM

GEM is very similar to windows in that it is an operating environment, working in conjunction with DOS. GEM is not as well used as Windows, and has therefore not received the same degree of support. One application that does use GEM is Xerox's Ventura Publisher, a desktop publishing system for PCs.

The problem experienced with many GEM applications, and especially with Ventura, is that they require very large amounts of memory to run. When a workstation is connected to the network, and has the appropriate drivers etc. loaded, there is just not enough space to run the application.

The only solution to these problems is to liberate an amount of memory, by using one of the techniques explained in Chapter 8.

1.11.6 OPERATING ENVIRONMENT PROBLEMS

Whichever operating environment is chosen, and there may well be more than one, it is of critical importance that the system manager/supervisor have an intimate knowledge of its workings. Most problems encountered in the network environment may either be traced back to the operating system, or may be avoided through the intelligent use of the operating system's facilities.

Any connection to a network consists of a number of software and hardware layers that interact with each other, and make no mistake, the operating system/environment is a major, if not the most important, player in that connection.

1.12 NETWORKED APPLICATIONS

When LANs were first conceived they were designed to allow organisations to reduce their expenses and investments in IT related subjects. They provided the ability to do this by allowing several different computers to share a range of common peripherals, typically printers, modems, disks etc. However, hardware prices have fallen a great deal since then, and now the emphasis on the use of networks is that they allow users to share data.

Unfortunately this is not as easy as simply linking a number of PCs together and running an ordinary application program. Networked applications have to be carefully designed if they are to offer the benefits of data sharing, as there are many different problems that may be encountered. These problems may not be noticed directly by the user, although in some situations a performance deterioration may be apparent. Despite the possible advantages of data sharing, there are many single-user applications that can be used on a LAN. It is important to examine both of these categories of application when considering LAN applications, as they are both relevant in modern organisations.

1.12.1 SINGLE USER APPLICATIONS

Single user applications do not necessarily mean that only one person can use the program on the network at a time; the terms actually means that only one person can access any data file using the application at a time. In this way they are very similar to applications run on standalone systems, and in many cases exactly the same applications software can be used.

Typical single-user applications include:
- Spreadsheets
- Wordprocessors and desktop publishing systems
- Computer aided design
- Financial and statistical analysis.

These systems are creative or analytical in orientation, and perform tasks that would usually be carried out by only one person anyway. Some systems, notably spreadsheet and word processors are becoming available in multi-user forms, but it is far more common to find them as single-user applications.

Relatively few problems are usually encountered with single user applications, and those that do occur are most often related to non-network specific issues, such as installation, hardware incompatibilities etc. This is to be expected, as the application is little different from its standalone counterpart, it is just accessing a disk drive in another room rather than one in the host computer.

Despite this apparent simplicity, the network operating system has to work almost as hard to control single-user applications as it does to control multi-user programs. In fact the network operating system is responsible for controlling every request for disk or printer access, and many other requests for such things as communications, mouse control etc. The operating system does this by mimicking DOS. For example, both NetWare and Banyan Vines take entire control of the system when the workstation is logged on to the network. Whenever the operating system detects a request of any form from the application, it services it immediately, without using any of the DOS routines that would normally be brought into use in a standalone system. This interruption of normal operation raises two issues:

- First, the network operating system is able to do whatever it wants when it receives the request, and it often uses this flexibility to take care of issues such as security, transaction tracking etc.
- Secondly, the network operating system must appear to behave as much like DOS as possible, otherwise there is a possibility that the application program will not function correctly.

This raises the problem of software compatibility. If the application cannot work in conjunction with the chosen network operating system then there is no way that it can be used on the network. It is in the interests of both the network vendor and the application designer to ensure that this does not happen. Inevitably the safest solution is to produce network versions of applications which have been designed and coded to take advantage of the features offered by the network operating system. More importantly, network versions of applications are generally more tolerant of how their requests for disk access, printer output, screen output, keyboard and mouse input etc. are handled.

From the users point of view all of this is transparent, and to all intents and purposes they will see no difference in using the application on a network or a standalone machine.

There are however three issues that need to be noted when considering the situation from the point of view of the supervisor, or the person responsible for managing applications programs on the network.

- First, when the application is purchased it is essential to ensure that it is in fact compatible with the firm's network. This means that it is compatible with both the hardware and the network operating system.
- Secondly, a scheme needs to be devised to cater for the possibility that the application may be executed on different hardware configurations. For example, one user may have a VGA display whilst another may be working with an EGA system. The problem of ensuring that the software functions on both systems

needs to be addressed, and the solution usually involves the use of batch files to ensure that the appropriate driver is loaded when the application is executed.
- The final problem relates to the configuration of the software. Many applications can be configured by the user, especially in terms of default settings used for routine operations. It is often found that different users require different configurations, and unless this issue is resolved severe confusion can result. As with the hardware configuration problem, the solution to this issue is to use batch files to ensure the appropriate defaults are loaded with the application.

1.12.2 MULTI-USER APPLICATIONS

Multi-user applications allow several users to access information from the same data files at the same time. More importantly, they allow several users to update information held in a data file at the same time. This form of concurrent file access introduces a whole array of problems that must be handled by a combination of the application itself and the network operating system. The advantages offered by multi-user applications far outweigh the problems, and it is now generally agreed that the future of the computer network, and possibly computing in general, lies in the direction of such systems.

As explained above, multi-user applications typically have to handle a number of problems and situations that do not occur with single user applications. Thus the software has to be written specifically to take advantage of the features offered by the network. Typical multi-user applications include:

- Databases
- Accounting
- Stock control
- Order processing
- Project planning
- Communications and electronic mail.

The way in which such applications handle multiple concurrent requests is relatively simple. Consider a database program which has four concurrent users, all of whom are accessing the main client database which contains 20,000 records. If user A requests a range of bytes from the database, the request is sent from the workstation to the server. A copy of the request data is then transmitted back to the workstation, and the server temporarily locks that area of the file. If user B now attempts to access the same area, on receiving the request the server will send a message saying that the area is locked. Depending on the precise programming techniques used, the application will then either wait for a short period, try again immediately, or report an error to the user.

This scheme takes care of the possibility that an area of data will be updated by two users at the same time. If such a situation were to occur then there would be no way to determine which changes were correct, as each would be different to the original data.

Such a scheme introduces its own loading on the server, and in severe cases this can significantly degrade the performance of the network. If this is thought to be a possibility, then it is advisable to purchase a dedicated database server. This is a machine similar to a file sever, except that it deals exclusively with database information. Database servers usually require specialist software if they are to be used effectively.

Modern accounting and electronic mail packages run on exactly the same basis as databases, except that the information that is handled is slightly different in format.
- Accounting packages contain tools for manipulating numbers and labels in data fields, and also allow files to be cross-referenced and sorted. They also provide excellent facilities for report production.
- Mail packages provide facilities for creating, writing and reading text files. They generally offer little in the way of sorting or analysis techniques, and very few contain facilities for report production. However, they do provide excellent tools for transferring data, both in the form of mail files and standard data files, and they allow these files to be placed almost anywhere on the network with great ease.

Other multi-user applications allow users to benefit from the fact that they are working together rather than on separate machines. Thus stock control, order processing, project planning and workgroup productivity applications allow users to combine forces much more easily than was ever possible on standalone machines.

1.12.3 MEASURING THE SUCCESS OF AN APPLICATION

Standalone applications are generally considered to be successful if they provide facilities that allow users to improve personal productivity. For example, few people would disagree with the fact that the two most popular PC applications, word processing and spreadsheets, allow users to improve their productivity, especially when contrasted with the manual systems of typewriters and ledger sheets.

Networked applications, and especially multi-user applications can be considered successful if they improve interpersonal productivity. This is based on the idea that one of the main objectives of introducing computers into modern organisations is to help individuals to work together more easily. Thus the network provides the route by which information can be shared, whilst the specific applications provide the methods and techniques for sharing and working with the information.

1.13 NETWORK MANAGEMENT

What exactly is network management? Is it simply a job? What does the network manager have to do? What do they need to know?

Questions of this type abound when the topic of network management is examined, although the answers are not so readily forthcoming. Network management is in fact not simply a job, it is more an approach to maintaining the operation of a network at an adequate level. Network management involves many routine tasks, such as monitoring usage, fault finding, installing new workstations, making backups etc., but it also involves the more important tasks of analysis and planning, so that the network can be expanded or modified when required. The network manager needs to have a broad knowledge not only of computer and network related facts, but also knowledge of how the organisation wants to use the LAN and what they expect to achieve from it.

Unfortunately many LAN managers are not particularly well suited to the task of network management. Many were not originally employed in such a role, and even now may not be so. Indeed many do not particularly cherish the idea of spending the rest of their working lives running around after the proverbial 'end-user'. However, bearing in mind that the average size of a local area network is a mere seven stations, most

organisations are simply unable to justify the expense of employing specialists to manage their LANs. In reality LAN management is a set of functions that someone has acquired by virtue of:
- The proximity of their desk to the file server
- Their knowledge of Lotus 123 or WordPerfect
- A lack of any other volunteers
- Their specialised training and skills in the field (least likely).

Fortunately most LAN operating systems have evolved to the stage where they can be installed and maintained by average PC users, thereby minimising the number of problems that the network manager will face. However, apart from things going wrong there is one other certainty about LANs; they grow, and as with the plant in the film 'Little Shop of Horrors' they consume resources at an ever increasing rate. The original configuration of the LAN's operating system often becomes hopelessly inadequate as the number of users and applications blossoms. The cry of "Feed me!" never lets up.

Obviously there are a plethora of consultants who will gladly share their wealth of opinion for a reasonable fee, but as with most industries an ounce of knowledge is worth a ton of opinion. What is really needed is knowledge of how the operating system can be configured so that it is simple enough to understand and maintain, yet is powerful and flexible enough to handle the majority of options that might be thrown its way.

Chapters 3 and 4 address this problem by illustrating how the LAN operating system can best be configured, and thus how the time spent looking after the network can be put to best use. Chapter 3 looks at the procedure that the network follows when users attach themselves (log-on). Chapter 4 examines the way in which network applications are loaded on the workstation and executed.

Chapter 6 continues along the general theme of network management by looking at some of the tools that are available to help the network manager maintain control of the network, and how the information provided by these tools can be used to maximise the performance of the system. Additionally the problems of planning future growth and usage rates will be considered.

Two final words to consider in conjunction with the topic of network management are *standardise* and *simplify*. These two words together form one of the most important factors that the network manager must consider. They tend to be bandied around by almost every manufacturer and supplier of incompatible products, and therefore the trick is not to take them at face value. For example it is often necessary to use fairly sophisticated techniques to simplify the end-users tasks. Therefore although the end product is a simplification of some aspect of the network, the steps required to achieve the desired result may be far from trivial.

In fact standardisation from a network point of view is not so much about hardware issues as software. In particular the standardisation and simplification is for the user's benefit, not for the benefit of the network manager. These two factors link in to the original discussion of the network, and the way in which it should appear to the user:
- First it should be consistent. If the network manager follows the guidelines laid down in Chapters 3 and 4 then the user interface will indeed be consistent and will adopt a standard format.

- Secondly it should be simple to use. Again if the guidelines are followed then the network will be simple to use. This will of course minimise the problems associated with user error, but will also have the hidden benefit of promoting use of the network and therefore furthering the business aims of the firm.
- Finally, the network should be functional. All of the major networks are functional if implemented correctly. They all have the capability to improve interpersonal computing, and thus provide the facility to enhance the business operations of the organisation.

1.14 SUMMARY

The variety of hardware that is encountered in the network environment is vast. Not only are there the PCs, XTs, ATs, 286s, 386s, 486s and 586s that are found in normal computer environments, but also stars, rings, trees, buses, repeaters, hubs, NICs, and many other network specific devices. Whilst the details of such devices are relevant in many situations, it is much more important for the troubleshooter to be familiar with the overall concepts behind networking, as this will help enormously in the identification of problems, both current and future.

2 The Nature of Network Problems

2.1 WHY IS NETWORK TROUBLESHOOTING DIFFERENT?

Most of the problems that are experienced in the day to day operation of computer networks are little different to those encountered by users of standalone machines. Typically they will take the form of loss of system functionality, or a degradation in the system's performance. Many of the causes of such problems can be traced directly to components of the system that are present in both networked and standalone systems. Thus all of the issues and techniques that are used in troubleshooting standalone personal computers are also valid in the network environment.

However, in certain situations the network will produce its own additional problems. These may manifest themselves in many different forms, for example a software product may execute perfectly on certain workstations whilst refusing to work at all on others. Other problems produce more obvious symptoms, such as an unacceptable loss of overall system performance when more than 80 users are connected to the network etc.

The problem faced by the network troubleshooter is how to identify the root cause of the problem, as the symptoms may exhibit themselves in a totally different area. Thus in addition to having the knowledge and skill to tackle the problem, the network troubleshooter must be able to use intuition, experience, and in many cases guesswork, to locate and isolate faulty components.

Whilst many of the problems are specific to particular network technologies, the methods and techniques that are used to identify, diagnose, isolate and remedy the causes are common to all systems. Therefore, although many of the examples and discussions in this book are based around Novell networks, the same principles apply to other systems.

2.2 A CATEGORISATION OF NETWORK PROBLEMS

The causes of all computer problems, whether they relate to a network or not, can be grouped into three categories:
- Hardware
- Software
- People.

42 CATEGORISATION OF PROBLEMS: HARDWARE

However, when dealing with networks, these categorisations are considerably wider, and contain a greater diversity of systems, than when working with standalone computer systems. The following sections examine these categories in greater detail.

2.2.1 HARDWARE

In the network environment, hardware relates to the computers used as workstations and file servers, backup systems and support peripherals such as printers, plotters etc. In addition, there are the network cards, cabling systems, connectors, interface boxes, transceivers, hubs, multi-station access units, repeaters, boosters and many more. These are all prime candidates for causing problems.

Despite the fact that the range of hardware implemented in any network is vast, it must still obey the fundamental rule that applies to any computing system:

All of the subcomponents must be compatible with one another, and must work reliably if the system is to be effective.

Ensuring that compatibility is maintained throughout the entire network can be difficult, although the task is somewhat eased by the standardisation of various types that is being applied in this area. Compatibility issues tend to cause problems when the network is first installed, or when it is modified in any way. Once the network is running on a day-to-day basis it is expected that any compatibility problems should have been fully resolved.

Figure 2.1 shows a diagrammatic representation of a simple network.

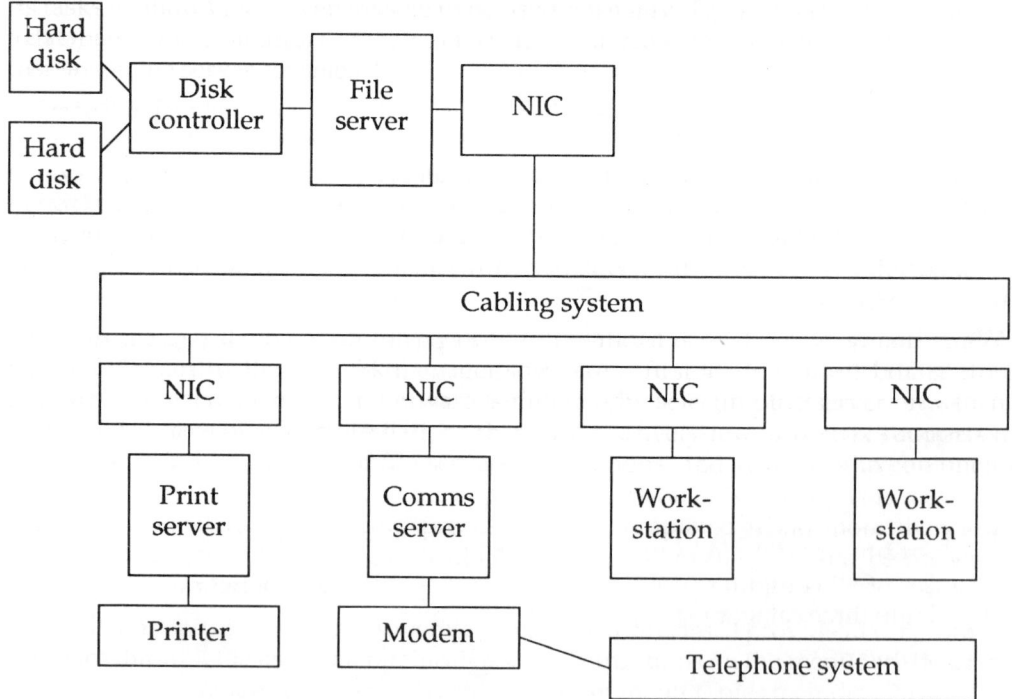

Figure 2.1 Diagrammatic representation of a network

Each component must be directly compatible with the devices to which it is connected; thus the network interface cards must be compatible with the workstations to which they are fitted, and with the cabling system to which it they are connected. This compatibility rule extends throughout the network.

The problem of ensuring that components are reliable does not have a simple solution either. Certain guidelines can be followed which will assist in reducing the number of failures, but rarely can they be prevented altogether:

- Devices and components should only be purchased from reputable suppliers and distributors.
- Components with extended warranty periods are likely to be more reliable than those with shorter guarantees, although this is not always true.
- Regular checks on the network will highlight any components or devices that are behaving erratically. Chapters 6 and 7 address this issue in more detail.

2.2.2 SOFTWARE

A network requires at least four levels of software to co-exist with complete compatibility if it is run effectively and efficiently. These levels are:

- Network operating system
- Workstation operating system
- Software applications
- Data.

The problems associated with configuring standalone PCs to work in the most efficient and effective way can be severe, but the task of installing and implementing these four levels of software, together with the diverse range of hardware, can be significantly more difficult. However, there is a certain level of standardisation that is applied to the software, which in many cases will ease the burden. Such standardisation does have a negative side though, often resulting in decreased flexibility and poor performance.

The following sections examine these software categories in more detail, and highlight some of the compatibility issues that must be addressed.

2.2.2.1 Network operating system

The network operating system (NOS) maintains overall control of the network. It is often comprised of a suite of programs which are executed on the file server, together with one or more programs or drivers that are executed on every workstation connected to the network. Some network operating systems, especially those designed for smaller LANs, do not require a dedicated file server to be present. In this case, the NOS will comprise a main program running in the background of a master workstation, together with a simple driver that runs in the background of every other workstation.

The network operating system determines how the network operates, and what facilities and features it offers to the users. It also effectively determines what applications software can be executed, and what workstation operating systems are supported. Thus it is effectively the key to the entire network's compatibility issues, as it must offer support for the desired applications and workstation operating systems, and must be compatible with the hardware on which it is running.

2.2.2.2 Workstation operating system

The workstation operating system determines what facilities are available to the user on the workstations, and how those facilities are presented. Common workstation operating systems include DOS, OS/2, Unix and Xenix, which are all capable of running on any PC compatible system, as well as the proprietary operating systems for workstations such as the Apple Macintosh, SPARC systems and NeXT cubes.

The workstation operating system must be supported by the network operating system, as the two work very closely. It must also support the desired applications software, as any programs that are run on a network are actually executed on the workstation rather than on the file server.

2.2.2.3 Software applications

It is the applications executed on the network that determine exactly what tasks and processes can be performed. Chapter 1 highlighted the many different types of applications that are available, although some are more often encountered than others. For example, over 95 percent of networks have some form of word processing and spreadsheet software available, whilst database and graphics software is provided on 85% or so. However, more sophisticated applications, such as detailed statistical packages, are found on only 15 percent of networks.

The applications must be compatible with the workstation operating system, and they should also be compatible with the network operating system if they are to be used in a trouble-free manner. This latter condition can sometimes be circumvented if necessary, although this will involve considerable time and effort on the behalf of the network administrator.

2.2.2.4 Data

Data is normally generated by the applications in use, and therefore there are relatively few compatibility problems in this area. However, in some circumstances it may be necessary to transfer data from other sources, which requires that it is compatible with the networked applications that will process it.

Alternatively, it may be possible to translate the data from the original format to a more convenient one for the network. Proprietary systems are available that allow this to be done with a minimum of effort, or alternatively there are many computer bureaux offering a similar service.

2.2.2.5 Software Interactions

All of these software levels interact to some degree, and therefore they should all be compatible with one another. Even minor differences can cause severe operational problems for the network, possibly resulting in failure of the entire system. Figure 2.2 illustrates the main areas of interaction between the different levels.

2.2.3 PEOPLE

No computer system is worth having if there is no one available with the skills to use it. With computer networks, up to three groups of people with different levels of knowledge and ability may need to be involved. These groups are the network design team, the network administration and the users.

THE NATURE OF NETWORK PROBLEMS 45

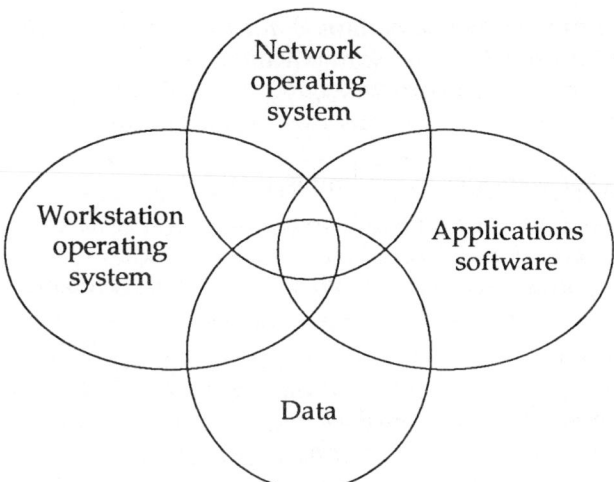

Figure 2.2   Interaction between software levels

2.2.3.1   The design team

The design team should be formed when the idea of installing a network is first raised. It is the responsibility of the design team to ensure that everything is correctly analysed, planned and drafted in terms of all major network decisions.

The design team needs to be drawn from all levels of the organisation, including:

- One or more members of top management, preferably those who have a vested interest in the success of the network implementation.
- Departmental heads who will be responsible for the staff that will use the network when it is fully operational.
- Members of the existing ISD, if there is one, who will have a more accurate picture of the degree of computer awareness within the organisation.
- The LAN managers and supervisors who will be responsible for the day to day running of the network.
- A number of staff members who will actually have to use the network when it is implemented.
- In some organisations, it may be appropriate to bring in outside consultants to assist with the planning and design of the network.

The planning stage is the most critical in the development of the network. Errors and misjudgments made at this level will be felt during the implementation and operational periods, and could have a serious effect on the efficiency and effectiveness of the final system. The planning stage will need to address issues such as:

- What does the organisation expect to achieve through the use of the network?
- For what reason is the network being implemented?
- Are top management aware of the likely costs involved?
- Do top management support the idea of implementing a network?

Once the key issues have been ascertained, the more detailed aspects of the network can be considered. The first issue is the applications that will be used on the system, as these are the most important determinant of the network's functionality. Consideration should be given to issues such as whether existing data needs to be transferred, whether existing software is suitable, and whether commercially available products can be used rather than having software specially commissioned.

Once the required applications have been chosen, appropriate network and workstation operating systems can be acquired that will support these products. Decisions will need to be made regarding the level of expertise that is to be assumed of the users, the type of interface that is required on the workstations etc.

Finally, once the software components have been selected, suitable hardware that is compatible with these systems can be chosen. Selection of hardware will need to take into account the physical size and positioning of the network, the requirements of the software applications and operating systems, user preferences etc.

If the planning and design stage of the network implementation is not completed correctly, there is a very high probability that problems will be experienced with the network once it is installed.

2.2.3.2 The network administrators

The network administrators or supervisors are responsible for the day to day operation of the network. It is their job to ensure that it is working efficiently and effectively, and therefore it is also their job to troubleshoot the system when problems occur.

The network administrators should have a good knowledge of computer hardware and software issues, and particularly of those issues relevant to networking. However, they should not be expected to be experts on every software product used on the network. They should be involved in the design and planning of the network, so that they can use their knowledge and experience to ensure that problems and bad decisions are avoided.

Problems most often occur with the network when the administrators are not supported by management. Ideally, these staff need to be kept informed of the latest developments, they need to have good access to information and products; they need to attend briefings and seminars on appropriate topics, and to do this they must have the backing of management.

2.2.3.3 Users

As mentioned previously, the causes of network problems can vary greatly. The problems may be due to hardware issues, such as physical failure of components or poor connections between different devices. They may be due to software issues, such as incorrectly configured or installed applications, conflicts between software systems etc.

However, when asked what is considered to be the biggest cause of network problems, many network administrators will say it is the end users. The problems experienced with the network may be directly due to their actions, for example when a user accidentally erases all of their files. Alternatively they may be indirectly due to the users, for example the problems caused when a user wants particular settings to be automatically chosen when using a certain application which are different to the settings required by everyone else in the organisation.

It must be realised that the network has been implemented for the benefit of the end-users, and without them the network manager probably wouldn't have a job. Unlike the computers that make up the network, the end-users are often unpredictable and in many cases this unpredictability is due to a lack of understanding of how the network has been designed to operate, which in turn leads to problems of users wanting to go beyond the original design limitations of the system. Other problems occur with users who have a fear of all things technical. Unfortunately this type of phobia is a reality, and is compounded by the unintuitive interfaces used on many computer systems and networks.

To counter these problems, the users need to be educated. They need to know what the network is, why it has been implemented, what the organisation expects to achieve through the network etc. Many users also feel more confident if they know some of the technical aspects relating to the system, such as where their data is stored, basic principles behind the operation of the system etc. All of this information will help them to appreciate why the network behaves as it does, which in turn will make them more patient when performance is suffering.

Users also need to know where to get help when problems occur, and it is the LAN managers responsibility to ensure that help is actually available for those who require it.

Many user related problems are due to the way in which the network operates, either because the system is too complex, or because it is not immediately obvious how the user can achieve the result they desire. It is the network manager's task to make the network and the workstations connected to it as easy to comprehend and use as possible. It is not necessarily their responsibility to teach every package to every user, although they should ensure that the users have access to appropriate training to a sufficient standard in the products they use. The network manager's primary responsibility is to present the offerings of the network in a manner that is (in order of importance):

– Consistent
– Simple To Use
– Functional.

This can be achieved in many different ways, some of which will be addressed in later chapters. If the network manager is efficient and effective, and implements the network in such a way as to comply with the above guidelines, the number of problems encountered will be significantly reduced.

2.3 TEN SITUATIONS OF NETWORK PROBLEMS

The following ten situations outline some of the more common problems that can be encountered with networks, and it is quite likely that readers will already have suffered with one or more of the scenarios. Each can be fully diagnosed and solved using the techniques and methods outlined in later chapters, although even at this stage it is expected that readers should be able to make an initial diagnosis as to the most likely cause of each problem, and whether it relates to hardware, software, people or a combination of these factors. A sample solution to each problem follows the question.

Note that some of these solutions are not necessarily simple, nor in some cases are they inexpensive. In fact it is often very difficult and expensive to fully resolve network problems, as the root cause may be due to the basic design of the system. Thus there are situations in which it is simply not cost effective to remedy the whole problem, and the most satisfactory result that can be achieved will involve a fine balance between cost and network reliability/performance. One of the skills required by a network troubleshooter is the ability to determine whether or not a problem can be economically solved, and if not, where the tradeoffs can most easily be made to achieve satisfactory results.

2.3.1   A DATA SECURITY PROBLEM

The problem:

> An EtherNet LAN is being used in conjunction with Novell Netware, supporting 62 terminals and over 3000 users in an academic institution. The majority (60 percent) of the users are students, 30 percent are either academic or research staff, and the remaining 10 percent are administrative staff.
>
> The network started out as a 12 terminal LAN for the express use of research staff, but has grown in a haphazard fashion over the last two years. Security is controlled through the use of individual access controls, with security equivalences used to simplify the task of allocating rights for students.
>
> Problems have recently been encountered with students gaining access to confidential data stored on the file server. This data is required by a number of academic and administrative staff, so must remain in a centralised position. The problems appear to have started when one of the students joined the academic staff in the role of network manager, although the person involved denies that they have changed the security rights of any of the students.
>
> *What is the likely cause of the security breach?*

The solution:

> The problems are due to the fact that security equivalences have been used to control access rights. When the new network manager was assigned supervisor rights, in order that he could perform legitimate network maintenance and monitoring work, any other students with security equivalence to this person also gained supervisor rights. Thus a number of unauthorised users now have access to any data or application on the network.
>
> To resolve the problem a new approach to allocating and maintaining security rights must be taken. This is covered in detail in a later chapter.

2.3.2   A NETWORK RELIABILITY PROBLEM

The problem:

> A metal fabrications company use a LAN on their shop floor in order to monitor and control workloads, order filling, warehouse stock levels etc. Four machine rooms have terminals, in addition to which each contains a number of milling machines, lathes etc. A coaxial based cabling system has been used in conjunction with ArcNet devices to give a tree topology.
>
> As soon as the LAN was installed a number of problems were noticed. Occasionally

the entire system would hang, requiring the server to be reinitialised before it could again be used. More common were intermittent problems with the terminals in the machine rooms, which manifested themselves in the form of either corrupt data transmissions, inability to use certain software at particular times etc. Cards have been swapped and machines moved around, and the original network vendor has been called in to double check the hardware and software. However, all of the machines work perfectly when tested, but refuse to work correctly in situ

What is wrong with the network?

The solution:

The problems experienced in this particular situation are due to an incorrect choice of cable when the network was first installed. Any medium- or heavy-duty machinery generates a great deal of electrical noise or interference, which will affect any electrical signals that are carried in nearby wires or cables. Twisted pair cable is extremely susceptible to interference of this form and cannot be used in such situations. Coaxial cable, contrary to some reports, is also quite susceptible to problems, and again should not be used near machinery of this type.

The solution to the problem requires a complete recabling of the shop floor section of the LAN. The only suitable cabling system in this particular case is fibre-optic, as it is totally unaffected by electrical noise. However, fibre-optic is currently the most expensive cabling option, and will cost many times more than coaxial to install.

2.3.3 INCORRECT PRINTER OPERATIONS

The problem:

A LAN manager is becoming frustrated with his users as they continually complain of problems in printing, either that the printers do not work correctly, or that the applications do not send their output to the correct printer.

The LAN applications have been set up to default to particular printers, in order that they make the best use of the available facilities. Thus the DTP system will use the laser printer, the spreadsheet uses the dot matrix and the CAD system uses the plotter.

Users are able to select other printers for each application simply by choosing the appropriate menu options from each program, and then telling the network to redirect the output to the appropriate device, again through a menu. However, very few follow this procedure correctly which results in the problems mentioned above.

How can the problems be overcome?

The solution:

It is not necessarily a good idea to install applications so that they automatically default to a particular printer, irrespective of the user or of the workstation in use. Two approaches could be taken in this particular situation to remedy the problem.

Either the network can be set up so that every application will always print to a local printer. Thus every user knows that their data will be printed on the nearest printer, whatever that is. This can cause problems if there is a wide mix of different printers in use.

Alternatively the network can be set up so that the user is forced to specify which printer they want to use before the application is executed. Thus the user will always know exactly where the data is being printed, and on which type of printer. This has the advantage of providing the ability to set the application up so that it formats its data correctly for the chosen printer.

2.3.4 BACKUP PROCEDURE REQUIREMENTS

The problem:

An ArcNet based LAN has been set up with a very large file server and over 100 workstations. The data stored on the server changes regularly, and is very important to the continued operation of the business. Therefore it is backed up to tape every evening. As the tape streamer is connected directly to the file server, it is necessary to down the network in order to perform the backup. All staff have been notified that this will occur at 6:30pm every evening, and that a warning will be issued by the system manager five minutes before the network is shut down. Unfortunately the network manager has on two occasions forgotten to post this warning, leading to several users losing data.

How can the likelihood of this happening again be minimised?

The solution:

The location of the tape streamer is perhaps not the most sensible, as it is impossible to backup the server while the network is operating. One solution is to move the streamer to one of the workstations, which will allow the backup to be performed without downing the network, although there will be a noticeable performance loss.

An alternative strategy is to make use of the time slotting capabilities offered by most network operating systems. These facilities allow the network manager to limit access by users to particular times. Thus it is possible to deny access to all users between the times of 6:30pm and 7:30pm, or whatever time span is required. The advantage of using this technique is that the system will automatically produce the warning message at a predefined time before it shuts down.

2.3.5 BACKUP RESTORATION

The problem:

A 330MB file server has just been destroyed in a computer centre fire. Also destroyed was the tape streamer, system unit and a number of workstations. Fortunately a full backup is available, which the network manager attempts to restore using a new tape streamer onto a brand new file server.

However, the backup appears to be corrupt with the software continually producing errors and refusing to read the data. A different tape streamer was tried and produced the same reports.

What is the most likely cause of this problem, and can it be remedied?

THE NATURE OF NETWORK PROBLEMS 51

The solution:

There are two equally likely causes of problems in this situation.

First, problems have been known to occur in reading a tape backed up with one streamer onto another one. This is due to minor mechanical adjustments which are different between the two devices. This can be overcome by calling in an engineer to make the adjustments so that the data can be restored correctly.

Secondly, there is no guarantee that the backup has not been corrupted. Certain combinations of backup hardware/software have been known to produce unreadable tapes, although they appear to work satisfactorily at the time. If the tape has been corrupted then it is possible that the data can be recovered, although it is unlikely. The only way to ensure that this does not happen is to attempt to restore a backup onto another machine. Obviously a secondary machine should be used for this operation in case the backup is corrupt and therefore cannot be restored.

2.3.6 RESTORING USER INFORMATION

The problem:

An academic institution has recently encountered problems with their file server which culminated in the server failing. A backup was reinstated and the majority of the data was intact. However, all of the passwords, access rights and security clearances associated with the users do not appear to be in force any longer. As there are over 4000 users on the network the recreation of this data is a long and tedious task.

Is there a practical way to reinstate this information?

The solution:

Most backup software will only make a copy of the data and program files on any disk, including file server storage media. As the user information is not stored in such a format on the majority of network operating systems, it is not backed up by the software. Therefore, there is no simple way to recreate the information if it has been lost.

Utilities are often supplied to get around the problem. For example, Novell's *BINDFIX* programs allow the network manager to control the Bindery information (the data relating to users accounts, passwords etc) so that it can be easily backed up and restored as necessary. Other operating systems provide similar facilities.

2.3.7 POWER FLUCTUATIONS

The problem:

Power fluctuations are causing major problems in a large consultancy organisation. The company is based in a rather old building, and the wiring system is inadequate for the loading placed upon it. Thus when the photocopier is switched on there is a temporary drop in the power supplied to nearby devices.

This is most noticeable when considering the computers, as several workstations have a tendency to lock up if nearby electrical equipment is used. The network manager is concerned that these problems may affect the file server, which has so far remained unaffected.

What can be done to improve matters?

The solution:

This problem can be tackled in two different ways. The first is really just a temporary solution, requiring the use of an uninterruptable power supply to power the file server. This will ensure that there is no data loss nor interruption of network operation due to the power problems.

However, there is a more fundamental problem in this particular instance relating to the condition of the overall cabling of the building. The only satisfactory solution is to have the building re-wired or alternatively move to new premises, as the power fluctuations will still affect the operation of the workstations.

2.3.8 SOFTWARE APPLICATIONS IN THE NETWORK ENVIRONMENT

The problem:

Certain software products which are essential to the functioning of a publishing business cannot be used on network workstations as they simply will not execute. They report a variety of errors, including invalid drivers, interrupt conflicts, fatal system errors and memory errors.

If the computers are disconnected from the LAN and used as standalone machines then the programs execute properly.

Can anything be done to allow the programs to run in the LAN environment?

The solution:

The problems are almost certainly due either to the network drivers conflicting with the software, or more likely the network drivers leaving an insufficient amount of memory for the programs to use.

If the drivers conflict with the software then it is very unlikely that the programs can be made to run on the LAN without upgrading or altering either the software or the network operating system.

If the problems are due to insufficient memory being available then there are a number of steps that can be taken to produce a solution. First, the amount of memory installed into each workstation can be increased to 640K or more as necessary. Secondly, all extraneous utilities, such as SideKick, can be removed. Thirdly, a utility can be used to load the network drivers into high memory, freeing more of the base 640K for the application to use.

2.3.9 CABLE DAMAGE

The problem:

An oil company has a network installed across a large campus on the South coast. Intermittent problems are caused by LAN cables being accidentally damaged or disconnected. The job of sequentially examining every section of LAN cable to find the damage is an immense task, so not surprisingly the LAN manager is becoming frustrated with the frequency of calls.

Is there any product that can be used to make his job easier?

The solution:

There are a number of network orientated products that allow problems such as this one to be easily identified and pin-pointed. The products take the form of both hardware and software, and use a technique known as Time-Domain Reflectometry (TDR) to locate cable breaks or disconnections. Additionally, many of these products are able to diagnose other faults in network cabling systems, even those that are not producing obvious symptoms.

2.3.10 A NETWORK VIRUS

The problem:

The town library recently suffered a virus attack on its network which affected data on the file server. After seemingly eradicating the effects of the attack from the file server of the LAN, the network manager was astonished to see the virus reappear only three days later. The speed of infection was amazing, corrupting over 1,800 files in a little over 20 minutes. The cleanup operation had taken three days before, so it looks as though it would take at least that long this time.

What special steps should the manager take when removing the virus from the network to ensure that it is not infected a third time?

The solution:

The problem with viruses is that they spread incredibly quickly. The most likely cause of reinfection in this particular case is that although it was removed from the file server and workstations, it may well have infected some of the floppy disks used by network users. Thus when they were used again at a later date, the virus was again able to infect the entire network.

To minimise the likelihood of this happening a second time, the following steps should be taken:

- The network should be isolated from all outside connections immediately. This means breaking all gateway, modem and dial-in connections that may have been made. This limits the spread of the virus to other networks.
- The network should then be shut down quickly, but in a controlled manner to minimise data loss.
- The virus should be eradicated from the file server, and from the hard disks of all network workstations. During this process none of the workstations can be used or the virus may reinfect the system.
- Any floppy disk that is likely to be used in a workstation must be checked for the existence of the virus. This includes floppies used before the first attack as well as more recent ones.

- The tape backups should if possible be checked to see if they are infected. If they are then they should be treated with great care, and if at all possible discarded completely in favour of older, uninfected, backups.

Once all possible sources of the virus have been checked, the operation of the network can be reinstated.

2.4 CAUSES AND EFFECTS

The most common causes of network problems have already been discussed above. However, the way in which these problems will be felt is also important. Generally speaking the problems associated with networks may affect the system in three different ways:

- Loss of functionality
- Inconvenience
- Causing future problems.

2.4.1 LOSS OF FUNCTIONALITY

Problems resulting in a total or partial loss of functionality are generally considered to be the most serious. They will significantly affect the operation of the network, and may even affect the overall continued operation of the organisation. Such problems can usually be overcome, although this may involve some trade off.

For example it may not be possible to connect 246 workstations to the chosen LAN and have all of them working reliably all of the time, so either the number has to be reduced or the intermittent loss of functionality of certain workstations must be accepted. Alternatively, a new LAN can be purchased which does indeed support the required number of nodes. This is a typical example of a loss of functionality due to a design/configuration problem, as a different LAN would have been chosen if it was thought likely that 246 terminals would be required.

Other problems that result in a loss of functionality may be due to hardware failures or operating system conflicts or incompatibilities. They may even be due to the applications that are in use. The ease with which such problems can be diagnosed and solved depends on many factors, not least the ability and experience of the troubleshooter, the configuration of the LAN, and the budget allocated for such repairs.

2.4.2 INCONVENIENCE

Problems that result in inconvenience are typified by comments relating to performance, or the lack thereof. Performance is certainly a secondary issue to functionality, but it also happens to be one of the most subjective areas of computing. Bearing in mind the relativity of the concept, there are few ways to objectively determine a network's performance. It may feel slower today than it did yesterday, but at what stage does the threshold of usefulness get crossed. One organisation's system may be slower than another's, but they are both unique and can seldom be compared directly to each other.

Performance can often be improved at relatively little cost (bar the consultant's fees) once the bottlenecks have been identified. Unfortunately users tend to measure network performance against the standalone 25MHz 80386 they have sitting at home, and the network manager usually has his bonus determined according to such objective measures. These are unrealistic, as most networks are not implemented to improve the efficiency of personal computing, but rather the efficiency of *inter-personal* computing.

2.4.3 FUTURE PROBLEMS

Many faults and incompatibilities in a network may not immediately be obvious, but over a period of time they become more and more dominant until they affect the operation of the entire system. This is typical of the situation in which the LAN is overstretched, and has too many workstations attached. As more and more use is made of such a network, the performance will worsen until finally the entire system crashes, possibly with disastrous consequences. If steps had been taken before the situation developed to this level, the network would have remained operational.

In fact it is often possible to get better performance out of a well thought-out and planned network than from a stand-alone machine. This is purely due to the way in which the network is designed, implemented and configured, in other words with suitable *foresight* and *forethought* network performance need not suffer. This leads in to another point, namely that there is a danger of network management preoccupying themselves with short-term issues, and being too restricted by current budgets, a situation which is doomed to failure. Whilst there is a need to manage the network on a day to day basis, it is essential to look to the future with special emphasis on anticipating the ways in which the network will grow and change. Failure to do this will lead to an unnecessary number of problems occurring later.

It is important to remember that the network only came into existence because it was seen as a solution to an already existing problem; mainframe technology was simply too expensive for most organisations, and PCs and mini-computers were unable to share either peripherals or data without sophisticated hardware and software. Thus the network provided an ideal solution at the time as it allowed organisations to invest in PC technology and gain a similar flexibility to that offered by the most powerful mainframes.

However, since those early days the complexity of personal computer LANs has increased dramatically. No longer is it simply a case of sharing peripherals and data files on an ad-hoc basis. Current networks offer a whole variety of features and facilities that allow users to do almost anything they want, from running multi-user applications to using *voice mail* to talk directly to other LAN users, wherever they may be.

Because of this volatility, which is inherent in the network environment, it is essential for network managers to continually re-evaluate the ability of the network to deal with both current and future requirements.

- Current requirements and problems can be addressed in a fairly straightforward way. New applications or workstations can be installed with relative ease, hardware and software failures can be tackled with existing tools and techniques.
- Future requirements may be more difficult to quantify. How is the network manager to know what new power-hungry applications will be required in two years time? How can they begin to estimate the number of new workstations that will be added to the LAN next year?

To successfully tackle these problems it will be necessary for the network manager to be regularly informed of all decisions taken by top management that may result in additional loadings on the system.

Inherent to the whole issue of being able to identify any future problem areas is the day to day monitoring of the network. It is only by monitoring various indicators and by understanding these indicators sufficiently that the network manager will be in a position to predict and prevent problems before they become an issue to the users.

Similarly the concept of regular monitoring will provide data which can be used as both a guide and a justification for the upgrading of the network's components. It will also provide a basis for the ongoing planning that should be an integral part of the network manager's job.

In fact the biggest mistake a network manager can make is to shortchange the planning. Networks are a strategic resource that must work in conjunction with other corporate resources, including the users. This is emphasised by the fact that among many network troubleshooters and consultants, it is generally agreed that

80 percent of network problems are directly attributable to inadequate planning and configuration.

Thus by designing and implementing a system in a logical manner, with sufficient flexibility to cope with future expansion and modification, the vast majority of network problems can be prevented. However, the design and implementation of a network is not a trivial process. It is not necessarily something that can be done in a few days, or even weeks, and very rarely can a series of predefined steps be followed that will produce a design for a network that is optimal.

Many suppliers currently offer to install newly purchased networks for the customer and to get them up and running as part of their overall service. Whilst this is a vast improvement on the days when they delivered a big box overflowing with disks and very thick manuals and left the network manager to it, it is still inadequate. 'Up and running' is a far cry from 'working efficiently'. Thus it is essential that the network administrator applies adequate time and effort to initial and ongoing planning and design for the network.

2.5 SUMMARY

The nature of network problems is a diverse area, ranging from hardware failure to configuration and software incompatibilities. In addition there are problems due to user ignorance and insufficient help and assistance from network suppliers and consultants, placing network managers in a situation beyond their scope and ability.

It is therefore essential for both users and supervisors to be aware of the potential problem areas, how to avoid them with good planning and forethought, and how to deal with the inevitable problems that will arise at some time.

3 The Network Access Procedure

3.1 INTRODUCTION

The relationship between a network manager and the end user can often become fraught. Indeed if it weren't for the end users there would be virtually no problems with the network at all! Unfortunately, it is impossible to take this drastic remedial step, and the problems caused by the end users will have to be accepted, or preferably prevented.

Prevention of user-related problems can most easily be achieved by configuring the network in a logical, easy-to-use way. Chapter 2 summarised this approach by stating that the network interface should be:

- Consistent
- Simple to use
- Functional.

This chapter deals with the techniques, methods and issues that the network manager needs to be aware of when configuring the network. In this sense, configuration refers to the software side of things, rather than the hardware interconnections. As this subject can be confusing when discussed only on a theoretical level, a number of examples have been included to illustrate specific points. These examples have been drawn from a network based on Novell's NetWare, and so make use of NetWare specific features. However, all the concepts are equally valid in any network environment, and many of the examples will differ only slightly when translated to other systems such as LAN Manager or Banyan Vines.

3.2 FOUNDATIONS

Architects spend hours planning, designing and drawing foundations for any building they are working with. Only if the foundations are solid will the building stand safely and resist the natural forces that are exerted upon it. Conversely, if the foundations are insufficient or defective, it is likely that the whole thing will come crashing down.

The same principle applies to computer networks. When the network is first installed, it must be configured both in terms of its hardware and software. This configuration phase should involve detailed planning that will highlight exactly what the organisation expects to gain from the network, how the network is to be used, how the users should access the network facilities etc. Once these issues have been resolved, the network can be set up in the most appropriate way to meet its goals, and hence the foundations of the software configuration can be set in place.

In the computer environment the foundations of the connection to the network may be found in three files:

- CONFIG.SYS
- AUTOEXEC.BAT
- SHELL.CFG

These files are often further supplemented by login scripts and a variety of batch files and menu systems. However, it is the contents of these three files that effectively determine how the network operates, and in particular, how it interfaces to the users. If they are correct from the start, then there should be few problems. Fortunately, if they are incorrect they can be modified with relative ease, unlike the architect who must destroy the building to alter the foundations.

While there may be the temptation to optimise the operations of all the various PCs attached to the LAN, doing so can often cause its own headaches as things quickly become more difficult to maintain and support. Thus whilst reading through the following discussion please bear in mind that it is often more useful to just have a couple of fairly standard, but not necessarily optimised, options in use.

Before anything else, the user needs to be able to access the local area network. This may seem like a statement of the obvious, but there is a big difference between simply attaching to the network and establishing a comprehensive user operating environment.

It takes time to set up a user environment, and while it is tempting to get users logged onto the system as soon as the network has been generated and installed, it is strongly advised that some time is spent establishing a user-friendly environment. Not all users are going to be hot-shot programmers who instinctively know how to translate the system manuals. In actual fact the majority of users on a network are not very computer literate at all.

A network's access procedures will determine the relative success or failure of a particular system, as users will be unlikely to make use of a poorly configured network.

As with people the intent of the workstation needs to be very precisely conveyed in order for the file server to be able to satisfy its requirements. If utilised to its true potential the network access procedure provides an excellent opportunity for clearing up many subtle problems way before they ever become an issue.

Before the actual examples are discussed two issues need to be explained, and they are:-

- Network drive mappings
- Network trustee rights.

3.3 NETWORK DRIVE MAPPINGS

The MAP command, or its equivalent, is the most crucial command available via the network operating system. It is absolutely essential that the basic concepts and usage of this command are understood. This section looks at the essential features of this com-

mand, with particular emphasis on the distinction between the two different modes of usage, namely
- Simple drive mappings
- Search drive mappings

3.3.1 SIMPLE DRIVE MAPPINGS

In this mode the MAP command is used to assign a drive designator to a volume and/or subdirectory on the file server. For example:-

```
MAP H:=SERVER1:SYS\PUBLIC\APPS\WP52
```

This command will assign the drive designator H: to the WordPerfect applications subdirectory on volume SYS of the file server SERVER1. In other words every time the user refers to the H: drive the operations performed will in fact happen to that specified subdirectory. Therefore H: is used as an abbreviation for the expanded subdirectory name.

3.3.2 SEARCH DRIVE MAPPINGS

While simple drive mappings are useful, search drives mappings are considerably more powerful in the network environment. They allow any file in the specified subdirectory to be accessed without referencing its DOS path name, irrespective of the setting of the current drive.

Whilst similar in function to the DOS PATH statement, the MAP command is not limited to .EXE, .COM, and .BAT files. In fact when logging into a file server, the login program replaces all DOS path assignments with appropriate NetWare search mappings.

Unfortunately the inherent power behind these search drive mappings leads many new network managers to define an excessive amount of them. This may be all very well when the network is small and only a couple of applications are supported, but as the network grows so too do the problems associated with this approach.

First, the network manager is restricted to a maximum of 16 search mappings and even this maximum is on occasions unobtainable. Secondly the operation of the network becomes unpredictable as files are executed and utilised from unintended source subdirectories.

Thus it is recommended that search mappings are grouped into two distinct categories:
- Generic search mappings
- Application specific search mappings.

Once this categorisation has been established, the two groups should be handled in totally different ways.

3.3.2.1 Generic search mappings

The generic search mappings should be defined up front for all users, and these definitions should not be altered or modified in any way whilst the user is connected to the network. Failure to observe this precaution may lead to unpredictable results. The generic search mapping group will usually consist of the following:-
- A mapping to the relevant DOS files

- A mapping to the subdirectory containing the batch files used to access the applications on the network
- A mapping to the subdirectory containing all of the commonly used utility programs
- A mapping to the \PUBLIC subdirectory which contains all of the Novell command-line utilities and programs
- A mapping to the \LOGIN subdirectory for the purposes of attaching to and detaching from the network
- A mapping to the Root subdirectory is usually included in order to handle those ill-behaved applications that insist on placing vital information about themselves in the Root.

It is important to understand how the LOGIN program modifies the user's current DOS PATH definition prior to executing the system Login script, and it is also important to understand the rules for inserting, deleting and overwriting search mappings. It should also be remembered that the search mappings are searched in a sequence corresponding to their search numbers, ie S1, S2, S3, etc. Thus S1 has the highest priority and will be searched first; S2 has the next highest priority and so will only be searched if the required files cannot be found on the S1 search path. Similar rules apply to search mappings S3 onwards.

3.3.2.2 Application specific search mappings

The generic mappings cater for all basic operations that will be required on all workstations, irrespective of which application is being executed. Once these have been established, all that is required when running an application is:

- Define any application specific search mappings prior to running the application of choice
- Remove the application specific search mapping definitions after finishing with that application.

The net result is that at no stage should there be any search mappings defined that are not required. Additionally at no stage should there be any need to exceed the maximum allowable number of mappings regardless of the growth rate of the network.

Examples of these procedures in practice are illustrated later on in this chapter.

3.3.3 CONTROLLING NETWORK DRIVE MAPPINGS

It is advised that the MAP INSERT command is not used. Doing so will destroy the generic nature of the set up unless extreme care is taken, and all the implications are fully understood. The reason for this is that MAP INSERT first moves S1, S2, S3 etc down one level and then creates a new S1 mapping. Thus the old S1 becomes S2, the old S2 becomes S3 etc. All the prioritisation that was implemented by defining the search mappings using the process outlined above has been lost.

A far better idea is to plan the network such that this command is never required, and the following sections illustrate how this can be achieved. This advice contradicts that given in most network management textbooks, but has been found to work in many different practical situations.

A drive mapping can be removed with the MAP DELETE command, which requires as a parameter the number of the drive mapping to be removed. For example, MAP DELETE S7: would delete search drive mapping S7, then move S8 onwards up one level. If MAP INSERT has been used there is no easy way to determine the number of the required mapping unless the system interactively checks the machine's current status.

There is one situation where the use of MAP INSERT is required, and that is when the users of the network have DOS PATH settings that they wish to retain during the network session, and subsequently restore after returning to standalone operation following logging out of the network. In such a situation, *all* the following examples should be changed so that every issuing of the MAP command reads MAP INSERT (with the obvious exception of any MAP DELETE commands). As discussed previously, the key point is to maintain standardisation across the network; choose a technique and stick with it throughout the entire network. If different methods are employed in different areas then it is almost inevitable that chaos will ensue.

3.4 NETWORK TRUSTEE RIGHTS

The network operating system allows the allocation or revocation of file and directory privileges either on an individual basis or on a group basis. Some of the specifics as to these privileges are discussed during the later chapter on security issues. At this stage however, it is important to have a brief look at the concept of trustee rights as they apply to the configuration of the users environment.

Again, the power of this feature is such that novice network managers are often tempted into an excessive application of individual trustee right assignments. This leads to inconsistent security procedures, and a situation which becomes difficult to both maintain and to troubleshoot.

The recommendation is again to categorise the rights that are required on the local area network. In this case the categorisation is simple, the two cases are:

- Trustee assignments that will only ever be granted to a single user
- All other trustee assignments.

3.4.1 INDIVIDUAL TRUSTEE RIGHTS

Individual trustee right assignments are easy to distinguish. There are ONLY two possible rights that need ever be granted to an individual user. They are:

- Full rights to a private or home subdirectory within which the user has the ability to store, erase, copy, execute or edit any file that may be kept there
- Read, open, and search rights to the subdirectory containing the user's private LOGIN SCRIPT file which is executed as they log into the network.

All other trustee rights should be acquired by virtue of the individual's membership of a relevant group.

3.4.2 GROUP TRUSTEE RIGHTS

Rather than spending hours specifying that each user has the ability to look at and use the files in the \UTILS subdirectory, it makes far more sense to simply assign those rights to the group EVERYONE once and once only.

Whilst this concept is easily understood, it is important that the network manager utilises exactly the same ideas on a more subtle level. For example even if at this stage in the corporation's life there is only one person who should ever be able to access the payroll file, it makes no sense to allocate trustee rights to that user on an individual basis.

People move on, and when they do it becomes a time consuming task to make a record of all the relevant rights that were given to that person, before transferring those trustee rights to the replacement personnel. Remember, the one thing that can be guaranteed is that the network will grow, and as it does more people will want or need access to currently installed applications.

It is much more efficient to simply add or remove a user from a group than it is to try and maintain a large set of individual security privileges. Additionally, security breaches can be more easily identified as it will not be necessary to wade through all the users individual assignments; all that is required is a quick search of appropriate groups to determine whether or not they contain unauthorised members.

An added advantage of this approach is that the addition of new users is accomplished in record time as privileges may be obtained simply by virtue of membership to a set of job-related groups.

The generic trustee rights assignments should be gathered together under the group EVERYONE invented for this specific purpose. The assignments should be constructed in such a way that additional rights are made available to the user by virtue of his membership to a particular group. It is wise to create and use these groups on an application specific basis.

A number of different utilities are available that allow the system to determine membership of groups on an interactive basis. Some of these are commercial products, whilst others are shareware or public domain. It is important to have access to such a utility in order to make the most of the grouping features offered by the major network operating systems. The examples given later in this chapter make use of such a shareware utility called NWHAT, which works with Novell NetWare systems. This simple to use utility allows batch files to be written in such a way that they are able to intelligently take appropriate actions based on a users membership to a particular group.

3.5 A TYPICAL NETWORK ACCESS PROCEDURE

Having discussed some of the concepts and issues to be borne in mind when setting up the network environment, the next step is to look at the actual practicalities of how to implement all those ideas. The various techniques and methods are illustrated with some practical examples. By necessity these examples have been constructed for use within a Novell networking environment, however as stated previously, it should be borne in mind that exactly the same principles apply to other network operating systems.

The examples have been developed specifically to illustrate the concepts that have been mentioned and should be used as a framework within which an environment can be constructed to suit particular requirements. Some of the techniques used in the examples may not appear to be consistent; this is intentional, as the examples have been produced to illustrate the various ways in which similar effects can be achieved. Thus before using this framework as the basis for an environment, it is recommended that a decision is taken regarding which techniques are to be used in each situation.

During the process of modifying and customising these routines, there are a few key points that should be considered. These ground rules help ensure that the ideas of standardisation and simplification are adhered to as much as possible:

3.5.1 PREVENTION IS BETTER THAN CURE

The examples presented will show how many network specific problems have been anticipated and catered for in advance of them occurring.

3.5.2 MODULARITY

The examples illustrate the use of a modular design. Generic routines are only coded once, thus enabling the network manager to concentrate on those aspects of the network that require special treatment, rather than continually re-inventing the wheel.

3.5.3 BLACK-BOXING

If a batch file takes longer than two minutes to put together (assuming the writers know what they are doing), then it is too complex and needs to be broken down into a number of simpler components. Complex files require complex maintenance and complex explanations. Control files should be as function specific as possible.

Similarly, a network menu structure should not contain more than seven to ten options. If it does it becomes unwieldy to use and more difficult to learn. If more options are required, then a series of sub-menus should be created that can show further detail to those people who require it. This is the concept of *black-boxing*. It is a programming philosophy which hides confusing details from those who do not wish or need to see them.

3.5.4 COMMENTED CODE

The idea of adding explanatory comments seems obvious. However as with regular backups, it tends to get overlooked as people rush to get the job done. It is perfectly true to say that a section of code will work without any comments at all (in fact it will probably execute more quickly too), but the real question is whether the code will be easily understood, and thus maintained six months later, perhaps by someone else.

With these points in mind, the following sections examine the key components of the software configuration that play a part in the network access procedure.

3.6 THE CONFIG.SYS FILE

Apart from the machine specific requirements, the CONFIG.SYS file needs to address a minimum of three issues.

3.6.1 FILES

Depending on the applications that will be running, it is necessary to specify the maximum number of open files that the workstation may handle at any one time. Three points to bear in mind are:
- Remember that the network itself is an application that needs consideration as well. In other words add at least two to the number of files required by the most demanding application that will be run on the workstation.

64   TYPICAL ACCESS PROCEDURE

- Due to a bug in certain versions of DOS 3.2, the FILES value should always be set to an odd number. Failure to do so can cause DOS to reserve the maximum allowable memory for file handles. However most memory checking programs will report no problem.
- If a multi-tasking environment is being used, such as Windows or DesqView, then sufficient provision should be made for situations in which multiple applications will be running.

3.6.2   BUFFERS

The number of buffers specified will also need to cater for the most demanding application on the network. A number of publications mention that because Novell has its own buffering system this value may be set to 0, thereby saving quite a large chunk of memory without incurring any performance penalty.

This comment is valid, although it only applies to networked hard disk drive accesses; if the application resides in part on a local hard or floppy disk drive, or even stores data locally, then extreme caution must be exercised when using a value of 0.

A second problem can occur if this option is pursued, and that relates to the installation of certain applications. For example, WordStar will refuse to install itself unless it is able to detect a sufficiently high value for the DOS BUFFERS. There are other packages that can give their own problems, however it may well be found that the system will work with significantly lower values than may at first be thought.

On a number of occasions it has been found that some of the larger ESDI and SCSI hard disk drives can cause major headaches with regard to DOS BUFFERS. For example, consider a system using a 380MB ESDI drive on a local station. Due to the fact that there are more than 1024 cylinders on the hard drive, it is necessary to increase the sector size in order to circumvent DOS limitations. This in turn affects the size of the BUFFERS created by DOS, and the net result is that each time the DOS BUFFERS value is incremented by 1, a massive 8K of memory is consumed. In such cases it is preferable to use a good disk caching system instead of a high BUFFERS setting, as this will most likely provide the best solution.

3.6.3   ENVIRONMENT SPACE

The DOS 3.3 default of only 160 bytes of environment space is not sufficient for the successful management of a network. This space is extremely useful for passing information between programs, and is used by many utilities to communicate with the system. Ideally it should be set to at least 512 bytes, which can be achieved through the SHELL command. This command was originally provided to allow a different command processor to be used with DOS, and as such requires that the name and path of the relevant file be specified. However, it is rarely used for this purpose, and is more useful for specifying various settings, such as the amount of environment space. The following command defines the command processor to be the COMMAND.COM file located in the C:\DOS subdirectory, and that 512 bytes of environment space should be allocated:

```
SHELL=C:\DOS\COMMAND.COM /E:512 /P
```

The /P parameter makes the change permanent, ie it remains in force until the system is switched off or rebooted, irrespective of what software is run.

Care must be taken when specifying the path for COMMAND.COM, and it is essential to ensure that it is from the same version of DOS that the system was booted with. If these rules are not obeyed then the system will not boot from the hard disk, and will have to be started from a floppy.

3.6.4 STACK SPACE.

On newer, faster machines, the space reserved for stack buffering is usually wasted. On such machines a few bytes of memory can be saved by including the following line in CONFIG.SYS:

```
STACKS=0,0
```

It should be noted that the intelligent use of a memory manager such as Quarterdeck's QEMM or Qualitas' 386-to-the-MAX for the 80386 based machines, can have a significant effect of the exact contents of the CONFIG.SYS, and indeed can result in significant memory savings via the relocation of the FILE and BUFFER space into high memory. Some of these issues are discussed in a later chapter.

3.6.5   A SAMPLE CONFIG.SYS

```
FILES=31
BUFFERS=25
STACKS=0,0
SHELL=COMMAND.COM /E:512 /P
```

3.7   THE AUTOEXEC.BAT FILE

The minimum requirements for an AUTOEXEC.BAT file are listed below. This example is ideally suited for use with diskless workstations, and if used on other workstations may require commands to change to the relevant subdirectories etc. If the user does not necessarily require access to the network services, then these commands may in actual fact reside in an ordinary batch file.

The '@' sign preceding the ECHO OFF statement is a feature available in DOS version 3.3 and higher. Just as the ECHO OFF suppresses a display of the commands following it, the '@' sign is used to suppress display of the command immediately following it on that same line, ie the words ECHO OFF will not be displayed on the screen as this batch file runs.

3.7.1   A SAMPLE AUTOEXEC.BAT

```
@ECHO OFF
CLS

REM ****************************************************************
REM *   It should be noted that with the introduction of the       *
REM *   newer shells you have the option to load the IPX and       *
REM *   NETx files into either extended or expanded memory, or     *
REM *   alternately you may load the NETx portion into high        *
REM *   memory using either DOS 5.0 or products like QEMM386,      *
REM *   QRAM or 386-MAX.                                           *
REM *                                                              *
```

```
REM *   It should also be noted that certain network interface   *
REM *   cards have the IPX routines stored directly within their *
REM *   own firmware which can additionally provide a useful     *
REM *   saving of conventional memory, eg Madge TokenRing cards. *
REM ***************************************************************
IPX
NET3

REM ***************************************************************
REM *   The following two lines should be omitted if you have no  *
REM *   need to load NETBIOS emulation. It should be noted that   *
REM *   the newer shells allow the removal of NETBIOS emulation   *
REM *   from your computers memory once you have finished using   *
REM *   it. Thus you should rather load it prior to running an    *
REM *   application that requires it, and then once you have      *
REM *   finished using that application, remove it from memory    *
REM *   using the /D parameter.                                   *
REM ***************************************************************

NETBIOS
INT2F

REM ***************************************************************
REM *   Depending on where you boot from, you may need to now     *
REM *   change to the drive containing the LOGIN.EXE program.     *
REM *                                                             *
REM *   In this case a 'dummy' user is logged straight into the   *
REM *   network for reasons we shall examine later.               *
REM ***************************************************************

LOGIN DUMMY
```

3.8 THE SHELL.CFG FILE

As the IPX, NETx and NETBIOS files are loaded from the AUTOEXEC.BAT listed above, the subdirectory is checked for the presence of a seldom used file, the SHELL.CFG file. It is a simple ASCII file containing a series of commands that can be used to change the default behaviour of the network.

If this file does not exist a number of default values are automatically assumed. If a SHELL.CFG file is used, then it is only necessary to specify the values that are to be changed; all others will assume their default values. The defaults values that are chosen are as follows:

3.8.1 IPX DEFAULTS

```
IPX SOCKETS = 20
IPX RETRY COUNTS = 20
SPX CONNECTIONS = 15
SPX ABORT TIMEOUT = 540
SPX VERIFY TIMEOUT = 540
SPX LISTEN TIMEOUT = 108
```

3.8.2 NETX DEFAULTS

```
CACHE BUFFERS = 5
FILE HANDLES = 40
PRINT HEADER = 64
PRINT TAIL = 16
EOJ = ON
HOLD = OFF
SHARE = ON
LONG MACHINE TYPE = IBM_PC
SHORT MACHINE = IBM
LOCK RETRIES = 3
LOCK DELAY = 1
READ ONLY COMPATIBILITY = OFF
LOCAL PRINTERS = (no default)
SEARCH MODE = 1
MAXIMUM TASKS = 31
TASK MODE = 1
SHOW DOTS = OFF
```

3.8.3 NETBIOS DEFAULTS

```
NETBIOS SESSIONS = 10
NETBIOS SEND BUFFERS = 6
NETBIOS RECEIVE BUFFERS = 6
NETBIOS RETRY DELAY = 10
NETBIOS ABORT TIMEOUT = 540
NETBIOS VERIFY TIMEOUT = 54
NETBIOS LISTEN TIMEOUT = 108
```

Although many of these values will only need to be changed in extreme circumstances, there are a few settings that every troubleshooter should be aware of:

- IPX RETRY COUNTS = number. If a lot of problems with lost packets are being experienced, then increasing this value may be of help.
- CACHE BUFFERS = number. This is worth increasing when the users' disk accesses typically involve the re-reading of large files.
- LOCAL PRINTERS = number. Used to specify the number of local printers attached to the workstation. Most valuable when set to 0 in order to prevent workstations with no local printers from hanging if the user presses the [SHIFT]-[PRINT SCREEN] combination.
- LONG MACHINE TYPE = machine name. Advantage can be taken of this command in the LOGIN SCRIPTS. There it is possible to code the scripts to make a decision based on the %MACHINE% variable. This is of extreme importance in the case where it is necessary to manage a number of different versions of DOS.
- SHORT MACHINE TYPE = machine name. Useful when using computers such as the Compaq or the AT&T that emulate an IBM colour graphics adapter on a monochrome screen. In such a situation many of the NetWare menuing utilities will be unreadable because of the colour translations involved. By default, colour

mappings are determined by the file IBM$RUN.OVL on the network. However if the short machine type is set to CMPQ, the file CMPQ$RUN.OVL is used instead, providing a black and white palette for use with these utilities. The maximum length of the entry is of necessity four characters.

- FILE HANDLES = number. If a multi-tasking environment such as DesqView or Windows is run, or the error messages 'unable to open file' or 'no file handles' are produced, then both the FILES in the CONFIG.SYS and the FILE HANDLES in the SHELL.CFG should be considered. The two settings work in similar ways, but relate to different aspects of the system. They also both require memory so should not be set to excessive values. Maximum is 256.
- MAXIMUM TASKS = number. The default of 31 is more than enough for single-tasking applications, however this setting may again be too low for use with either DesqView or Windows. The minimum is 8 and the maximum is 128.
- SHOW DOTS = ON. If you plan to use Windows with the network, and have already installed the new shells and the new versions of the network utilities, then the value of SHOW DOTS needs to be set to ON. This will allow users to see entries for the '.' current directory, and '..' parent directory via Windows.

3.8.4 A SAMPLE SHELL.CFG FILE

```
CACHE BUFFERS = 10
LONG MACHINE TYPE = MITAC_PC
FILE HANDLES = 51
MAXIMUM TASKS = 51
```

3.9 THE SYSTEM LOGIN SCRIPT

All network administrators and troubleshooters should already know what Login scripts are. Therefore they will not be covered in great detail here. Despite their apparent simplicity, they are of great importance to the network access procedure. Just as the CONFIG.SYS and AUTOEXEC.BAT files are automatically executed when the user boots up their PC, a series of commands contained in a file known as the LOGIN SCRIPT are executed when a Novell network is accessed. To be a bit more precise Novell allows for two different login scripts to be executed when the network is accessed.

- First off the mark is the SYSTEM LOGIN SCRIPT which should contain the commands applicable to every user of the network. This is a generic login script, and is executed first.
- Secondly, NetWare allows for individual USER LOGIN SCRIPTS which contain commands applicable only to a particular user. The appropriate user login script is executed after the system login script.

Contrary to what is believed by many LAN managers and supervisors, there is little need for individual login scripts. Whilst they offer a greater degree of flexibility and make it easier for users to configure the system in exactly the way they want it, the use of individual login scripts has a number of inherent disadvantages, including the following:

- It is inevitable that some users will modify their login scripts, possibly bypassing certain safeguards that were initiated by the system administrator.

- The network will grow and change, possibly requiring the modification of every individual login script.
- By using individual login scripts, the original concepts of standardisation and simplification are being abandoned.

By using only a standard system login script, the occurrences of the above problems can be minimised. Fortunately, it is not necessary to sacrifice flexibility to gain these benefits, as it is possible to produce an interactive system login script that takes different actions depending on who is logging in, where they are logging in from etc. However, in order to produce this flexibility, it will be necessary to produced a somewhat sophisticated script. This need not mean that it is overly complex though; by breaking it down into a number of logical steps the problem can be simplified. This is the idea behind modularity, one of our key concepts defined earlier.

Examination of the sample system login script listed below will show that there are no complex routines or concepts (at this stage). Appropriate comments have been included in the code to explain exactly what each section does. Once execution is complete, a short batch file is run which ultimately calls the menu system from where application can be accessed. It is in essence a very simple setup, and all the elements of the login procedure have been kept as straightforward as possible. At this stage we are only interested in laying secure foundations for the network. These can always be built upon if necessary.

3.9.1 A SAMPLE SYSTEM LOGIN SCRIPT

```
REM ************************************************************
REM * The following line sets up an environment variable with   *
REM * the name of the currently active file server. This is     *
REM * useful in situations where a backup file-server needs to  *
REM * be accessed in preference to the standard file-server.    *
REM * The program access batch files have been written so as    *
REM * to automatically search the server named in this          *
REM * variable for application files.                           *
REM *                                                           *
REM * PS. Backup file servers are not such a dumb idea.         *
REM *     Correction, backups period, are not such a bad idea.  *
REM ************************************************************
DOS SET SERVER="NET1"

REM ************************************************************
REM * The error displays on the map commands are suppressed    *
REM * via the lines below, as are the display of the command   *
REM * as it is executed. The "MAP DISPLAY OFF" works much      *
REM * like the DOS "ECHO OFF" in batch files.                   *
REM ************************************************************
MAP DISPLAY OFF

REM ************************************************************
REM * Various environment variables are setup below. The       *
REM * following environment variables will be used for printer *
REM * setups. In later sections I will illustrate the best     *
REM * way to use these variables to enable you to get the most *
REM * out of the LAN's print queues.                            *
REM ************************************************************
```

70 THE SYSTEM LOGIN SCRIPT

```
DOS SET BANNER="NB"
DOS SET FFEED="NFF"
DOS SET QNAME="LOCAL"
DOS SET TABS="NT"
DOS SET TIMEOUT="25"

REM **************************************************************
REM * The following environment variable is used by software     *
REM * packages to identify the user and the user's home          *
REM * subdirectory.                                              *
REM **************************************************************

DOS SET USER="%LOGIN_NAME"

REM **************************************************************
REM * Map to the user's home sub-directory. Note the             *
REM * exception for the "SUPERVISOR". DOS subdirectory names     *
REM * longer than eight characters are permissible under Novell  *
REM * but they can cause all sorts of headaches and should be    *
REM * avoided at all costs.                                      *
REM **************************************************************

IF LOGIN_NAME#"SUPERVISOR" THEN BEGIN
    MAP F:=\DATA\%LOGIN_NAME
END

IF LOGIN_NAME="SUPERVISOR" THEN BEGIN
    DOS SET USER="SUPER"
    MAP F:=\DATA\SUPER
END

REM **************************************************************
REM * The first line sets up drive "F" as everyone's default     *
REM * drive. The next two lines assign some drive letters to     *
REM * other volumes on the file server for ease of access.       *
REM **************************************************************

DRIVE F:
MAP G:=NET1/VOLUME1:
MAP H:=NET1/VOLUME2:

REM **************************************************************
REM * The various search mappings are set via the lines below.   *
REM * The precedence in which the sub-directories are searched   *
REM * is determined by the order of these mappings. It is not    *
REM * recommended that the settings listed below are changed.    *
REM *                                                            *
REM * NOTE. It is a good idea to reserve Search mappings 7       *
REM * and higher for use as application specific mappings.       *
REM * They are created and removed as required by the program    *
REM * access batch files. I will be covering the topic of        *
REM * program access fully in a later section.                   *
REM **************************************************************
```

THE NETWORK ACCESS PROCEDURE

```
MAP  S1:=\
MAP  S2:=\PUBLIC\%MACHINE\%OS\%OS_VERSION
MAP  S3:=\MENU
MAP  S4:=\UTILS
MAP  S5:=\PUBLIC
MAP  S6:=\LOGIN

REM  ***************************************************************
REM  * The COMSPEC variable specifies where the DOS command         *
REM  * processor is located. PS. When experimenting with this       *
REM  * command leave a PC Logged in at all times in case you        *
REM  * hash it up and need to make a correction. Your machine       *
REM  * will hang with the message "Invalid command processor"       *
REM  * and your ability to access the network will be severely      *
REM  * curtailed.                                                   *
REM  *                                                              *
REM  * Please ensure you put ALL the relevant DOS files into        *
REM  * the correct subdirectory...                                  *
REM  *                                                              *
REM  *              eg    F:\PUBLIC\IBM_PC\MSDOS\V3.30               *
REM  ***************************************************************
COMSPEC=S2:command.com

REM  ***************************************************************
REM  * Clear the screen. Can you believe this syntax ???            *
REM  ***************************************************************
#COMMAND.COM /C CLS

REM  ***************************************************************
REM  * The following command displays a text file on the screen    *
REM  * in order to welcome the user to this network. The last      *
REM  * line of the $LAN.TXT file has a centred message stating     *
REM  * that the user should "Press a key to continue". Thus        *
REM  * the pause output is directed to the NUL device as its       *
REM  * message is redundant. The main reason for doing this is     *
REM  * that I am horribly image conscious and I dislike            *
REM  * anything resembling DOS. The entry "CLS" is passed to       *
REM  * the DOS command processor in order to clear the screen.     *
REM  *                                                              *
REM  * When this option is not necessary, it can be REM'd out.      *
REM  ***************************************************************
FDISPLAY \MENU\$LAN.TXT
#COMMAND.COM /C PAUSE > NUL
#COMMAND.COM /C CLS

REM  ***************************************************************
REM  * All the necessary set-up commands have now been             *
REM  * executed. All that remains is for the script to             *
REM  * terminate "gracefully" and transfer the user into the       *
REM  * menu system that he/she will be using to access the         *
REM  * various facilities available on the LAN.                    *
REM  *                                                              *
REM  * The command "PCCOMPATIBLE" ensures that the subsequent      *
REM  * "EXIT" command will operate correctly on machines that      *
```

```
REM * are not true-blue IBM PC's and for which you have      *
REM * changed the LONG MACHINE TYPE in the SHELL.CFG file.   *
REM ***********************************************************
PCCOMPATIBLE
EXIT "pre_help.bat"
```

3.10 THE PRE_HELP.BAT FILE

It may well be required that each workstation load certain TSRs or memory resident programs. This cannot be done from within either the login scripts or menuing system and so it is for this purpose that a batch file is run between these two stages in order to provide a suitable opportunity for these programs to be loaded.

The reason for splitting this file from the HELP.BAT file (see below) is that not all TSRs are intelligent, and if executed from the command line twice will actually install themselves twice in memory. Thus the workstation will end up with multiple copies of the TSR in memory, thereby wasting precious space.

3.10.1 A SAMPLE PRE_HELP.BAT FILE

```
@ECHO OFF
CLS
PROMPT $P$G

REM ***********************************************************
REM * Display a wisecrack from the "HI" database. A touch of  *
REM * humour as they log into the network serves two very     *
REM * important functions:-                                   *
REM *     1)  Removes some of the impersonality of the system,*
REM *     2)  Catches the users attention in case you need to *
REM *         display some important news on the screen. In   *
REM *         which case it would be shown as a result of the *
REM *         FDISPLAY command in the login script.           *
REM ***********************************************************
HI
BATCHMAN waitfor 2

REM ***********************************************************
REM * Generic TSR's loaded for all machines. eg  LANASSIST.   *
REM *                                                         *
REM * Load lanassist :   - memory resident portion            *
REM *                    - authorised users only              *
REM *                    - chat window                        *
REM ***********************************************************
LA +N /C > NUL

REM ***********************************************************
REM * Specific TSRs loaded for some machines. Eg. MOUSE.      *
REM *                                                         *
REM * NWHAT utility is used to check the physical machine/card*
REM * number, which can then be used to decide whether the    *
REM * driver is required.                                     *
REM ***********************************************************
NWHAT -physical
```

```
SET ACTION=NO
IF %NWHAT%==AA3400020445 SET ACTION=YES
IF %NWHAT%==BD3D00120375 SET ACTION=YES
IF %NWHAT%==0000000000F5 SET ACTION=YES
IF %ACTION%==NO NEXT_STEP

F:\UTILS\MOUSE
SET NWHAT=
SET ACTION=

:NEXT_STEP
REM ************************************************************
REM * Exit to HELP.BAT                                           *
REM ************************************************************

HELP
```

3.11 THE HELP.BAT FILE

The reason for creating a file called HELP on the file server is that this provides an easy to remember way for users to return to the menuing system as if they had just logged in. The one thing that *every* user tries if they are in difficulty is to type HELP, and with a HELP.BAT file present this will have the effect of returning them to a common starting point – the menu system.

The batch file can be run irrespective of the users current subdirectory as a path will have been set to the /MENU subdirectory within which this file should be located.

One point to consider is that Novell's NetWare comes with a file called HELP.EXE which contains on-line network manuals and information. It is recommended that this file is renamed as NHELP.EXE, in keeping with other network specific commands such as NCOPY and NPRINT. In this way the user is prevented from unintentionally accessing the NetWare Infobase instead of the Menuing System.

3.11.1 A SAMPLE HELP.BAT FILE

```
@echo Off
CLS

REM ************************************************************
REM * The following two lines ensure that the user is returned  *
REM * to his own private subdirectory prior to execution of any *
REM * programs from the menu system. The "user" variable was    *
REM * set in the system login script.                           *
REM ************************************************************

F:
CD \DATA\%USER%

REM ************************************************************
REM * "MENU MAIN" command calls the NOVELL menu utility which is*
REM * documented fully in the manuals. The menu system run in   *
REM * this instance has its details stored in an ASCII file     *
REM * named "MAIN.MNU". This file can be edited as and when     *
```

74 SYSTEM RESPONSE DURING THE LOGIN PROCESS

```
REM *  alterations need to be made to the menuing system. A    *
REM *  sample file is located in the \PUBLIC sub-directory of  *
REM *  your network.                                            *
REM ***************************************************************
MENU MAIN
```

3.12 SYSTEM RESPONSE DURING THE LOGIN PROCESS

The majority of the login process is transparent to the user due to the extensive use of ECHO OFF etc in the batch files and scripts. However, there are two particular displays that are produced for the benefit of the user.

- The first is the welcome screen produced by the system login script. This displays an appropriate message when the user first gains access to the LAN.
- The second is the response from the HI database, which will encourage the user to watch the screen during the login process. This could be temporarily replaced by a different message screen if it is necessary to notify all users of some important information, such as the fact the the server will be down for repair etc.

The two displays are shown in Figures 3.1 and 3.2 below Note that the output from the HI program is a one or two line quip, which is sited in the centre of the screen.

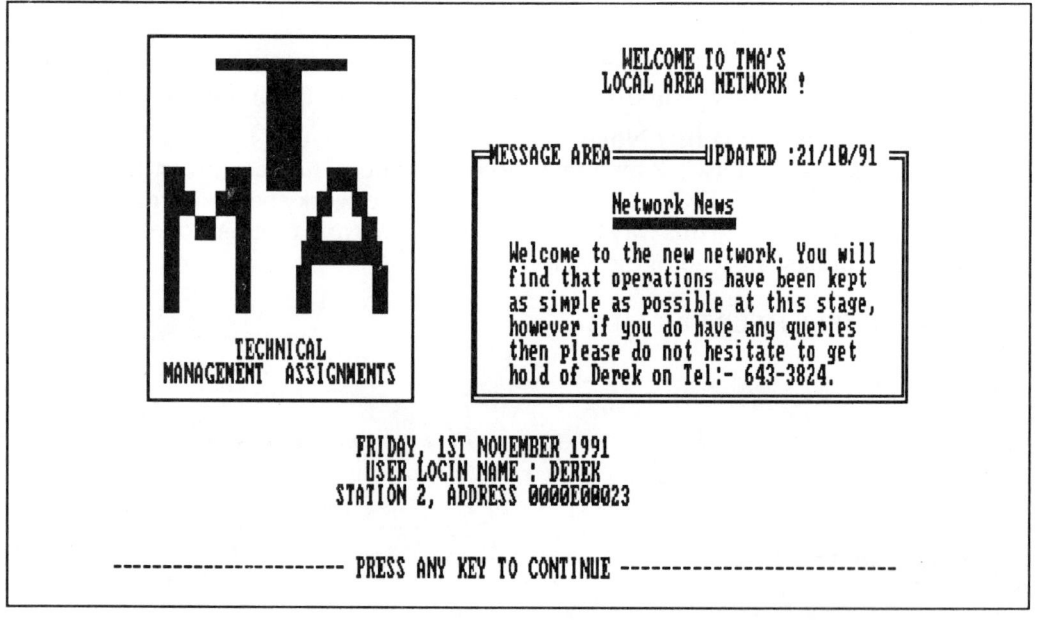

Figure 3.1   Message screen displayed when logging in

```
Skip's Lament:
    Given any problem containing N equations,
    There will be n+1 unknowns.
```

Figure 3.2   Typical message produced by HI

3.13 SUMMARY

When a user switches on a workstation and logs into the network there are only two issues which are directly of interest to him/her:

- First, how they can gain access to their data which is stored on the network. It is for this purpose that the login procedure is followed, as the user must supply the necessary password and account numbers to ensure that they alone can access their own data. The login process also establishes a record of the user in the system, so that they may access any application programs to which they have the necessary rights. The discussions and examples provided in this chapter have illustrated a comprehensive design concept which can be employed to make this process as consistent and error free as possible.

- Secondly the user needs to be able to access one or more application programs. By far the best way of providing this facility is through the use of a menu system, which may be constructed using DOS batch files, or by using a proprietary package, and this topic is examined in Chapter 4.

It is essential that these two steps are kept as simple as possible, as users will be discouraged from using the system if an excessive number of commands are required for each operation. Similarly, the number of user-generated errors will be significantly reduced if the interfaces employed by these systems are consistent.

4 The Application Access Procedure

4.1 INTRODUCTION

At this stage of the proceedings the user will have been able to log into the network, and will be looking at the menuing system in preparation for running the application of their choice.

This chapter looks at the issues related to application access. The exact treatment of this issue is largely dependent on the menuing system chosen for use on the particular network. The example files that are listed have been developed based on the assumption that the MENU utility that is supplied as a standard part of the Novell NetWare Operating System is being used.

Novell's MENU utility allows individual menuing systems for each user on the network to be set up. This practice is contrary to the recommendations that have been made throughout the previous chapters, and thus it is important to bear in mind that the following discussion will be limited to the creation and implementation of a single generic menu structure for all users on a network.

All of the same programming philosophies that were mentioned in the previous chapter are equally applicable to this discussion.

Application access is handled via two distinct mechanisms:
- the MENU utility itself
- complementary batch files.

4.2 THE MENU UTILITY

Whilst this section concentrates on a discussion of Novell's MENU utility and how it can be used to best effect, the discussion and concepts should prove valuable irrespective of the menuing system or the network operating system that is being used in the organisation. One menu utility is much the same as any other menu utility, and similarly the problems that need to be overcome when setting up and maintaining a menu utility tend to be fairly common across the spectrum, whether it be a DOS batch-file driven menu system (arguably still the most effective method), or the 'SupaDupa Menu System' from 'SupaDupa Software'.

Novell's MENU utility is fully described in the manuals provided, but there are still a

78 THE MENU UTILITY

few issues relating to this menuing system that the troubleshooter needs to be aware of. Additionally there are some guidelines that should be followed when constructing the menu system for users. These are discussed briefly, before examining an example .MNU file that has been created to fit in with previous philosophies and recommendations. These are discussed in the following categories:

- The various versions of the MENU utility
- Black-boxing and the MENU utility
- Making changes to the .MNU file.

4.2.1 THE VARIOUS VERSIONS OF THE MENU UTILITY

Novell currently distributes version 1.22 of their MENU utility, a version which is fully functional, yet has a couple of shortcomings. The most serious shortcoming of the menu system is that it has a TSR component which is not removed fully prior to executing any external programs. This has three implications for the network manager:

- No TSRs may be loaded from within the menuing system
- Less conventional memory is available for use by the applications
- It may not be possible to run the MENU utility from within itself.

The fact that TSRs cannot be loaded from within the menuing system can, in part, be solved via the PRE_HELP.BAT file which has already been discussed. Unfortunately it seems to be increasingly popular for applications to make use of their own TSR component in order to maintain a tighter control over the environment in which they operate. The menuing system itself is a prime example of such an application.

The fact that the menuing system does not remove itself completely when running other batch files and/or programs from within itself can be a fairly critical problem. The extra 11KB of memory held by the menuing system can be just too much when added to the 70KB or more already claimed by the network drivers and shells. This memory grabbing usually results in nothing more serious than inconvenience due to slowed performance on systems with large numbers of applications, and large unwieldy .MNU files which are a problem from the maintenance perspective. That said, it is still a cause of great irritation to those who have to manage the system.

A few privileged industry insiders will be aware that Novell has actually made an updated version of the MENU utility available to its user base. What Novell has not done is tell all its users how to get hold of the new version, or even that it exists. This version of the MENU utility will remove more of itself from memory prior to running any external programs, and even allows the loading of TSRs while it is operational, however those TSRs should be removed from memory before re-entering the menu system otherwise memory fragmentation will result. Version 1.23 of the MENU utility addresses the first two problems directly, however it does have a shortcoming of its own.

It's shortcoming is of a minor nature in comparison to the problems that it solves. It is not possible to LOGOUT from the network without incurring the wrath, and associated screeds of error messages, of the DOS command processor. Fortunately the errors are harmless despite the ominous rumblings, and indeed it is possible to get around this problem by logging a 'dummy' user, with no rights, onto the system instead of actually logging out.

Novell recently started shipping yet another version (2.30) of their MENU utility. This version solves the 'logout' problem, but has an enormous appetite for memory (92K) and does not work on XT systems.

To its advantage Novell's own MENU utility does not cost a cent extra and utilises the same interface as do all of Novell's other utilities, thus the entire networking environment begins to take on a more standardised look and feel. Indeed, more and more network utilities are beginning to utilise the same code library (C-WORTHY) as Novell in order to make their user-interfaces conform to Novell's standards.

To its disadvantage, Novell does not seem to have put much effort into the continuing development of this utility, and by industry standards it leaves a lot to be desired. Among the issues that would greatly benefit from improvement are the:

- Ability to run the same menuing system on machines that are not logged into, or even attached to, the network, in order to retain consistency throughout the enterprise.
- Ability to maintain a central menu script that allows different users to see different options, rather than keeping, and having to maintain, individual scripts for all the users that need one.
- Incorporation of the ability to test for group membership from within the menu system, in order to show different options depending on a particular user's privilege rights etc. Novell's own utilities incorporate this feature, in that different options are shown relative to the user's security level.
- Ability of the menu system to *completely* remove itself from memory prior to executing an external program.
- Ability to call sub-menu script files rather than having to store every possible option within one gargantuan script file, thus allowing complete modularisation of the application access procedures without needing to leave the format of the script files.
- Ability to monitor software usage on the network and report on its findings. These reports could provide valuable support information when preparing budget requests and operational reports.
- Ability to limit access to software in accordance with licensing agreements for that software. For example, limit the usage of Harvard Graphics to a maximum of 10 users at any one time.
- Despite the clean and efficient style of the user-interface that Novell currently provides, many users would prefer a menu system based on the Windows interface. This idea is further enforced by LAN Manager, which uses such an interface to make the task of managing the network much easier, and almost enjoyable!

Many systems make extensive use of Novell's menuing system despite its shortcomings, although there are some excellent programs available which are worth consideration. The better ones address many of the above items, but in choosing a suitable system it is also important that it should fit in with what the rest of the organisation is doing. There are a sufficient number of industry-standard interfaces without the network manager complicating the matter any further by adding to the user's learning curve.

80 DESIGNING A MENU SYSTEM

4.2.2 BLACK-BOXING AND THE MENU UTILITY

Unfortunately Novell's MENU utility can prove sluggish on older machines, especially if the .MNU file is at all large.

Most texts, including the NetWare manuals, suggest that the system is set up to execute applications directly from within the .MNU file without utilising batch files. They imply that the .MNU file should, in effect, replace any batch files that may otherwise be used.

It is absolutely essential that a 10000 line .MNU file is avoided, if only for no other reason than the fact that there is no way of commenting, and thus understanding, this file. The situation is compounded by the fact that there is no way of setting up a series of .MNU files, each relating directly to a single menu, and therefore the entire menu system must be based on a single .MNU file. As longer .MNU files mean slower performance, it is essential that as little detail is kept in the file as possible. Thus the only way to effectively manage the menuing system is to call batch files which contain the commands required to get the application running.

These batch files can at least be *black-boxed* so that any generic functions are themselves contained in separate files. Thus a series of generic support batch files are created for use together with the menuing system. This may appear somewhat confusing, but the following examples should clarify the situation.

4.2.3 MAKING CHANGES TO THE .MNU FILE

Before considering the example files, a quick word of warning is appropriate. If users are logged into the network, and are under the control of the MENU utility, there is no way that the .MNU file can be changed directly. This file becomes locked by the network operating system during use. Two implications arise from this situation:

- Once set up, there will be no opportunity to randomly meddle with the system.
- If changes do need to be made, the following procedure must be performed in order to minimise disruption to the users:

    - Copy the current .MNU file to a new file. eg
      COPY MAIN1.MNU MAIN2.MNU
    - Edit the new file and make the required changes.
      EDIT MAIN2.MNU
    - Edit the HELP.BAT file at the line that calls the MENU utility. For example, change the line that reads 'MENU MAIN1' to 'MENU MAIN2'. Any users who subsequently access the system will be presented with the new options.
    - After a period of between a couple of hours and a couple of days, depending on how long it takes for all the users to logoff from the system, the old "MENU1.MNU" file will no longer be locked and can subsequently be deleted.

4.3 DESIGNING A MENU SYSTEM

Before a menu system of any kind can be created, it is essential to first plan on paper what options are required, how they should be ordered and grouped into submenus, as well as how the conditional subroutines will work that support these options. Failure to take sufficient care at this stage can lead to clumsy and repetitive code, and a system that is inflexible and difficult to maintain.

Menu options should be organised in a logical way; similar applications should be grouped into submenus, each of which is accessed via one main menu. This hierarchical menu structure ensures that there is not an excess of information on screen at any one time whilst still providing for quick and easy access to any desired option.

The use of flowcharts and flow diagrams is a useful approach that can be adopted for planning batch files etc. Figure 4.1 shows a simplified flowchart outlining the main steps performed by the menu system shown in this chapter.

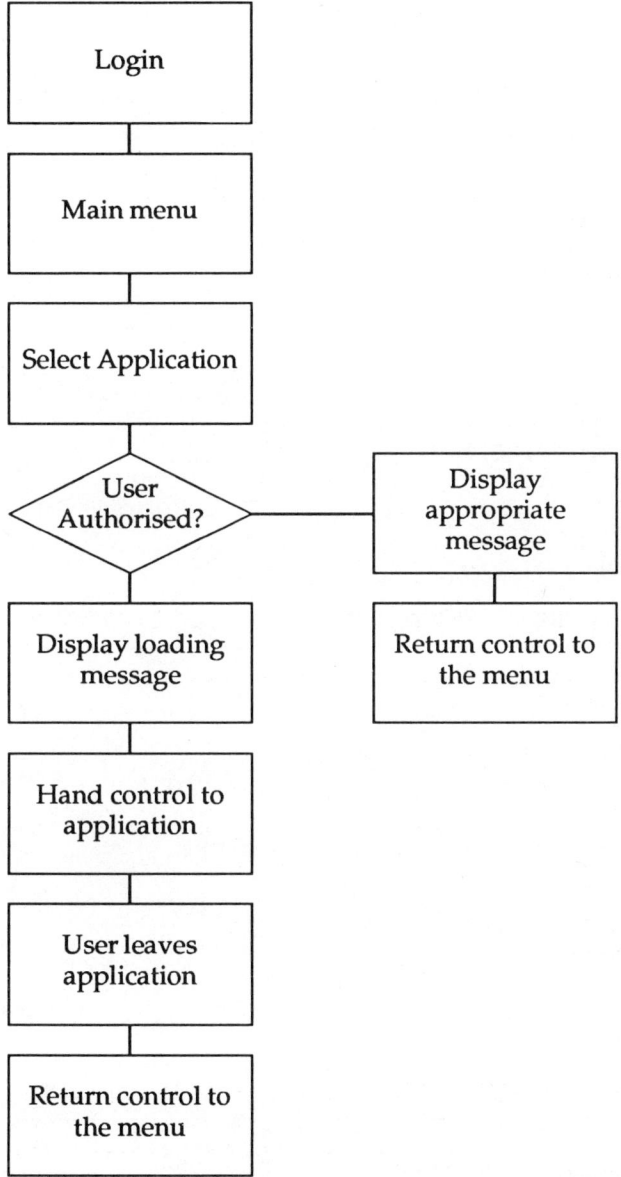

Figure 4.1   Flowchart for the access procedure

4.4 A SAMPLE EXTRACT FROM A MAIN.MNU MENU FILE

The MAIN.MNU file is used by the Novell MENU utility. It is essentially a text file, although it contains commands that will be executed by the system under certain conditions. The following listing shows an extract from a typical menu file.

```
%MAIN MENU,10,15,0
0. Printer Selection
     %Printer Selection
1. Word Processing
     %Word Processing
2. Spreadsheets
     %Spreadsheets
3. Presentation Graphics
     %Presentation Graphics
4. Database Management
     %Database Management
5. General Utilities
     %General Utilities
6. Communications
     %Communications
7. Novell NetWare
     %Novell NetWare
Q. Logout
     !Logout
%Printer Selection,4,70,0
0. Re-direction Status
     @echo off
     $showcap.bat
1. Local Printer
     @echo off
     echo CONFIGURING PRINTING FOR QUEUE : LOCAL PRINTER
     echo -----------------------------------------------
     echo Please wait - returning to menu system ...
     set qname=LOCAL
     $setcap.bat
2. BH Area Printers
     %BH Area Printers
3. CE Area Printers
     %CE Area Printers
Q. Logout
     !Logout
%BH Area Printers,9,62,0
0. Re-direction Status
     @echo off
     $showcap.bat
1. Local Printer
     @echo off
     echo CONFIGURING PRINTING FOR QUEUE : LOCAL PRINTER
     echo -----------------------------------------------
     echo Please wait - returning to menu system ...
     set qname=LOCAL
     $setcap.bat
```

THE APPLICATION ACCESS PROCEDURE   83

```
2. BH Area LASER
    @echo off
    echo CONFIGURING PRINTING FOR QUEUE : BH_LASER01
    echo ---------------------------------------------
    echo Please wait - returning to menu system ...
    set qname=BH_LASER01
    $setcap.bat
3. BH Area EPSON
    @echo off
    echo CONFIGURING PRINTING FOR QUEUE : BH_EPSON01
    echo ---------------------------------------------
    echo Please wait - returning to menu system ...
    set qname=BH_EPSON01
    $setcap.bat
Q. Logout
    !Logout
%CE Area Printers,9,62,0
0. Re-direction Status
    @echo off
    $showcap.bat
1. Local Printer
    @echo off
    echo CONFIGURING PRINTING FOR QUEUE : LOCAL PRINTER
    echo ---------------------------------------------
    echo Please wait - returning to menu system ...
    set qname=LOCAL
    $setcap.bat
2. CE Area EPSON
    @echo off
    echo CONFIGURING PRINTING FOR QUEUE : CE_EPSON01
    echo ---------------------------------------------
    echo Please wait - returning to menu system ...
    set qname=CE_EPSON01
    $setcap.bat
Q. Logout
    !Logout
%Word Processing,10,22,0
0. Printer Selection
    %Printer Selection
1. WPerfect 5.1
    @echo off
    !wp51.bat
2. WPerfect Tutorial
    @echo off
    !wptut.bat
Q. Logout
    !Logout
%Spreadsheets,10,21,0
0. Printer Selection
    %Printer Selection
1. Lotus 123 2.2
    @echo off
    !lotus.bat
```

THE MAIN.MNU FILE

```
2. Quattro PRO
     @echo off
     !qpro.bat
3. Quattro PRO - 123 mode
     @echo off
     !qpro123.bat
Q. Logout
     !Logout
%Presentation Graphics,9,21,0
0. Printer Selection
     %Printer Selection
1. Harvard Graphics 2.12
     @echo off
     !harvard.bat
2. Draw Applause II
     @echo off
     !applause.bat
Q. Logout
     !Logout
%Database Management,10,20,0
0. Printer Selection
     %Printer Selection
1. dBASE III Plus
     @echo off
     !dbase3.bat
2. dBASE IV
     @echo off
     !dbase4.bat
Q. Logout
     !logout
%General Utilities,12,29,0
0. Printer Selection
     %Printer Selection
1. Change Login Password
     @setpass
2. PC Tools Deluxe 6.0 - DOS Shell
     @echo off
     !pcshell.bat
3. Memory Usage Info
     @echo off
     !memchk.bat
4. Network Login Info
     @echo off
     !whoami.bat
5. Virus disk-checker
     @echo off
     !vseek.bat
9. Run a DOS command
     @1"Enter Command "
     @echo off
     echo PRESS ANY KEY TO RETURN TO MENU SYSTEM ...
     pause   nul
Q. Logout
     !Logout
```

THE APPLICATION ACCESS PROCEDURE 85

```
%Communications,9,20,0
0. Printer Selection
     %Printer Selection
1. WPerfect Elec. Mail
     @echo off
     !wpmail.bat
2. Beltel
     @echo off
     !beltel.bat
Q. Logout
     !Logout
%Novell NetWare,13,29,0
0. Printer Selection
     %Printer Selection
1. Session Management
     @Session
2. File Management
     @Filer
3. Volume Information
     @Volinfo
4. System Configuration
     @Syscon
5. Network Game : SNIPES (Single player)
     @snipes SINGLE @1"ENTER Level of play (1-10)"
6. Network Game : SNIPES (Multi-player)
     @snipes MULTI @1"ENTER Level of play (1-10)"
Q. Logout
     !Logout
```

The precise displays that will be produced when such a menu system is running will obviously differ depending on the menuing system in use and the way it has been configured. However within any given network, the appearance of the menu should be consistent and logical, so that the user can easily find the option they require. Figures 4.2 to 4.4 show some of the displays produced by the MAIN.MNU file listed above. Notice that *every* menu has the first option as Printer Selection and the last option as Logout. Also note that submenus do not completely overwrite the previous information.

4.5 BATCH-FILE PROCESSING

The various batch files are either called directly by the menu system, or by other batch files. They perform a whole variety of tasks from running applications to displaying message screens and checking various information about the user.

A special form of typographical convention has been used for naming these files:

– Support files have their names prefixed by a $ sign
– Other batch files have their names prefixed by a ! symbol.

This means that the names will not conflict with the names of any applications programs or utilities. The technique also has the added advantage that the network users will be unlikely to execute the batch files directly, and so will only access the applications through the menu system. This further enhances the control and management that is inherent in this approach to network configuration.

86 BATCH FILE PROCESSING

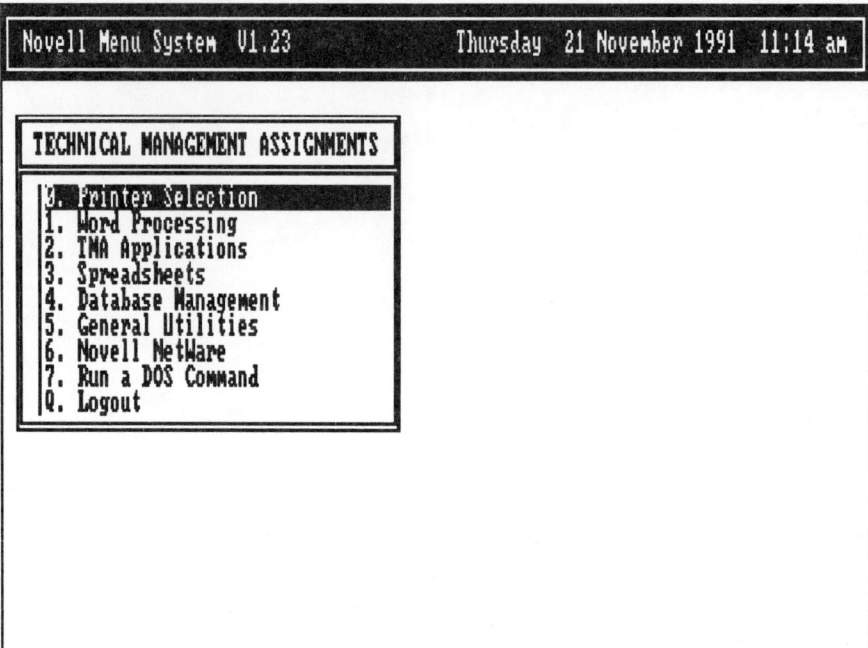

Figure 4.2   Main menu display

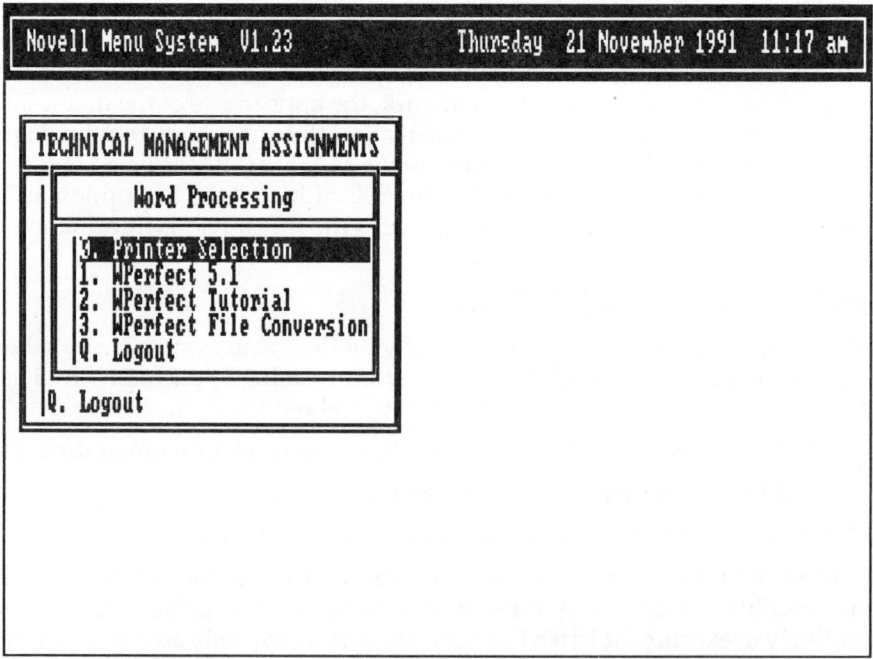

Figure 4.3   Wordprocessing sub-menu display

THE APPLICATION ACCESS PROCEDURE 87

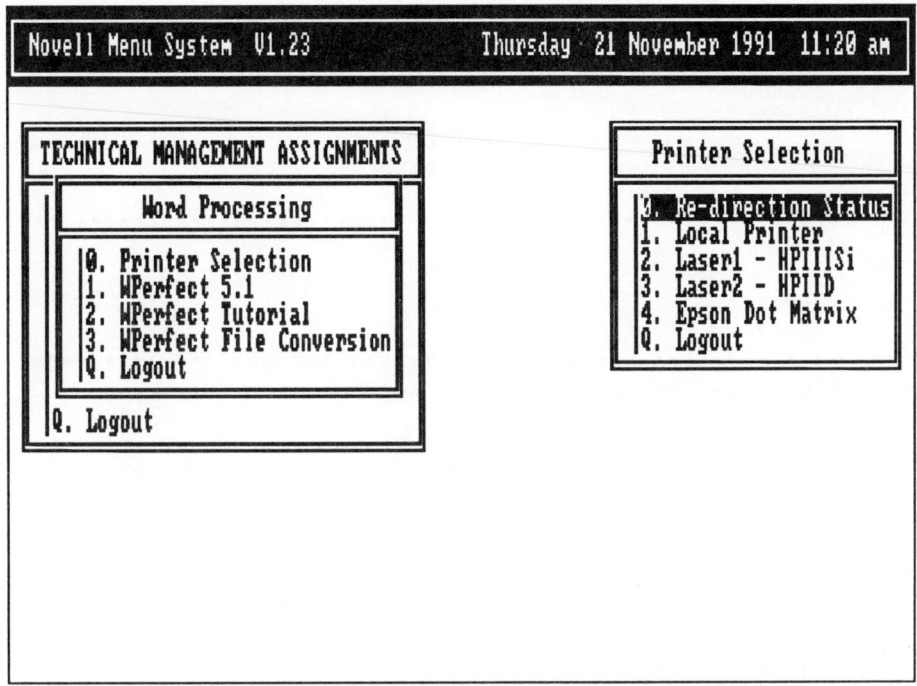

Figure 4.4   Printer selection menu display

The batch files listed in the following sections make use of a number of different utilities. For example, the Norton Utilities Batch Enhancer program (BE) is used in many situations to improve the appearance of the screen by drawing boxes or displaying messages, and to obtain user input in response to questions. Similarly the NWHAT utility is used to gain certain information relating to the users membership of certain groups etc. Whilst these utilities are not essential in such situations, they considerably simplify the coding required in the batch files and enhance the overall appearance of the system.

4.5.1   A SAMPLE APPLICATION ACCESS BATCH FILE – THE !WP51.BAT FILE

This batch file is executed when WordPerfect is selected from the main menu. It is the primary batch file that will take control of the system and perform all the necessary tasks, including the following:

–   It ensures that the user is permitted to access the application.

–   It informs the system that it requires the printers to be set up in the most appropriate way for WordPerfect.

–   It defines the temporary search drive mappings that are required by WordPerfect.

–   It runs the WP.EXE program, together with any appropriate parameters.

Once the user exits the application, the batch file again takes control and reverses the above process by resetting the printer status, removing the search drives and returning control to the menu system.

88 BATCH FILE PROCESSING

```
@ECHO OFF
CLS

REM ****************************************************************
REM *                                                              *
REM *                    WORDPERFECT 5.1                           *
REM *                     (!wp51.bat)                              *
REM *                                                              *
REM ****************************************************************

F:
CD \DATA\%USER%

REM ****************************************************************
REM * Test whether the user is authorised to use this package.     *
REM *                                                              *
REM * For extra information on ERRORLEVELs and the NWHAT utility   *
REM * please refer to an earlier section on "Configuration         *
REM * Management and DOS Environment Variables."                   *
REM *                                                              *
REM * NB : If the user is a member of the group xxxx_exclude,      *
REM *      they are not allowed to use this package.               *
REM ****************************************************************

NWHAT -member WPERFECT_EXCLUDE
IF ERRORLEVEL 2 GOTO YES_AUTH
IF ERRORLEVEL 0 GOTO NOT_AUTH


:NOT_AUTH
REM ****************************************************************
REM * User is a member of the group, so is NOT authorised.         *
REM ****************************************************************

COMMAND /c $notauth
GOTO END


:YES_AUTH
REM ****************************************************************
REM * User is not a member of the group, so IS authorised.         *
REM ****************************************************************
REM ****************************************************************
REM * Display message to the screen via a batch file. The name of  *
REM * the application name must be sent as a parameter, but,       *
REM * because normal spaces are ignored when used as part of a     *
REM * parameter string, the [ALT 255] character must be used       *
REM * instead in order to centre your message on the screen.       *
REM *                                                              *
REM * The total length of the application name is 35 characters.   *
REM ****************************************************************

COMMAND /C $loading           WORDPERFECT 5.1
```

THE APPLICATION ACCESS PROCEDURE

```
REM ****************************************************************
REM * Set up the capture command via a batch file. The following   *
REM * environment variables were setup in the LOGIN SCRIPTS.       *
REM *         - QNAME (Printer queue name selected by user)        *
REM *         - BANNER (Set up as a default)                       *
REM *         - FFEED (Set up as a default)                        *
REM *         - TABS (Set up as a default)                         *
REM *                                                              *
REM * The following defaults must be overridden...                 *
REM *         - TIMEOUT (because WordPerfect is "Network Aware")   *
REM ****************************************************************

SET DEF_TIMEOUT=%TIMEOUT%
SET TIMEOUT=0
COMMAND /C $setcap

REM ****************************************************************
REM * Set up the search mappings required to run this application  *
REM ****************************************************************

MAP S7:=%SERVER%/belvol01:\soft\WP51 > NUL
MAP S8:=%SERVER%/belvol01:\soft\WP51\LEARN > NUL


REM ****************************************************************
REM * Run executable program with applicable switches etc., but    *
REM * specify the search drive to run it on, rather than rely on   *
REM * the search path to do the work for you. This has two         *
REM * advantages:                                                  *
REM *     1)  Increased loading speed of the application; and,     *
REM *                                                              *
REM *     2)  Obviation of the problem of possibly having a file   *
REM *         sitting in another subdirectory being loaded in      *
REM *         preference to the intended application.              *
REM ****************************************************************

T:WP /NT=1 /D=g:\OVERFLOW /U=%WPUSER%

REM ****************************************************************
REM * Reset current drive to F:, in case the user or the software  *
REM * has reset the current drive to one of the search mappings,   *
REM * which might cause the failure of the following commands.     *
REM ****************************************************************

F:


REM ****************************************************************
REM * Display a message to the user informing him that the         *
REM * application is in the process of being unloaded.             *
REM ****************************************************************

COMMAND /C $unload
```

```
REM ***************************************************************
REM * Restore the status of the capture command to its default    *
REM * behaviour, and clear any unnecessary environment variables  *
REM * from memory.                                                *
REM ***************************************************************

SET TIMEOUT=%DEF_TIMEOUT%
SET DEF_TIMEOUT=
COMMAND /C $setcap


REM ***************************************************************
REM * Delete all search mappings that were set up, remembering to *
REM * perform this action in sequence from high-low because when  *
REM * you delete S7, S8 of consequence becomes S7.                *
REM *                                                             *
REM * Thus, as an alternative you could delete S7 twice to        *
REM * achieve the same effect, but I believe that using this      *
REM * technique reduces the understandability of your code, and   *
REM * complicates later management of your environment.           *
REM ***************************************************************

MAP DEL S8: > NUL
MAP DEL S7: > NUL

REM ***************************************************************
REM * The label END is included as a pointer for the GOTO listed  *
REM * in the code above.                                          *
REM ***************************************************************

:END
REM ***************************************************************
REM * Reset the current directory to the user's private           *
REM * directory, in order for the menu system to resume           *
REM * operation. This action is of extreme importance when using  *
REM * some menu systems, including that offered by Novell itself, *
REM * because that menu system will fail if restarted from a      *
REM * different subdirectory.                                     *
REM ***************************************************************

F:
CD \DATA\%USER%
```

4.6 THE MENU SYSTEM SUPPORT BATCH FILES

Several support batch files are executed during the selection, initialisation and loading procedures. The following sections show the code required by each.

4.6.1 THE $LOADING.BAT FILE

This batch file simply displays a message on screen to tell the user that the application is being loaded from the network. It is very important to reassure the user in this way, and to show them that their machine is actually working correctly, especially on heavily loaded networks where it can take up to 45 minutes to load some applications!

```
@ECHO OFF
CLS

REM ***************************************************************
REM *                                                             *
REM *                     $LOADING.BAT                            *
REM *                                                             *
REM ***************************************************************
REM * This batch program displays a message to the user           *
REM * whenever an application program is loaded.                  *
REM *                                                             *
REM * The NORTON UTILITIES 4.50 (Advanced) batch enhancer         *
REM * program (BE.EXE) is used to produce the message, and       *
REM * must be present in the \UTILS subdirectory.                 *
REM *                                                             *
REM * The user passes the following parameters into this file     *
REM * from the application specific batch file eg. !WP51.BAT      *
REM *    - application name (max of 35 characters, and centred    *
REM *      using [ALT]-[255])                                     *
REM ***************************************************************
REM ***************************************************************
REM * Display box # 1, with main message                          *
REM ***************************************************************

BE WINDOW 5 10 11 65
BE ROWCOL 8 20 "PLEASE WAIT ... LOADING APPLICATION."

REM ***************************************************************
REM * Display box # 2, with application name.                     *
REM ***************************************************************

BE BOX 12 20 14 55
BE ROWCOL 13 21 ""
ECHO %1

REM ***************************************************************
REM * Display more info to the user.                              *
REM ***************************************************************

BE ROWCOL 15 30 "USER NAME : "
ECHO %USER%
BE ROWCOL 16 33 "SERVER : "
ECHO %SERVER%
BE ROWCOL 17 26 "PRINTER QUEUE : "
ECHO %QNAME%
BE ROWCOL 18 28 "SCREEN TYPE : "
ECHO %VMODE%
BE ROWCOL 20 1 " "
```

4.6.2 THE $UNLOAD.BAT FILE

This batch file displays a message on screen to say that the application is being removed from memory. In most situations this message will only stay on the screen for a relatively short period of time.

```
@ECHO OFF
CLS

REM ****************************************************************
REM *                                                              *
REM *                       $UNLOAD.BAT                            *
REM *                                                              *
REM ****************************************************************
REM * This batch program displays a message to the user            *
REM * whenever an application program is being unloaded.           *
REM ****************************************************************
REM ****************************************************************
REM * Display box with message                                     *
REM ****************************************************************

BE WINDOW 5 10 11 65
BE ROWCOL 8 19 "PLEASE WAIT ... UNLOADING APPLICATION."
BE ROWCOL 12 1 ""
```

4.6.3 THE $NOTAUTH.BAT FILE

This batch file is only executed if it is found that the user does not have access rights for the chosen application.

```
@ECHO OFF
CLS

REM ****************************************************************
REM *                                                              *
REM *                       $NOTAUTH.BAT                           *
REM *                                                              *
REM ****************************************************************
REM * This batch program is executed if the user attempts to       *
REM * load an application which he is not authorised to use.       *
REM ****************************************************************
REM ****************************************************************
REM * Using NORTON's Batch Enhancer (BE.EXE), explode a window     *
REM * display a message and also beep twice.                       *
REM ****************************************************************

BE WINDOW 5 10 12 65
BE ROWCOL 8 16 "YOU ARE NOT AUTHORISED TO USE THIS PACKAGE."
BE ROWCOL 9 16 "        APPLICATION CANNOT BE LOADED."
BE BEEP /D4 /F1000 /R2
BE ROWCOL 13 19 "PRESS ANY KEY TO RETURN TO THE MENU ..."

PAUSE > NUL
CLS

:END
```

4.6.4 THE $NOTYET.BAT FILE

There may be situations when it is impossible for a user to load a given application, either because it has temporarily been removed from the system, because the maximum permitted number of users are already using it, or for a number of other reasons. This batch file takes care of this situation by displaying an appropriate message.

```
@ECHO OFF
CLS
REM ****************************************************************
REM *                                                              *
REM *                        $NOTYET.BAT                           *
REM *                                                              *
REM ****************************************************************
REM * This batch program displays a message to the user            *
REM * whenever an application program is not yet available for     *
REM * use.                                                         *
REM *                                                              *
REM * the NORTON UTILITIES 4.50 (Advanced) Batch Enhancer          *
REM * program (BE.EXE) is used to produce the message, and         *
REM * must be present in the \UTILS subdirectory.                  *
REM *                                                              *
REM * The user passes the following parameters into the batch      *
REM * file :                                                       *
REM *    - application name (max of 35 characters, and centred     *
REM *      using [ALT]-[255]                                       *
REM ****************************************************************
REM ****************************************************************
REM * Display box # 1, with main message.                          *
REM ****************************************************************

BE WINDOW 5 10 11 65
BE ROWCOL 8 20 "SORRY... THIS APPLICATION NOT AVAILABLE."

REM ****************************************************************
REM * Display box # 2, with application name, pause for a short    *
REM * while (5 secs), and then return to the menu system.          *
REM ****************************************************************

BE BOX 12 20 14 55
BE ROWCOL 13 21 ""
ECHO %1
BATCHMAN WAITFOR 5
```

4.7 THE PRINTER CONTROL SUPPORT BATCH FILES

Most applications require the printer to be initialised in a specific way, perhaps by having the timeout set to a certain value, or by having page size, alternate character set etc specified. These settings can be specified with the $SETCAP.BAT file, and displayed on screen with the $SHOWCAP.BAT file.

4.7.1 THE $SETCAP.BAT FILE

```
@echo Off
CLS
REM ****************************************************************
REM *                                                              *
REM *                        $SETCAP.BAT                           *
```

```
REM *                                                              *
REM ****************************************************************
REM * This file sets up the printer capture command for all       *
REM * printing on the lan. It can be called in 2 ways :           *
REM *         1. When the user is selecting a printer             *
REM *                                                              *
REM *         2. When an application is loaded up.                *
REM ****************************************************************

IF %QNAME%==LOCAL GOTO LOCAL_MODE

:LAN_MODE
REM ****************************************************************
REM * The following section is to capture printing to a queue     *
REM * chosen by the user.                                          *
REM ****************************************************************

CAPTURE Q=%QNAME% TI=%TIMEOUT% L=1 %FFEED% %TABS% %BANNER% > NUL
GOTO END

:LOCAL_MODE
REM ****************************************************************
REM * The following section is to reset printing to the local     *
REM * printer.                                                     *
REM ****************************************************************

ENDCAP > NUL
GOTO END

:END
```

4.7.2   THE $SHOWCAP.BAT FILE

```
@ECHO OFF
CLS

REM ****************************************************************
REM *                                                              *
REM *                       $SHOWCAP.BAT                           *
REM *                                                              *
REM ****************************************************************
REM * This batch program displays the current capture settings.   *
REM ****************************************************************

ECHO ----------------------------------------------------------------
ECHO CURRENT DEFAULT PRINTER QUEUE = %QNAME%
ECHO ----------------------------------------------------------------

CAPTURE SH

ECHO.
ECHO ----------------------------------------------------------------
ECHO PRESS ANY KEY TO RETURN TO MENU ...
PAUSE > NUL
```

4.8 APPEARANCE OF THE SYSTEMS DURING EXECUTION

Figures 4.5 to 4.7 show the displays produced by some of the support routines.

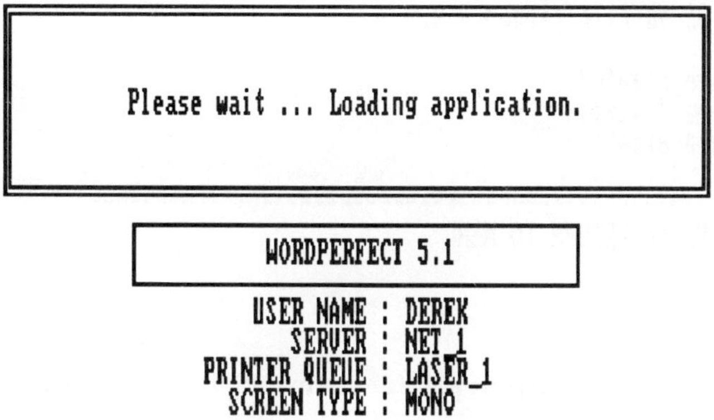

```
┌─────────────────────────────────────────┐
│                                         │
│      Please wait ... Loading application.│
│                                         │
└─────────────────────────────────────────┘

            ┌──────────────────────┐
            │    WORDPERFECT 5.1   │
            └──────────────────────┘
                 USER NAME : DEREK
                    SERVER : NET_1
             PRINTER QUEUE : LASER_1
               SCREEN TYPE : MONO
```

Figure 4.5   Loading WordPerfect ($LOADING.BAT)

```
┌─────────────────────────────────────────┐
│                                         │
│      Please wait ... UNLOADING APPLICATION.│
│                                         │
└─────────────────────────────────────────┘
```

Figure 4.6   Unloading WordPerfect ($UNLOAD.BAT)

```
-----------------------------------------------------------
   Current default printer queue =
-----------------------------------------------------------

Novell Capturing all output to LPT1, and rerouting it to print
queue LASER_01 on file server RSA.

LPT1 : capture enabled
LPT2 : capture disabled
LPT3 : capture disabled

-----------------------------------------------------------
   PRESS ANY KEY TO RETURN TO MENU ...
```

Figure 4.7   Current printer status ($SHOWCAP.BAT)

4.9 SUMMARY

This chapter has given a comprehensive example of how an application access system may be designed and structured. Care has been taken to maintain flexibility by modularising the process and breaking it down into a number of small, simple subroutines.

This approach means that additional routines can be added, and existing routines modified, with a minimum of effort and disruption to the LAN.

5 Troubleshooting Software Related Problems

5.1 GENERAL GUIDELINES

Network problems relating to software can be among the most difficult to identify and remedy, not only because the symptoms can be so varied, but also because in some situations there is simply no ideal solution. Thus the rectification of such problems can be a long drawn-out affair, with no overall guarantee of success.

The first stage in diagnosing software based problems is to determine whether the problem relates to data or programs. If it is the data that is corrupt, it can either be replaced with a backup or an attempt at recovery of the original information may be made. The approach required for data recovery is little different in the network environment than on a standalone system, and further details on the processes of data recovery are provided in *PC Data Recovery and Disaster Prevention* (Harris & Nugus, 1991).

If it appears that the problem is related to the programs and executable files then it is necessary to determine whether or not the situation is due to a conflict, and if so attempt to identify which category of conflict the problem falls into.

If the problem is not due to a conflict, then it is likely to be due to the effects of corrupt software or incorrect installation. The best approach in this case is to reinstall the software and reconfigure the required options.

One other potential source of problem that may exhibit the symptoms of software failure is a virus attack. It is essential that routine anti-virus procedures are adopted in any computer environment and especially with a network. More detail is given on this issue in Chapter 9 as part of a discussion on security issues.

5.2 CONFLICTS

As discussed above, the cause of many network problems often relates to conflicts. A conflict may take one of three forms:

- Conflicts between the network operating system and the application software
- Conflicts between the workstation hardware and the software
- Conflicts between co-existent software systems.

The following sections discuss the three different categories.

5.2.1 NETWORK/SOFTWARE CONFLICTS

Some software is simply not network compatible, ie it can never be made to work on a network. Typical examples of such products include systems which require a 'key disk' to be present before the program will execute, as well as programs which modify their own executable files when they are first installed. The requirements of such programs cannot be satisfied by the network; for example, it is impractical to insert the key disk into the floppy drive of a workstation in order to execute the program.

Other software can be more flexible, but the installation of such products onto a network is often time consuming and difficult. Database systems fall under this heading, as they tend to require certain programs, overlays and data files to be held open whilst the program is executing. Thus the user must be given exclusive rights to the program, thereby excluding other users from accessing the application at the same time.

The legal issues behind the use of such systems on networks are very complex. Systems employing key disk techniques do so in order to maintain a degree of copy protection, although the key disk requirement can occasionally be circumvented by using special software techniques. However, this will almost certainly infringe the licence agreement, and therefore break copyright law. The simultaneous use of such a product by two or more users is certainly in breach of the agreement, and therefore makes the organisation liable to prosecution. Any product that is licensed for multiple users will usually be *network-aware*, and should exhibit very few problems in a network environment. Being network-aware will also usually mean that the program can detect when the licensed number of users are connected, and will not allow additional people access.

One last fact to note in terms of network/software conflicts is whether or not the software is compatible with the particular network in use. If it is not, then the results can be entirely unpredictable, as the programs will have been written and optimised with the facilities of a particular network in mind. Thus the use of such a system on incompatible network hardware, or the use of an unsuitable network operating system, may cause either total or partial loss of functionality. In some cases this can result in extensive loss or corruption of data.

5.2.2 HARDWARE/SOFTWARE CONFLICTS

When an application is installed it will usually require the user to specify the hardware configuration of the system that it is running on. Thus it may be necessary to specify the video adapter (CGA, EGA, VGA, Hercules etc), the printer (dot matrix, laser etc), and even in some cases the particular make of computer that is being used. Thereafter, whenever executed the software will load appropriate drivers automatically depending on the choices made at installation time.

Obviously there are no problems in using this technique for applications running on standalone machines. However, when using such applications in the network environment difficulties can be encountered due to the diversity of hardware and software that is certain to be encountered. Thus, whilst the application may be required to run on a variety of PCs, XTs, ATs etc, each of which may be using a CGA, EGA or VGA adapter, it might be that it can only be installed for one particular configuration.

This will obviously lead to problems unless steps are taken to correct the situation. Chapters 3 and 4 dealt with the configuration issues that should be addressed in order to overcome the hardware compatibility problems that are sometimes experienced.

SOFTWARE TROUBLESHOOTING   99

However, this approach does not work in all situations, as some software does not make use of appropriate driver techniques. Thus it may be necessary to approach the problem in a different way.

Without re-designing the software, there are two primary techniques that can be applied to enable software to be used on the network.

- The hardware can be standardised for those users wishing to use problematic applications. In many organisations this can be achieved by shuffling existing equipment and will therefore require only a minimum of extra investment. However, this approach will limit the use of the product to those workstations that comply with the hardware specifications.

- The software can be installed several times on the file server, using different configuration settings for each installation. For example, a firm wants to use a CAD system on terminals equipped with EGA, VGA and Hercules display adapters. The software provides no simple way for this to be achieved, and so the application is installed three times. The EGA version is situated in a directory called CAD_EGA, the VGA version in CAD_VGA, and the Hercules version in CAD_HERC. Batch file techniques are employed to automatically select the appropriate version of the software depending on the hardware configuration in use.

Whilst this approach will allow the CAD system to be used on any workstation equipped with a EGA, VGA or Hercules adapter, it does introduce its own problems. First, the batch files that execute the appropriate software have to be fool-proof, and there may be difficulties in getting the batch files to work with certain hardware combinations. Secondly, and more importantly, it may be necessary to purchase three copies of the application, depending on the licence agreement. However, in cases where the software will not run at a satisfactory level on the network, the system vendor may be willing to compromise and allow special dispensation to install the program a multiple number of times.

Another problem with the above approach is that a significant amount of disk space on the file server will be required to hold the multiple copies of the package – some CAD systems currently exceed 12MB in size. Some packages provide a facility for installing the software with multiple driver files. This allows the program to be installed once, but executed in several different ways for different hardware configurations. Lotus 1-2-3 is an example of such a system.

The issue of printer selection and configuration is normally addressed by the network operating system. If using the techniques discussed in Chapter 4, then it is necessary for the user to specify a printer before using any application. Thus the data that is to be printed will be automatically routed to the specified printer, irrespective of the settings selected for the application. However, problems can occur even in this operation, as printer data usually contains formatting codes which produce special effects such as different fonts, emboldening, italicising, graphics etc. These special codes differ greatly between printers and therefore data formatted for one particular printer will usually appear as garbage if it is sent to a different one. There are again two ways in which this problem can be solved:

- The task of ensuring that an appropriate printer is selected can be left to the user. This provides a greater amount of flexibility but can cause problems with users who are unfamiliar with the different printers.

- The batch files that execute the application can automatically choose a particular printer. Thus the data will always be formatted in a particular way, and will always be produced on the same printer. This technique is extremely inflexible, and limits the appearance of the printed information to the capabilities of the chosen device. Also if the chosen device fails then it may require a considerable amount of work before users can again print their data using a different printer.

There may be situations in which it is difficult to determine whether or not hardware/software conflicts have occurred. In such cases it is advisable to try and run the system and software on a standalone basis, so that there is no interference between the network, the software and the hardware of the computer. If problems persist then they cannot be due to the interaction of the network and therefore must be caused by the hardware/software configuration. However, if the problems cease then further investigation will be necessary, as they may have been due to the interaction of the network and either the hardware or the software.

5.2.3 SOFTWARE/SOFTWARE CONFLICTS

Some software products require exclusive control of the computer system before they will function correctly, and so there can be no other software programs resident in the computers memory (except the operating system). The conflicts between the different software products in such cases can be due to one of two factors:

- Conflicts between memory usage
- Conflicts between interrupt usage.

5.2.3.1 Memory usage conflicts

These are caused when two different software products attempt to use the same area of memory. The problems are minimised by the operating system, which allocates specific areas of memory for each program, although poorly-written or memory-hungry systems will often exceed the specified boundaries. Also, programs which make use of undocumented DOS features, or those which access the PC hardware directly, may cause problems of this kind.

5.2.3.2 Interrupt usage conflicts

An interrupt is a special signal generated when a particular event occurs. An event may be a request from a part of the PC for attention, such as the disk drive, or it may be a signal from a device to say that it has received some data, such as the keyboard or the communications port. Alternatively it may be a regular signal, such as the clock tick.

These interrupt signals are monitored by software products, and when one occurs a software routine is automatically executed. Thus when a key is pressed, an interrupt signal is generated which causes the DOS keyboard handler routine to be executed. When the timer tick interrupt occurs the routine to update the system date and time is called.

Furthermore these interrupts can be redirected by applications and other programs to cause non-standard routines to be executed when the specific interrupt occurs. Typical of such products are the pop-up utilities such as SideKick and SuperKey. They both remain dormant in memory until an appropriate interrupt occurs to activate them. This interrupt may be a keyboard interrupt, the clock tick interrupt, or the dedicated interrupt that occurs when the Print Screen key is pressed.

If two such programs attempt to use the same interrupt for their own routines then a conflict will occur, and one or both of the programs will fail to operate correctly. Generally speaking the program that is executed first will be the most likely to fail, and the one that is executed last is most likely to operate correctly. This is because of the way in which the programs take control of the interrupt system.

Program that remain in memory in this way are said to be TSRs, or Terminate-Stay-Resident programs. There are many different types of TSRs, from the obvious ones such as the pop-up utilities which includes SideKick and SuperKey, to the lesser known ones such as the DOS kernel, the network driver software and the device drivers that are required for almost every peripheral installed in the computer. If there are conflicts between any two of these systems then problems will be experienced.

5.3 RESOLVING SOFTWARE PROBLEMS

The discussion above has outlined the major causes of problems that are encountered in terms of the applications and network software used on the network. Some of the causes can be circumvented, and in some situations the software can simply be reconfigured. However, there are certain situations in which further action must be taken. The following sections describe the procedures that may be required to remedy such problems.

5.3.1 REINSTALLATION

In certain cases it may be necessary to reinstall the software in order to get it to work properly. Installation of software can be quite a time consuming task as many products are now supplied in archived form, so that they can fit onto a smaller number of diskettes. This means that the files have been compressed and must therefore be uncompressed as part of the installation procedure. Other applications, notably graphics and DTP, create font files, etc, as they are being installed. These files can take in excess of 30 minutes to create. Whilst this is not a problem if the package is only installed once, it can quickly become very tedious if it has to be re-installed a number of times.

During the installation process the system will almost certainly want to know what devices are connected to the computer, especially the display adapter, mouse and printer. The exact choice of these details is dependent upon exactly how the network software is to be used. If the product is to be installed for a particular configuration then exact details of the configuration should be to hand. If it is to be a more flexible configuration then the exact details of the choices made at this point may be less important, as appropriate driver files for the relevant devices will be copied and executed by the batch file when the application is called.

Some software requires that certain interrupt numbers and memory addresses should be specified. Software of this type often works with a particular device such as a scanner or specialist option card, and the addresses relate to the actual card. These systems are rarely network compatible and often have to be installed on a workstation's local drive.

Note that it may be necessary to reinstall the software several times before it works correctly on all workstations, especially those workstations that have non-standard displays or mice. In such cases a trial-and-error approach is often adopted. However, this is not the best technique as it can waste a great deal of time; it is far more productive to spend a few moments searching out the manuals for the system in question to determine exactly what the peripherals are compatible with.

5.3.2 SINGLE USER PRODUCTS

Single user products are very rarely network compatible, and are certainly not designed for concurrent use by two or more people. They often employ copy protection techniques that may require a key disk, or may modify the original source files when they are installed.

The installation of such products onto a network may be in breach of the licence agreement, although there are some systems which do permit this to be done. If this is the case then the exact technique that is required is dependent upon the software. One of the most popular ways to circumvent the protection techniques is to use a product such as COPYIIPC, which includes two programs to overcome the key-disk requirements of many products.

5.3.3 MEMORY HUNGRY PRODUCTS

One of the problems encountered by many network managers is that the applications required by the users cannot be executed on the network workstations due to memory constraints. Typical of such programs is Ventura Publisher, which requires so much of the computer's 640K base memory that it won't run on networked workstations.

The methods that can be used to overcome these problems are numerous. Many of the products and methods discussed in Chapter 8 can be used to release more memory for the applications themselves. The release of DOS version 5 should also help the situation by freeing up even greater amounts of memory. Common sense steps can be taken such as removing all non-essential TSRs from memory (this may require the workstation to be re-booted).

Ultimately it may be that the application simply cannot be executed on a networked workstation, as with Ventura, although future developments will more than likely overcome the problem using new techniques and products. For example, Ventura for Windows will run on any system that can run the Windows operating environment. As Windows now works satisfactorily on most networks, making use of extended memory in workstations, a practical way of using Ventura is available.

5.4 PRODUCT SPECIFIC PROBLEMS

The following sections describe some of the typical problems that can be encountered when working with networked software. Three examples are considered:

- Lotus 1-2-3
- Harvard Graphics
- dBASE IV

The problems discussed in conjunction with these three packages will be common to the majority of networks, but the list is not exhaustive. Thus it may be possible that further difficulties will be encountered when using these systems with certain configurations.

5.4.1 Lotus 1-2-3

When Lotus is installed it requires the user to specify the hardware configuration of the system in use. In particular it needs to know the display adapter and printer that are being used. These choices predominantly affect the production and display of graphs, although in certain cases they can cause other problems. The specifications are stored in a special file on disk, known as a driver file. In Lotus Release 2.X, these files have an extension of .SET, whilst in Release 3.X the extension is .DCF, although the filename can be specified by the user.

Because the settings are specified at the time of installation, the product will not initially work on all different hardware configurations. To overcome the problem the installation routine must be executed again, and new driver files created that are appropriate to all the different hardware configurations that may be in use. These should be named appropriately, for example the file CGA.SET may contain driver information relating to systems equipped with a colour graphics adapter.

By default, Lotus will always choose the driver file called 123.SET. However, it can be forced to use another one when the program is executed by using the command 123 <filename.SET> where <filename.SET> is the name of the required driver file.

This process should be automated by the batch file that executes the application. It must first determine the configuration of the host workstation, and then either issue an appropriate 123 <filename> command, or copy the appropriate driver file to 123.SET and then simply issue the 123 command to execute the program.

To make the process as simple as possible it is suggested that all versions of 123 be installed for the same printers. Lotus actually allows 8 or more different printers to be selected during installation (depending on the release), which should be more than sufficient for most situations.

5.4.2 Harvard Graphics

Due to anomalies in the design of certain versions of Harvard Graphics it is not possible to run the program in the way that it is first installed. Before it can be executed on a workstation, it is important that the files are temporarily copied into the user's data directory. This will ensure that any changes made by the user to the configuration of the software will not affect other users of the system.

There are in fact a number of files that should be transferred to make the system operational. These are as follows:

- HG.OVL
- HG.EXE
- HG.HLP
- HG.DIR
- All files with a .FNT extension.

Once these have been copied to the appropriate subdirectory the program can be executed with the HG command.

A problem that should immediately be obvious is that of security. If all the files that are required for the program to operate are copied to the user's directory then they can be copied and pirated for private use. The chances of this happening can be minimised by having the batch file delete all the above files when the user exits from the application. Thus rather than have a number of COPY commands to replicate the files as was necessary before the program was executed, a number of DELETE or ERASE commands should be included to remove the files afterwards.

5.4.3 dBASE IV

dBASE IV is one of the better behaved application programs when considering networks. It is not necessary to replicate the program files, nor is it necessary to specify driver files etc in order to get the system running.

The only problem that does occur, and it is common to many other products as well, is that dBASE has a tendency to create files for its own use. These are not related in any way to the data files created by the user, nor are they essential for the operation of dBASE when it is next executed. However, as they may be created for every user, they can quickly consume large amounts of storage space and so it is necessary to delete them once the package has been exited.

The files are named CATALOG.CAT and UNTITLED.CAT, and can be removed with DELETE or ERASE commands. Failure to do this will in no way impede the operation of the program, but may lead to overuse of the file server storage media.

The creation of temporary files by software applications is quite common, WordStar and WordPerfect being two further examples. The names of these temporary files are often given in the manuals that accompany the software. For example the WordStar temporary files have extensions of A, B, C etc.

5.5 SUMMARY

This chapter has focussed on how software installed on the file server or workstations of a network can produce problems. Some of the problems can be identified and diagnosed using the principles that apply to standalone systems, and more detail on this topic can be found in *Troubleshooting, Maintaining and Upgrading PCs* (Nugus & Harris, 1992).

It is the area of conflicts that is more specific to the network environment, and it is essential that due care is given to the installation and configuration of software. The keeping of documentation with configuration notes including interrupt and memory usage, software installed and its availability to each workstation on the network will make the modification, upgrading and installation of new software much easier to control.

6 LAN Management Software

6.1 WHY IS LAN MANAGEMENT SOFTWARE NECESSARY?

The network manager is responsible for performing many different tasks on a day to day basis. These vary from monitoring network activity and usage, to solving particular hardware and software based problems. In many cases it is impossible for these tasks to be performed without the use of certain tools and programs.

Programs that are used in these situations generally fall into four categories:
- Network Utilities
- Network monitoring/analysis systems
- Network fault diagnosis systems
- User assistance systems.

6.2 NETWORK UTILITIES

Many network operating systems provide the network manager with only a minimal amount of information relating to the technical aspects of the system. Thus when system and application access batch files are created, for example, it is impossible in some situations to design them to cater for all different workstations.

Third party network utilities allow the supervisor, or any other user for that matter, to gain detailed technical information about many different aspects of the network, the current user account, and the chosen workstation. Typical data produced by these utilities includes:
- The ID, or node address, of the workstation
- The account number and ID of the user
- The user's full name
- Which groups the user is a member of, and what rights the user has
- The hardware configuration of the workstation, in particular its display adapter and port configuration.

Examples of how such utilities may be used to enhance the flexibility of the system have been shown in the chapters on Configuration Issues, Network Access Procedure, and the Application Access Procedure.

These applications are available from a number of different sources. Many are sold by network dealers and vendors under the general title of Network Support Software. However, very high quality utilities can be obtained from other sources, most notably shareware clubs and organisations.

6.3 NETWORK MONITORING/ANALYSIS SYSTEMS

These products are designed to allow detailed information on the network usage to be collated and analysed, in order to determine current usage, performance and efficiency levels. The software can provide information on trends in the usage patterns, which in turn will alert the network manager to the necessity to expand or modify the network in some way.

6.3.1 Monitrix

An example of such a system is Monitrix from Cheyenne Software. Monitrix works only with Novell based LANs, in particular with either *Advanced NetWare 286* version 2.12 or later, or *NetWare 386* version 3.0. The system runs on the file server in the form of a NetWare *Value Added Process* (VAP) or *NetWare Loadable Module* (NLM), and effectively stays very much in the background. Thus it does not impose any undue loading on the file server while it is operating.

Whilst the two versions differ in technical aspects, for example the NLM consumes only 36K RAM whilst the VAP requires 64K, they operate along very similar lines from the user's point of view. The main aim of the utility is to collect network traffic statistics and monitor network nodes, disks and printers. At the same time Monitrix is performing its tasks, it allows the server console to be used normally. The statistics can be stored in a database for later analysis, or they can be viewed in real-time by calling up the Monitrix display on the server console.

Once the data has been recorded, Monitrix allows hard-copy reports to be generated. Alternatively dBASE format data files can be created etc. The use of the dBASE format allows the network manager to create specific reports for use in particular applications. For example, the statistics can be translated through the dBASE format into one of many different spreadsheet formats for further analysis. The statistics produced in either hard-copy or dBASE form give the network manager a full spectrum of information on the network and file server activity.

Whilst the installation of Monitrix is not automatic, it is relatively easy and straightforward. Typically, the network manager software is first loaded onto the hard drive, and then the network monitor software is initiated by selecting the server on which it will run. In terms of system limitations there are relatively few; Monitrix supports the use of an unlimited number of file servers and stations, and will work in conjunction with any NIC that is supported by the appropriate version of NetWare. This means that the overall installation and setup process can be completed in no more than a few minutes, and due to the inherent flexibility of the system there should be no serious problems encountered.

Monitrix is one of the easiest to operate programs in its class. It provides a very intuitive interface through the use of hierarchical menus. The options on the menus are described to give the user an idea of what each achieves. Main menu topics include:

- Node configuration

- Topology and Statistics
- Connectivity check
- Report/Export

Node Configuration provides information on each station and each user logged on to the LAN. This includes the version numbers of the SPX and IPX, the board type and the board settings for each station.

Topology and Statistics produces a graphical display of the interconnected LANs, and provides statistics on the activity of each node for the LAN managers use.

Connectivity check is a point to point test of transmissions. This includes information on source and destination addresses, workstation users, packet sizes, number of diagnostic packets, number of packets received, number of transmit errors and the amount of elapsed time.

Report/Export provides all the facilities required for producing either hard-copy or dBASE formatted reports.

Other features include a communication statistics menu that allows data on SPX, IPX, drivers, DOS, file server process and network bridges to be accessed. Statistics for these areas are displayed both in terms of numeric values and bar graphs that indicate the number of transmit and receive packets.

Any problems or complications that arise in interpreting the data produced by the system can be resolved by referencing the manual. This is very well written, and should serve to answer 95 percent of user queries. It also contains a comprehensive glossary of the terms used for each of the statistics, which goes a long way to helping the network manager understand exactly what the network is doing.

6.4 NETWORK FAULT DIAGNOSIS SYSTEMS

These products are designed to help in the identification and diagnosis of network problems. Many of the products in this category also provide statistical data on network usage, performance and efficiency. However, unlike the less sophisticated monitoring and analysis products discussed above, the fault identification systems use this information in a more technical way, alerting the manager when faults and problems occur in network transmissions.

6.4.1 WatchDog Network Monitor

This product is produced by Network General Corp., who also produce *Sniffer*, one of the more advanced hardware diagnostic tools.

Unlike many of the other software diagnostic tools, WatchDog is selective in terms of the hardware and software with which it will operate. In particular, it is supplied complete with its own Ethernet interface card, as the drivers used by the software have been written specifically for this device. It can be installed on any workstation on the network, and requires DOS 3.1 or above. In terms of the network operating system WatchDog is very much more flexible than its competitors, because it is not restricted to working only with Novell NetWare.

The WATCH program runs in foreground mode on the host workstation, and allows the user to do such things as view statistics and generate reports. When WATCH is executed, it also executes a background routine called WATCHDRV which continually monitors network traffic. If it detects an error condition then it notifies the user with a 'bark' from the loudspeaker, and displays an appropriate message on the screen. The actual criteria for determining whether or not an error condition has occurred can be user-specified in terms of either the entire network or for individual workstations.

WatchDog will collate statistics on up to 1024 network stations, although it does not operate across internetwork bridges. Therefore a second WatchDog system will be required on bridged LANs.

WatchDog is a very comprehensive product in terms of the statistics that it collates and analyses. The issues on which it reports information include:

- The number of error packets
- Protocol usage
- Packet size distribution across the network
- Traffic overloads
- Intruder detection
- Which applications users work with
- How long each user access a given program
- How much stress each user places on the LAN.

These statistics can be viewed either numerically, or as graphical bar charts, both of which are informative and easy to read. All statistical information can be logged to a file on disk for later analysis. Thus when faults are reported it is a simple matter for the network manager to compare the current statistics with past values in order to try and identify the root cause of the problem.

These statistics can also be analysed to produce information on trends and patterns. This is a significant help to the network manager in determining where bottlenecks are likely to occur, and in which direction the network should be expanded to counteract these problems.

6.5 USER ASSISTANCE SYSTEMS

These products are designed to allow the network manager to monitor current users' activities. Many of the products allow the supervisor to see exactly what each user is doing, and in many cases they also permit the supervisor to take control of the user's keyboard as well. Thus if a user is experiencing difficulty in performing some activity in a given application package for example, then the supervisor can show the user exactly which steps they should take to achieve the desired results.

6.5.1 LAN Assist

LAN Assist is a user assistance/monitoring system produced by Fresh Technology. It is actually the first in a suite of three programs, its companions being entitled MAP Assist and Print Assist. The three programs effectively allow the supervisor (or any other user) to take control over any workstation, local drive, or printer that is connected to the network.

LAN Assist works through the use of two programs. A kernel program can be run on any workstation that will allow the main system to later take control or monitor workstation operations. By running this kernel on every workstation when the user first logs in, the supervisor can ensure that they have access to every user that logs on to the network.

At a later point the supervisor can invoke the main LAN Assist program, and choose from a list of users. The supervisor's screen then displays an exact replica of the chosen user's display, and whenever the user's screen changes, so does the supervisor's. Thus the two systems are effectively showing exactly the same data. Similarly, any keystrokes entered by the supervisor will be effected on the user's workstation, thereby allowing the supervisor to take control and issue commands etc.

Other features provided by LAN Assist include chat windows, to allow the supervisor and user to communicate with each other, as well as many other monitoring facilities.

MAP Assist works in a very similar way, but rather than allow the supervisor to take control of the workstation, it allows the local disks on that station to be directly accessed. Thus any data on those devices is made available to the supervisor.

Print Assist allows the supervisor to take control of any networked printer, usually to the exclusion of any other network user.

In the above discussion of the three products the term supervisor should be applied very loosely. In general, any user having access to the main LAN Assist programs will be able to use the full functionality of any of the systems. This can cause obvious problems. For example LAN Assist can be used to remotely reboot any workstation or other network node. Thus it is theoretically possible for a user to reboot the supervisor's workstation, or alternatively destroy their files or lock them out of the system in some way. This problem has been solved on the latest release of LAN Assist, and the supervisor can specify that users should no longer be granted this power.

6.6 SUMMARY

Good monitoring procedures greatly assist network managers to spot potential problems early, sometimes before the user has felt any hint of trouble. Performance monitoring, if acted on correctly, can mean that improvements in the network structure and/or capacity can be made before the system degrades to an unacceptable level of functionality.

Using utilities such as Lan Assist help network managers troubleshoot user problems by allowing almost mini-training sessions to be conducted. Furthermore, these sessions can be performed on-line, in real situations where the user is experiencing real problems.

7 Troubleshooting Component Faults

7.1 INTRODUCTION

Preceding chapters in this book have tended to concentrate on the problems that may be encountered with the software aspects of a local area network, and have examined in some detail a variety of measures that may be taken to combat such situations. However, it should be remembered that the hardware components of the system may also fail, and it is equally important to address the topic of troubleshooting such component failures.

It is important to realise that all the issues, methods and techniques that apply to the troubleshooting of standalone PCs are equally relevant in the network environment; the key difference is that there are a whole host of additional problems that may be encountered due to the network specific components. Therefore in addition to performing specific checks on certain pieces of equipment, it will be necessary to consider the network as a whole in order to try and identify the root cause of the problem. In some situations this may be very different from the device that is exhibiting the symptoms.

7.2 A STRUCTURED APPROACH

Most important is to approach any troubleshooting situation in a structured, orderly manner. Figure 7.1 shows a basic flowchart that illustrates the steps for approaching most faults and involves both the user who actually noticed the symptoms and the troubleshooter. It should be possible for the user to perform these simple checks without any assistance from the troubleshooter. When the steps in Figure 7.1 have been covered and the fault has still not been remedied the system should be handed to the control of the troubleshooter. A second flowchart is supplied for the basic procedures required from this point and this master flowchart references a number of further charts which deal with problems specific to particular components. If from the reported fault the troubleshooter is of the opinion that the fault most likely lies with a particular component such as a local disk drive or a workstation's power supply, having checked for obvious problems, it might be appropriate to move directly to the specialist flowcharts rather than to pursue all the preliminary checks listed below.

7.2.1 SPARE PARTS

At various points in the following pages it is suggested that components are substituted with compatible parts that are known to function for test purposes. If these components

112 A STRUCTURED APPROACH

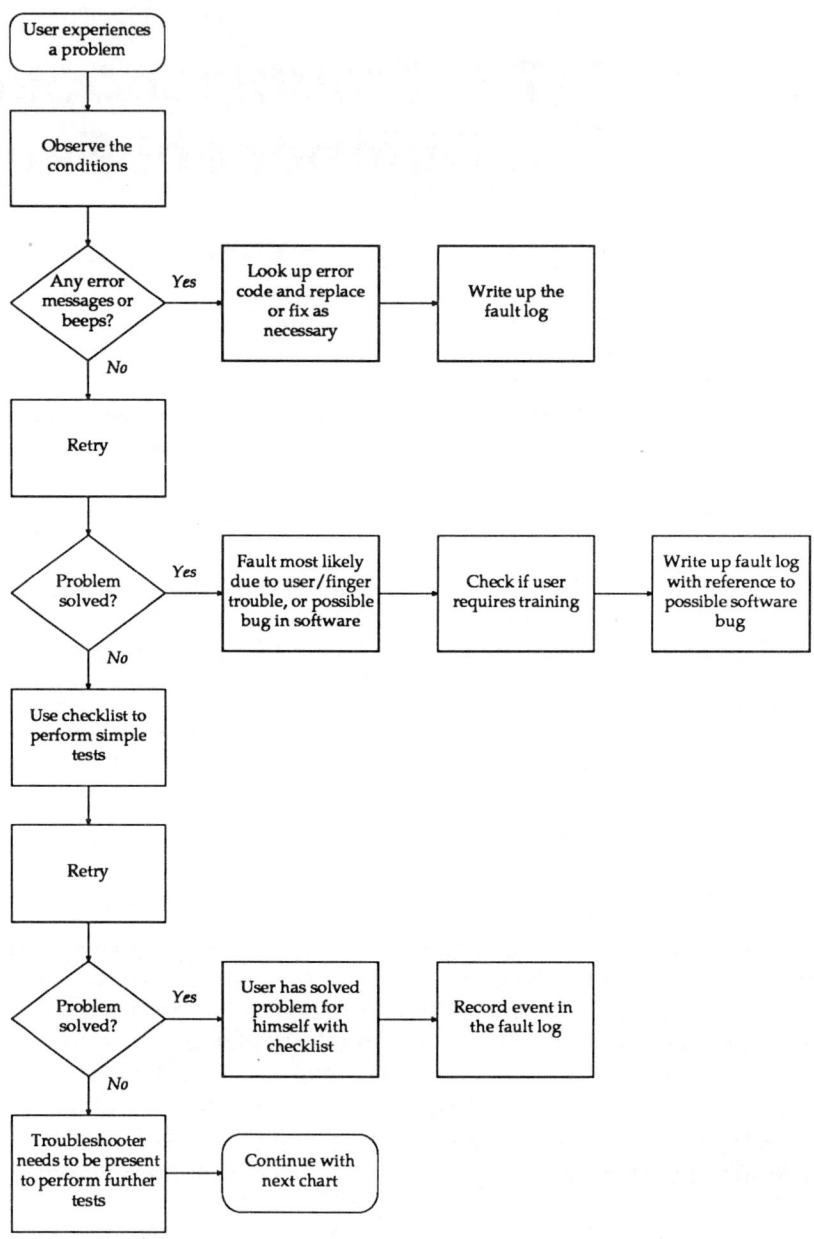

Figure 7.1   Basic troubleshooting flowchart

solve the problem a permanent replacement can be made. It will obviously depend on the size of the support department as to the amount of spare parts that can be held. A popular approach in larger organisations is to have one or two 'phantom' machines, which are fully configured systems that are on the company's asset register but which are not designated to an individual or department. The phantom machines may be specially purchased or they may be systems that have been released due to user upgrades. These systems can be used either as substitute systems if a workstations fails so that users can continue working whilst the troubleshooter endeavours to solve the problem, or they can be used as 'part swappers' in order to test potential failed components on other machines.

In addition to phantom machines, if possible retain redundant parts when upgrading components such as disk drives, memory chips etc, as the old parts may be useful in an emergency situation to restore a system to use, even if only to enable data to be transferred. It may, of course, not always be cost effective to do this as many suppliers will give special prices on new equipment if the old is traded in.

The idea of keeping spare parts also applies to network specific components such as NICs, cables, hubs, repeaters etc. These are as likely to fail as any other component, but their failure may affect the entire network rather than just the user of a single workstation. Therefore it is essential to be able to remedy any such problem in a minimum amount of time. This is especially relevant to the file server, as if this fails then it is most likely that the entire network will fail. Therefore it is essential that spares are kept for the file server. This includes all of the previously mentioned devices, as well as devices such as preformatted and tested hard disk drives, RAM chips or SIMMS etc.

The following list summarises the general spares that any network support department should hold. It is important to note that it will be necessary to hold several of each part to cater for the possibility of multiple systems failing at the same time. Furthermore, the troubleshooter should be aware of the differences between the systems in use in the organisation. For example, what type of cabling do the disk drives in each type of computer require? What speed RAM is installed in the server?

- Cables of all types for both network and and non-network purposes
- Power supplies, suitable for use in workstations and the file server
- Memory chips, SIMMs and SIPs
- Network interface cards for workstations and the file server
- Floppy disk drives and controllers for workstations
- Display cards and monitors
- Hard disk drives and controllers for the file server, and if necessary for the workstations
- Parallel and serial interface cards that are required by printer or comms servers
- Keyboards.

The following sections support the flowcharts and give guidelines that will help in the identification of most types of fault. Note that some problems are specific to particular network technologies, and therefore later sections in this chapter cover some of the typical faults and fault finding devices applicable to Ethernet, ARCnet and Token Ring.

7.2.2 DON'T PANIC

When a user reports a fault it is quite likely that the system has failed in the midst of some critical work – it is also quite likely that the data involved is not fully saved and thus the user is likely to be panicking. It is too easy to say "calm the user down", but at least keep calm yourself and prepare to ask the correct questions in order to most speedily ascertain the source of the problem.

7.2.3 OBSERVE THE CONDITIONS

Information that is usually easy to ascertain from the user is exactly what was happening when the fault occurred. This involves asking questions such as "Did the fault exhibit as the system was switched on?" "Was a program running?" "Were you entering information at the keyboard?" "Were you attempting to save or retrieve a file?" "What command were you attempting to issue?"

Eyes, ears and nose are all useful detectives when trying to ascertain the source of a problem. Users must be encouraged to understand what the lights on their computer represent in order that questions such as "Were the disk drives' lights on?" "Is there a power light showing?" "Did the system beep, flash or display any kind of error message on the screen?" can be asked. If a local disk drive is failing due to a fault with the motor or other moving parts, it may make unusual sounds when trying to access data on the disk. Finally, in some circumstances, usually those connected with power faults, there may be a smell of burning material.

Warning

If a user reports any kind of evidence suggesting power problems, ensure immediately that all mains power has been disconnected from the workstation, but do not allow the user to touch the computer further.

If the user is able to report some useful observations, such as seeing an error code or message displayed on the screen or hearing a series of beeps, it may be possible for the fault to at least be diagnosed, if not repaired without needing to proceed further along this flowchart. Error codes and messages that relate to workstation hardware problems will often enable the troubleshooter to isolate the problem at least to a major component such as the disks, monitor, keyboard etc. A full listing of these can be found in *Troubleshooting, Maintaining and Upgrading PCs* (Nugus and Harris, 1992). Once the component has been identified, the appropriate flowchart for that area should then be consulted in order to further diagnose the problem. In fact, in some cases the error message is so specific as to report the chip that has failed.

Error messages relating to the network can often be more confusing. Whilst it is true to say that many errors are detailed fully in the manuals for the network operating system, it is also true that many others are not. For example, certain versions of Novell Netware may, under extreme circumstances, produce a 'GPI Interrupt' error message. Although references to this error may be found in some textbooks, what it means in real terms is that the operating system cannot perform the requested operation but it doesn't know why! In other words this is a catch-all error message that caters for unforeseen problems. Therefore diagnosing the cause of this fault is far from easy. Other network components, such as NICs can also produce similarly cryptic error messages.

7.2.4 WRITE DOWN WHAT HAPPENED

Users must be encouraged to record problems on paper. This should include a list of all the conditions observed at the time of the system failure. Users should have a checklist that they can answer at the time a fault occurs. Figure 7.2 is an example of such a checklist.

Checklist to be Completed in Case of System Failure

- What were you trying to do at the time of failure?
- Are there any error messages being displayed?
- What is your workstation doing that it shouldn't be?
- What is your workstation not doing that it should?
- What parts of your system appear to still be functioning?
- Which indicator lights are still on?
- Is any unit smelling, or are any devices unduly hot?
- Can you run a software program, or issue a command, other than the one that was attempted at the time of the failure?
- Have you changed your SETUP, CONFIG.SYS or AUTOEXEC.BAT files?
- Have you installed a new version of DOS onto your workstation recently?
- Have you recently installed new software onto a local drive?
- Have you installed any new peripherals into the workstation?
- Has anyone different had access to your system recently?

Figure 7.2 User checklist

In some cases the act of completing the checklist can lead to a problem diagnosis and maybe even repair. This will largely depend on the experience of the user. For example, if a user had changed CONFIG.SYS it is likely that he or she has enough knowledge to be able to change this file again and in some cases to thereby rectify the fault. Of course, a little knowledge can be a dangerous thing, and the user may not be able to get the system back into a working order. It does, however indicate to the troubleshooter where the source of the problem lies.

7.3 ROUTINE CHECKS

In addition to the checklist of questions in Figure 7.2, users should be supplied with a few basic routines that they can perform before reporting a fault, as shown in Figure 7.3.

If any of the points in the checklist show a potential problem, it is of course important to retry after correction. Furthermore, as many faults are due to finger trouble or user error, it is often advisable to coach the user through a retry exercise. However this will depend to some extent on the nature of the problem. For example, if it is suspected that the workstation has been attacked by a virus, the user should leave the system alone as any attempt to access the network facilities may result in further problems. At this stage the troubleshooter should tackle the problem with appropriate virus detecting software.

> **Main system**
> - Is the power cable properly connected to the wall socket and to the PC, and is the wall socket switched on?
> - Is the network cable connected to the NIC?
> - Is the connection properly made, ie is the cable fixed in place or is it just loosely connected?
>
> **Monitor**
> - If there is a separate power source, is it connected and powered on?
> - Are the contrast, brightness and colour buttons correctly set?
>
> **Keyboard**
> - In the case of switchable XT/AT keyboards, is it correctly set?
>
> **Local disks**
> - If working with floppy disks, are disks inserted correctly and is the drive door properly closed?
> - If experiencing write problems with floppy disks, are there write protect tabs in place?

Figure 7.3   User guidelines for routine checks

Even if a retry procedure does not solve the problem, it might cause it to re-exhibit, which in turn can help the troubleshooter diagnose the cause. If the problem is related to a floppy disk, it is always worth trying another disk and even another disk drive before attempting more in-depth diagnostics.

If the problem is remedied when the user retries the operation, then it may be worth making a quick note of the circumstances under which the problem occurred. The reason for this is that although it is possible that the fault was due to user error or finger trouble, it is also possible that it is due to an intermittent hardware or software problem. Recording when it occurs will make it easier to identfiy the underlying cause.

7.4 PROBLEM REPORTS AND FAULT LOGS

It is important to maintain a detailed log of all faults encountered, relating to both hardware and software, including a description of the action taken to remedy the fault. This should be a two tier operation with a fault log and a problem report.

The fault log is a brief description of the problem as it was reported and there should be a fault log for every computer installed in the firm. Figure 7.4 is an example of such a log. Notice the reference to the computer by name and by serial number. The fault log may either be kept in the troubleshooting department, or it may be left with the computer.

A separate problem report should also be kept that outlines more details of the problem and the steps that were necessary to solve it. Figure 7.5 shows a typical problem report for the last fault listed on the fault log.

FAULT LOG

MACHINE MODEL: TANDON 386/20   **SERIAL #:** 1-0889-54723

Date fault Occurred	Details of Fault	Date Fault Reported	Name	Date Fault Fixed	Name	Problem Report Ref.
11-1-91	Would not boot from C: drive at all	11-1-91	J. Anderson	11-1-91	P. Thomas	110191/0134
27-1-91	Bad data written to floppy by A: drive	28-1-91	J. Anderson	28-1-91	P. Snellings	280191/0279
15-3-91	Printer will not work at all.	15-3-91	H. Barnton	15-3-91	P. Thomas	150391/044
23-5-91	Would not boot from C: drive at all	23-5-91	J. Anderson	23-5-91	P. Thomas	230591/0529
24-5-91	Lost files & corrupt data on C: drive. WP5 cannot read it's own data files	24-5-91	J. Anderson	30-5-91	P. Thomas	300591/0624

Figure 7.4   Computer system fault log

PROBLEM REPORT

Reference: 300591/0624

Date and Time Fault Occurred: 24-5-91, 10:30 AM

Details of Problem: WORDPERFECT 5 CANNOT ACCESS ITS DATA FILES. SOME ARE CORRUPTED, SOME ARE LOST COMPLETELY.

Location of System: FLOOR 3, MARKETING OFFICE, JOAN ANDERSON'S DESK

Networked (Yes/No): NO

Hardware Configuration: TANDON 386/20, 80MB HARD DRIVE, TWIN FLOPPIES, HPLJ PRINTER, VGA DISPLAY.

Software Configuration: MS-DOS 3.2, WORD PERFECT 5.1, VENTURA PUBLISHER, 1-2-3, COMMS SOFTWARE. APPROX 25MB OF DATA FILES.

Operation Attempted: TRIED TO LOAD WORD PERFECT DATA FILES.

Details of Remedial Procedure: RECENT HISTORY OF HARD DISK PROBLEMS. AGREED TO CHANGE HARD DISK UNIT
- REMOVED SEAGATE 80MB MFM UNIT
- INSTALLED SEAGATE 110MB MFM UNIT.

RE-INSTALLED SOFTWARE + DATA FILES ONTO NEW DISK.

TESTED WITH MULTIPLE READ/WRITE OPS.

RETURNED 30-05-91

Figure 7.5 A typical problem report

It is surprising how often problems recur and in time keeping problem reports make solving future problems much quicker and easier. If for any reason it is impractical to use a manual system such as that shown in Figures 7.4 and 7.5, there are a number of software packages available now that allow this data to be stored on a computer, thus making cross referencing and fault finding even easier. In larger organisations a database interrogation system could be developed that cross-references with the asset register.

All the flowcharts in this chapter end a successful diagnosis and repair with the instruction to write up the fault log and problem report.

7.5 HAND CONTROL TO THE TROUBLESHOOTER

At this point in the troubleshooting flowchart it is likely that it is no longer possible for the user to solve the problem his/herself, either alone or with the troubleshooters help. Instead the troubleshooter will have to look more closely at the system in an attempt to identify the failed component or peripheral.

The first step is for the troubleshooter to attempt to identify the scope of the problem:

- Is the problem confined to a single workstation?
- Is the problem confined to a particular section of the network?
- Is the problem affecting the entire network?

To determine the scope of the problem it will be necessary for the troubleshooter to run a number of tests, to see if the problem can be replicated on any other workstations.

If the problem appears to be confined to a single workstation, then it is most likely that there is some form of hardware problem with that particular PC. The flowcharts in Figures 7.6 and 7.7 can be followed to identify the cause. Before opening up the workstations system box, it is worth checking the SETUP, CONFIG.SYS and AUTOEXEC.BAT files (if the system will boot up) and also any software on local drives can be checked to ensure that it has been correctly installed. These checks should already have been incorporated in the checklist above, but it is wise not to entirely trust the judgment of the user and as the basic setup of a system is a common source of problems, it is always worth double-checking. It is also advisable to run the diagnostics disk that should have been supplied with the computer to see if any errors can be detected this way. Proprietary utilities might also be useful at this stage to check things such as the disk drive spindle speed or the presence of bad sectors on the disk. When all external checks have produced nothing helpful, the next step is to open up the system box and investigate inside. Figures 7.6 and 7.7 show the flowcharts that the troubleshooter should pursue from this point..

If the problem appears to affect more than just one workstation then it is most likely to be due to the transmission media. This includes not only the actual cabling system, but also devices such as active hubs, passive hubs, repeaters, multistation access units, terminators etc. However, it could also be due to component failure in the file server itself. If the transmission media is deemed to be the cause, the flowcharts in Figures 7.17 and 7.18 should be followed. If it is thought that the file server has in some way failed then the flowcharts in Figures 7.6 and 7.7 can be followed, as the file server is just a PC, albeit a rather high-spec one.

The following sections outline some of the key issues that need to be addressed during the troubleshooting process.

120 HAND CONTROL TO THE TROUBLESHOOTER

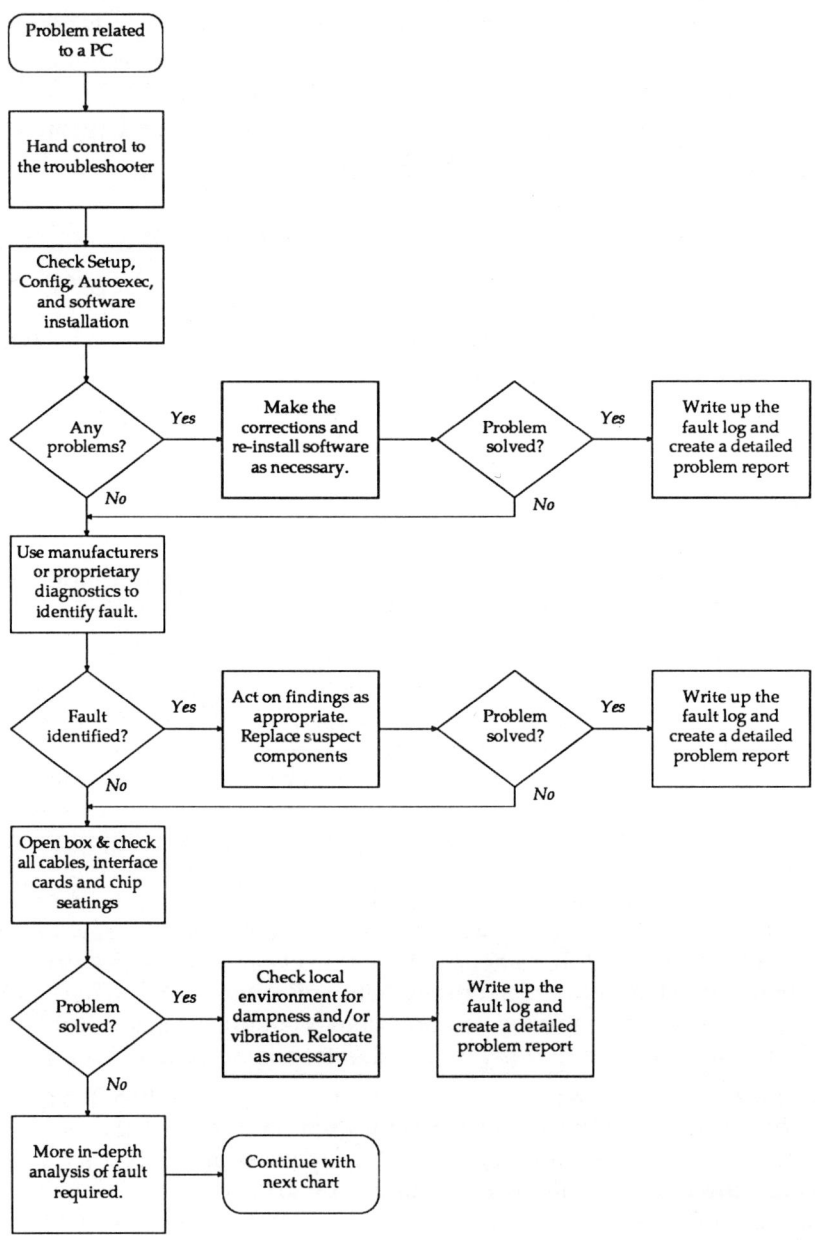

Figure 7.6 More detailed troubleshooting flowchart

TROUBLESHOOTING COMPONENT FAULTS 121

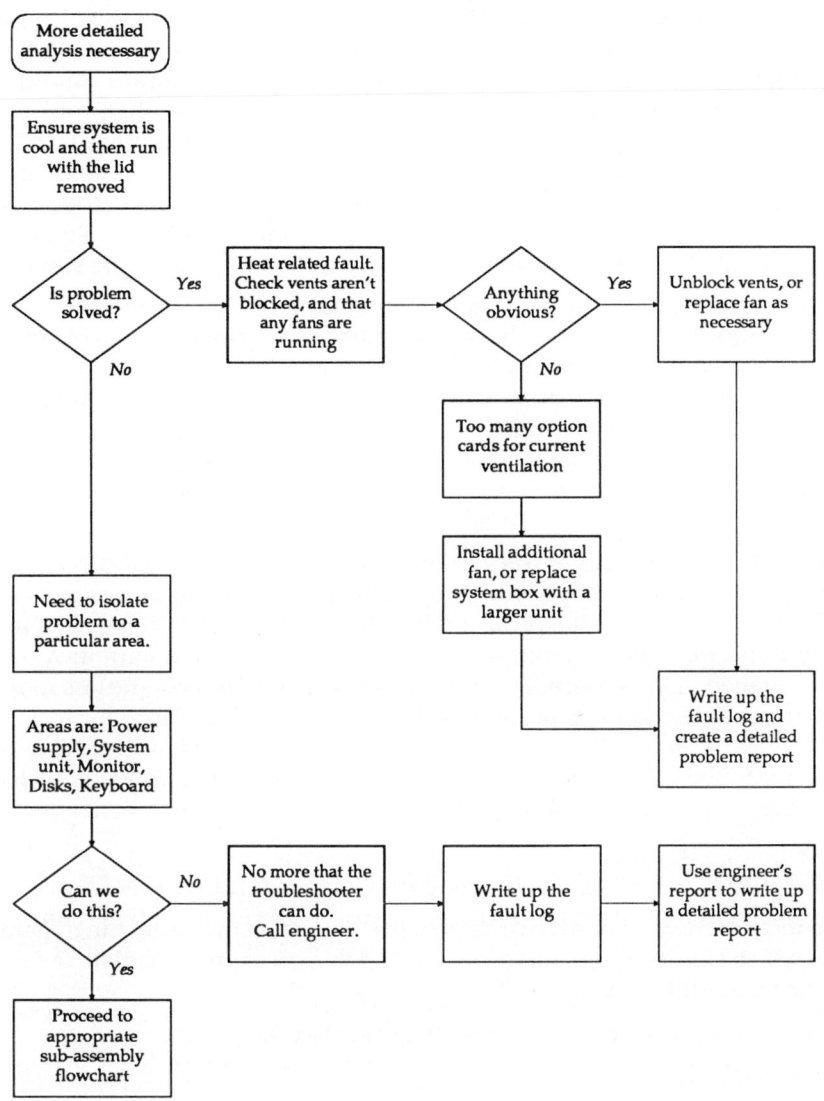

Figure 7.7   More detailed troubleshooting flowchart

122 THE POWER SUPPLY

7.6 HEAT AND MOISTURE

It is surprisingly common to find interface cards and chips not properly seated into their sockets on the motherboard. Chips in particular are prone to a disease called 'chip creep', the main cause of which is vibration. Moisture is a problem area as well, causing corrosion of the chip pins, which in turn leads to bad connections. Therefore if cards and chips can be pushed more firmly into their sockets, and this appears to solve the problem under investigation, it is important to check the environment that the computer is located in. Stacked systems with printers on top of the computer is generally not recommended as this can produce both excess heat and undue vibration. Computers in hot rooms without air conditioning can be prone to humidity and dampness. If it is not possible to improve the air conditioning, the purchase of a portable dehumidifier can help the situation.

Heat can cause problems in other ways. In particular it can be responsible for a range of intermittent faults. For example if the vents on the system box are blocked, then there may be insufficient circulation of air inside the system. This can lead to the disk drive motor overheating which in turn causes the casing of the drive to overheat and ultimately in an extreme case the disk surface itself. The power supply can also overheat if the vents are blocked or if the internal fan fails, which can lead to intermittent power problems, or in an extreme case to complete power supply failure. These heating effects can also affect chips on the motherboard which can then fail.

To test for heat related problems the system should be cool and then run for a period of time with the lid off, and perhaps with an additional fan to ensure components cannot overheat. If this seems to solve the problem, but the vents and fans in the system are all clear and operating well, the problem is then likely to be associated with the number of option cards installed in the system. The more option cards in the box, the less room there is for the air to circulate and thus the ventilation supplied with the original specification cannot cope with the load. The problem can sometimes be solved by installing an additional fan into the existing system. However, in a very overcrowded system it is usually preferable to transfer everything into a larger system box with better ventilation.

7.7 DIAGNOSE A PARTICULAR PERIPHERAL OR UNIT

At this stage most of the prospective problems that can affect the system in general have been assessed. If the fault still has not been isolated it is necessary to isolate the problem to a particular area of the system.

The five areas of the system that have been categorised here are:
- the power supply
- the disk drives
- the system unit
- the monitor
- the keyboard.

7.8 THE POWER SUPPLY

Figure 7.8 is a flowchart illustrating the troubleshooting steps that can be followed to ascertain whether the power supply unit (PSU) in the system is at fault.

TROUBLESHOOTING COMPONENT FAULTS 123

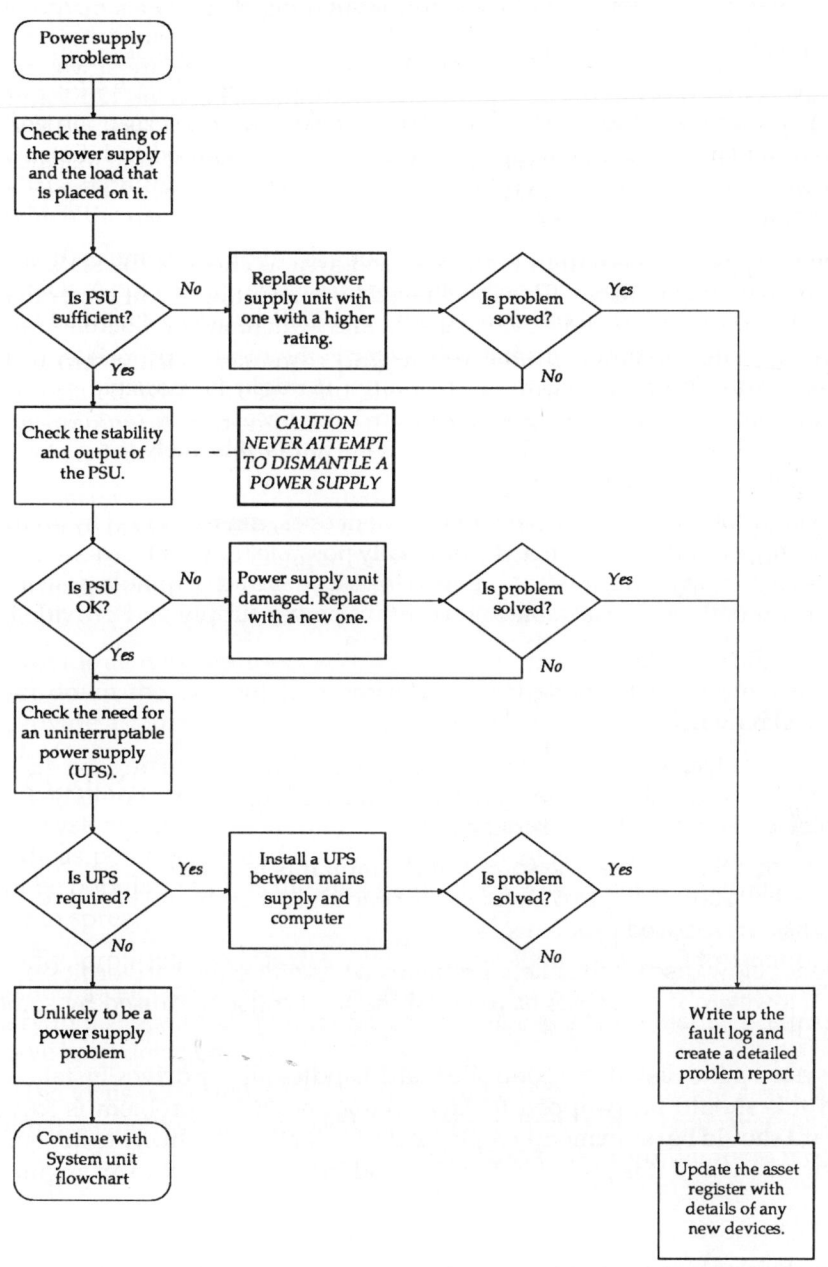

Figure 7.8   Flowchart for diagnosing power problems

124 DISK DRIVES

Computer systems require different power supplies depending on their configuration. For example an XT with few option cards installed does not require as much power as a 486 system with several option cards. When troubleshooting the power supply, the rating of the power supply is one of the first things to check and if the system is underpowered a replacement power supply should be installed. Generally speaking, most systems based around the 8086/8088 processor will require power supplies of between 120W and 180W. Those based around the 80286 will require 150W–250W, whereas 80386 and 80486 will typically require 200W–300W of power. These figures are for normal systems; file servers supporting multiple disk drives and many option cards may need higher ratings, sometimes as much as 350W or 400W.

If the ratings appear to be within limits the next area to check is the stability of the power supply in terms of output. This is achieved by connecting a volt meter to each of the connectors coming from the power supply and watching for fluctuations in the output value. For this purpose a digital volt meter is the most appropriate. If this test shows a single wire in one connector to be faulty, it might be possible to swap this connector for another unused one and thus avoid the necessity of purchasing a new power supply. If however, several wires are showing faults, it is likely the power supply unit itself is faulty and it should be replaced.

Some power problems, and especially intermittent ones, can be caused by an unstable mains power supply. If this is suspected it is usually possible for the Electricity Company to test the supply. In any case, it is advisable to install an uninterruptable power supply (UPS) which will both ensure a stable and constant power supply and provide backup power in the case of total power failure.

7.9 DISK DRIVES

The stability and output of the power supply can also exhibit by causing the disk drives to fail intermittently and thus the section above on checking power should be followed when troubleshooting disk drive problems.

If power is not deemed to be the source of the fault it is necessary to establish which drive or drives have failed. Figure 7.9 shows the procedure that should be followed when diagnosing disk drive based problems.

The sections below discuss the likely problems when either the hard or floppy drives are at fault. However, if all drives have failed the fault must be caused by something common to all drives.

In some systems the disk drive controller card handles all the drives installed in the system and this should be swapped for a working one. If the problem is solved the controller card should be permanently replaced, but if not then it is likely to be something on the motherboard and it is probably time to hand the system over to an engineer.

7.9.1 FLOPPY DISKS

Always begin by checking the condition of the disk media in another working system. If it fails in the other system, format a new disk and try using this in the original system. If it works, it is either the media that is faulty, or the disk drive is corrupting the media. If the disk still does not work, then the problem is more likely to be connected with the drive unit. Figure 7.10 shows the procedure that should be followed to identify the problem.

TROUBLESHOOTING COMPONENT FAULTS 125

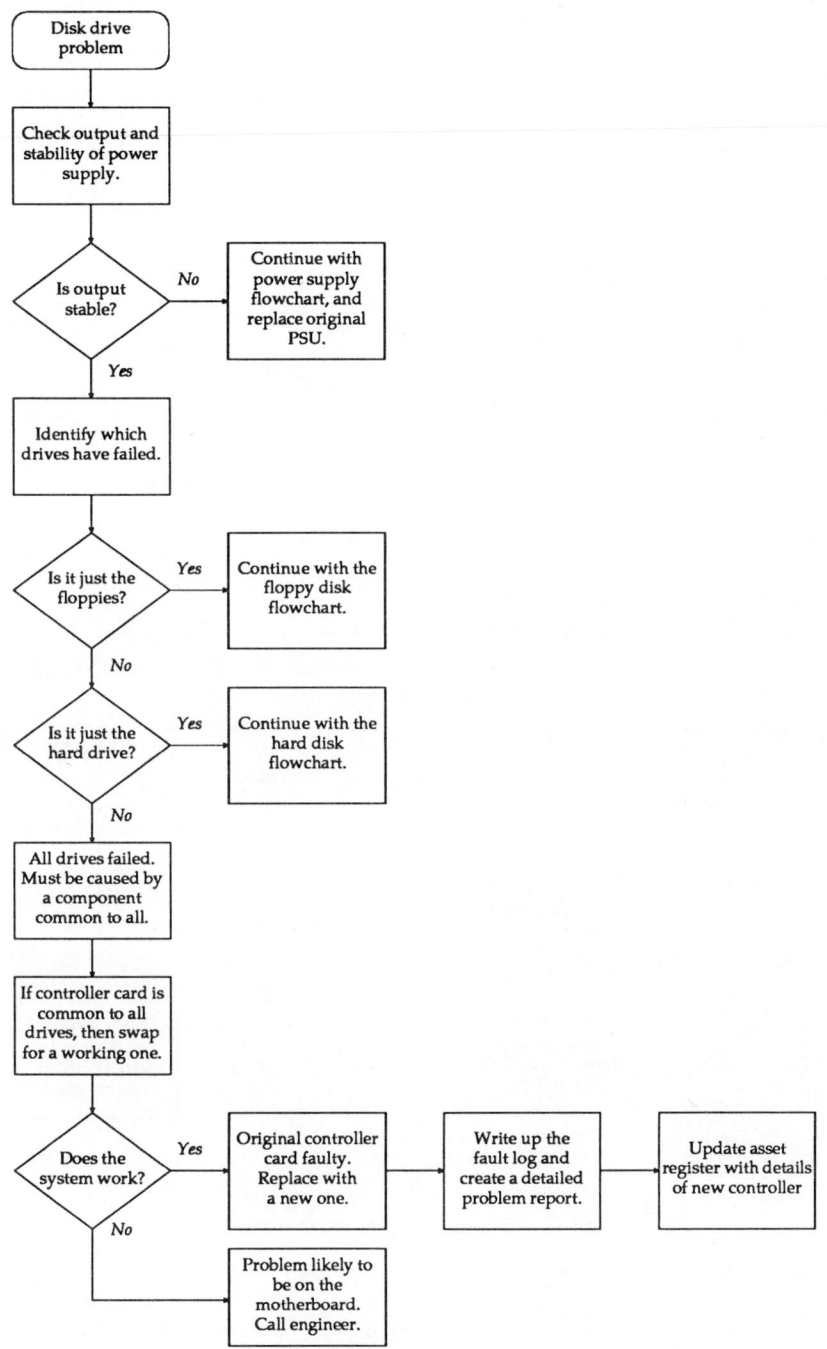

Figure 7.9 Flowchart for diagnosing disk problems

126 FLOPPY DISK PROBLEMS

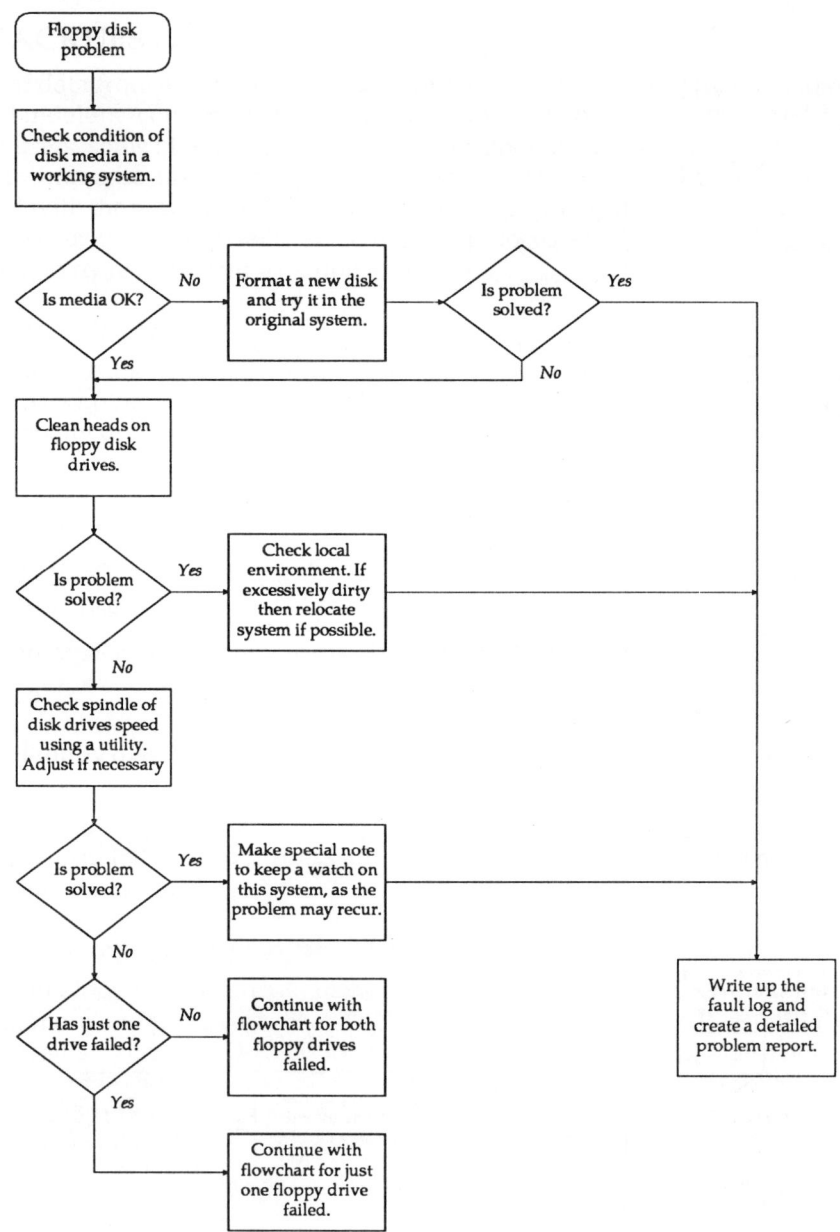

Figure 7.10 Diagnosis of floppy disk problems

TROUBLESHOOTING COMPONENT FAULTS

Around 80 percent of floppy disk drive failures are due to dirty heads on the drive. In much the same way as it is recommended to clean audio tape drives and video tape drives, it is also important to regularly clean the heads of floppy disk drives. There are two ways to do this. Either a proprietary drive cleaning kit may be used which involves placing a few drops of cleaning solution onto a special disk and then inserting the disk in the drive and making the drive turn. Alternatively the heads can be manually cleaned with a cotton bud and cleaning solution. This would normally only be necessary if a drive had been badly neglected and the disk cleaning kit was not able to clean the heads.

The problem is to decide how regularly the cleaning operation should be performed. Factors that influence this decision include the environment the computer is located in and the amount of usage the disk drive has. If the computer is located in a factory or in some other dusty environment, the heads will gather dust more quickly than on a computer in a clean office environment. Similarly, if the computer operator smokes (which should be strongly discouraged in any case), this will cause the heads to clog up with ash and tar and cleaning must be performed more regularly. With regards disk drive usage, much of the dirt that accumulates on the drive heads comes from the floppy disks and thus the more disks that are inserted in the machine, the more likely particles will gather on the drive heads.

Some drive cleaning kits suggest cleaning every day. This is definitely too often and will be detrimental to the life of the disk. Once a week should be the most frequent period and once a fortnight or once a month should be adequate for most environments. When using drive cleaning kits there are a few guidelines which should be followed:

- The cleaning disk should have a series of boxes on it indicating the number of times it may be used before replacement. It is important not to exceed the recommended number of uses as re-using the same disk too many times will cause dirt to be transferred from the cleaning disk back onto the heads.
- Use only the recommended amount of cleaning solution.
- Do not allow the cleaning disk to spin in the drive for more than about 30 seconds. Entering a DOS command such as DIR will cause the disk to spin whilst the system tries to read information from it. When the system cannot read the disk it will stop spinning and display the Abort, Retry, Fail message on the screen.

There is a problem with this approach to making the disk spin which is that entering DIR always causes DOS to search the first track of the disk and thus it is only the outmost part of the cleaning disk that is ever used. Various utilities are available which spin the disk for approximately 30 seconds whilst at the same time moving the head back and forth across the read/write area to ensure that the cleaning disk is uniformly worn.

7.9.1.1 Spindle speed

Another common culprit for faulty floppy disk drives is an incorrect spindle speed setting. The recognised standards are 300 or 360RPM, depending on the type of drive. There are a number of spindle speed test utilities and these will identify the tolerance limits for the spindle speed. If a disk drive is outside the tolerance range it can usually be brought back into line by adjusting the drive whilst it is running the test utility.

Faulty spindle speeds are often the cause of intermittent disk drive problems, and in

128 DISK DRIVE FAILURE

particular can exhibit when users of two machines exchange disks, as a disk formatted and used on a faulty system alone will sometimes function without problem. If, however, an attempt is made to use that disk on another system it may not work. Similarly, a disk from another machine that is within the tolerance range will quite likely not work in the faulty machine.

7.9.1.2 Identify which drive

The above techniques for floppy disk drives are fairly routine and would normally be performed on both drives. If the problem in hand still has not been solved it is necessary to be clear whether both floppy drives have failed or whether the problem can be isolated to one or other drive.

Both Drives

If neither floppy drive appears to function, it is reasonably safe to assume that the problem must be with a component common to both disk drives. Therefore the areas at most risk are the power supply, the ribbon cable connecting the drives to the controller card, the controller card itself or possibly, but least likely, a problem on the system board. Figure 7.11 shows the procedure that should be followed. It is assumed at this stage that all power supply related faults have already been examined; if this is not the case, refer back to the power supply section.

The simplest area to check first is the cable connecting the drives to the controller card. It is quite common to run two floppy disk drives from a single controller card and to connect the drives via a single ribbon cable with two connectors along it. To test this cable a replacement one should be tried. If this does not solve the problem the next step is to swap the controller card itself.

> Warning
>
> *Care must be taken when swapping a controller card from another machine that a compatible card is used.*

Although it is just possible that both the floppy disk drive units have failed and if circumstances allow, they could be swapped out for alternative ones, it is more likely that the failure is on the motherboard and the troubleshooter has gone as far as possible. The engineer should be called at this stage.

One Drive Failed

If it is possible to isolate one or other floppy disk drive it is necessary to establish which component has failed. It could be, as with both drives, the cable or the controller card, but it could also be the disk drive unit itself. Figure 7.12 shows the procedure that should be followed to identify the faulty component.

To test for the drive being at fault, the cables for drive A and B can be swapped. If the faulty drive now functions, either the cable or controller card is at fault. In this case each should be substituted and the system tested. If the problem persists the fault is likely to be on the motherboard and an engineer should be called.

If the drive still does not function after swapping the cables, the drive unit itself is at fault and should be replaced. Note that as the price of floppy disk drives today is quite

TROUBLESHOOTING COMPONENT FAULTS 129

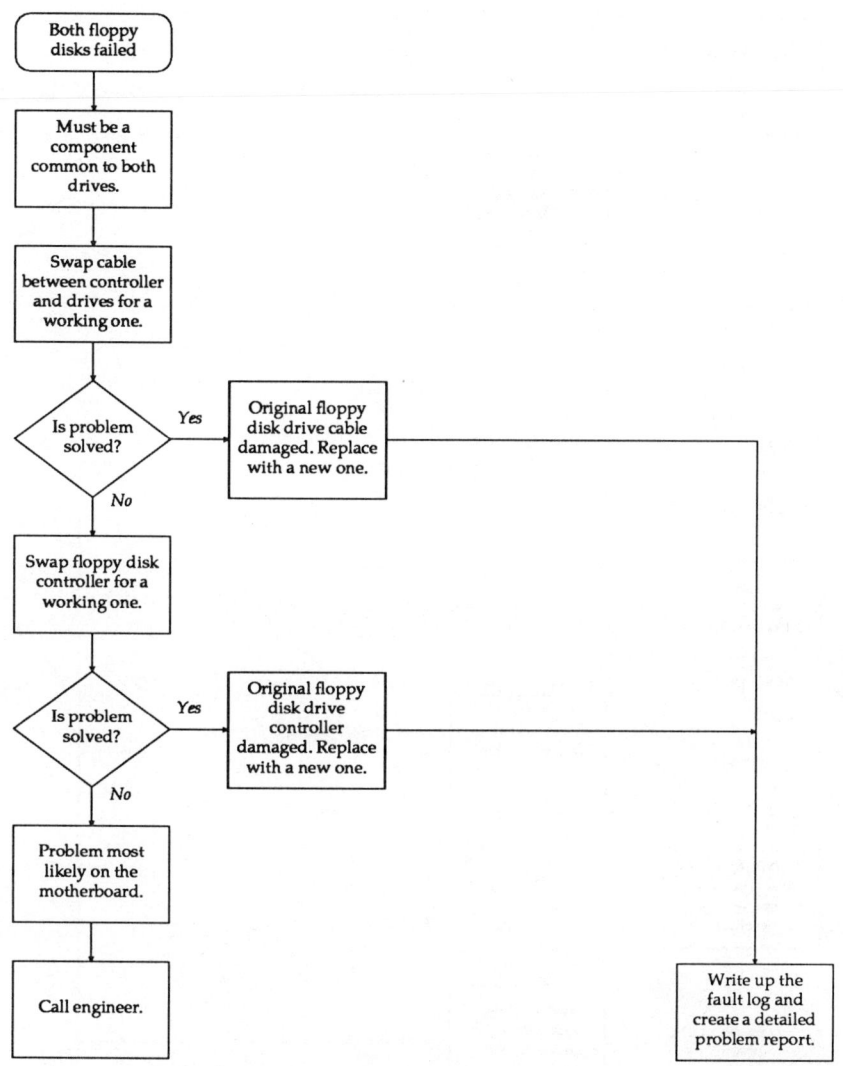

Figure 7.11 Floppy disk problems – both drives

130 FAILURE OF ONE DRIVE

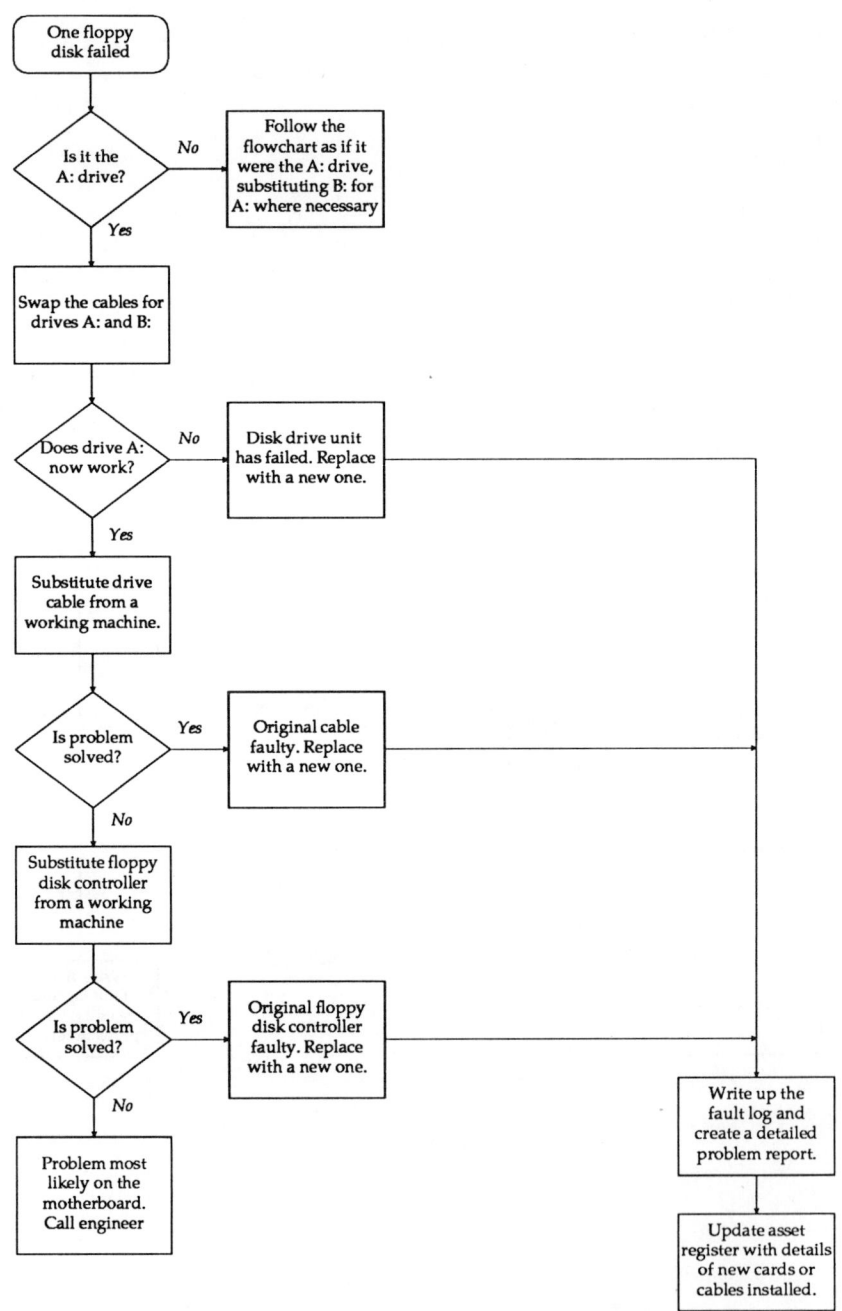

Figure 7.12   Floppy disk problems – one drive

TROUBLESHOOTING COMPONENT FAULTS 131

low it is usually not worth further investigating the fault on the drive for repair purposes.

7.9.2 HARD DISK PROBLEMS

As with floppy disk drive problems, failures connected with a hard drive can be with the power supply, the cables, the controller card, the drive itself or the motherboard. Figure 7.13 shows the procedure required for diagnosing hard disk problems.

Assuming power supply associated problems have been checked using the power supply section of the troubleshooting guide, the next area to check is the connector cables. These can be substituted with alternative compatible cables and the machine tested. If this does not solve the problem the disk controller card can be substituted.

> **Warning**
>
> *If it is thought likely that the drive itself has failed, on no account should an attempt be made to open up the drive as not only would this invalidate any warranty that might be on the equipment, but it will almost certainly render the drive useless.*

If it is possible to substitute another drive, this should be tried and if the system works a replacement drive can be permanently installed. If the problem persists it is likely to be a motherboard failure and an engineer should be called.

7.9.2.1 Integrated drive electronics

A new form of disk drive technology is becoming increasingly popular on modern PCs. Integrated Drive Electronics (IDE) refers to systems that have the majority of the controller logic for a disk drive on the drive itself and on the motherboard, thus negating the need for a complex drive controller card. If this type of drive gives problems, there are less components that can be substituted and it may be necessary to exchange the drive unit in order to see whether the drive or the motherboard is at fault.

7.10 SYSTEM BOARD

Figure 7.14 shows the flowchart that should be followed when suspecting a fault is connected with the motherboard itself.

Although it should already have been done in the early stages of the troubleshooting procedure, the chip seatings, interface card and cable connections should all be double-checked and the system re-tried.

It is likely that by the time the troubleshooter reaches this stage a number of other checks will already have been performed in an attempt to isolate the source of the problem. Therefore, it has proved difficult to isolate the problem with the computer configuration as it is currently set.

The next step is therefore to strip the system to the simplest possible configuration. This means removing any expanded memory cards, communication or network adapters and any other interface cards not essential to the operation of the system. Before attempting to test the machine, make sure that any dip switches or jumpers have been adjusted as necessary and that the SETUP, CONFIG.SYS and AUTOEXEC.BAT have been revised accordingly. If the system now works, the problem is likely to either be incorrectly set switches, SETUP or CONFIG files or to be due to a faulty peripheral card.

132 HARD DISK PROBLEMS

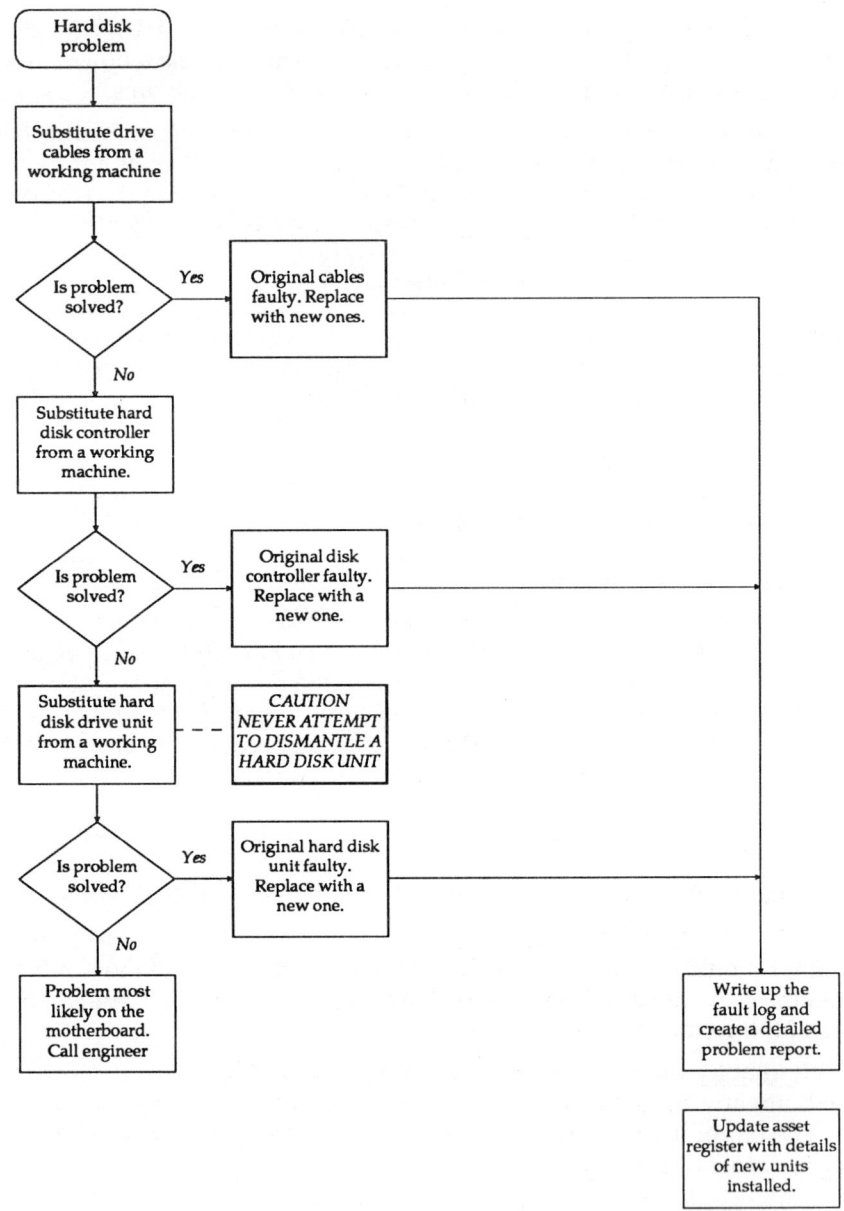

Figure 7.13   Diagnosis of hard disk problems

TROUBLESHOOTING COMPONENT FAULTS 133

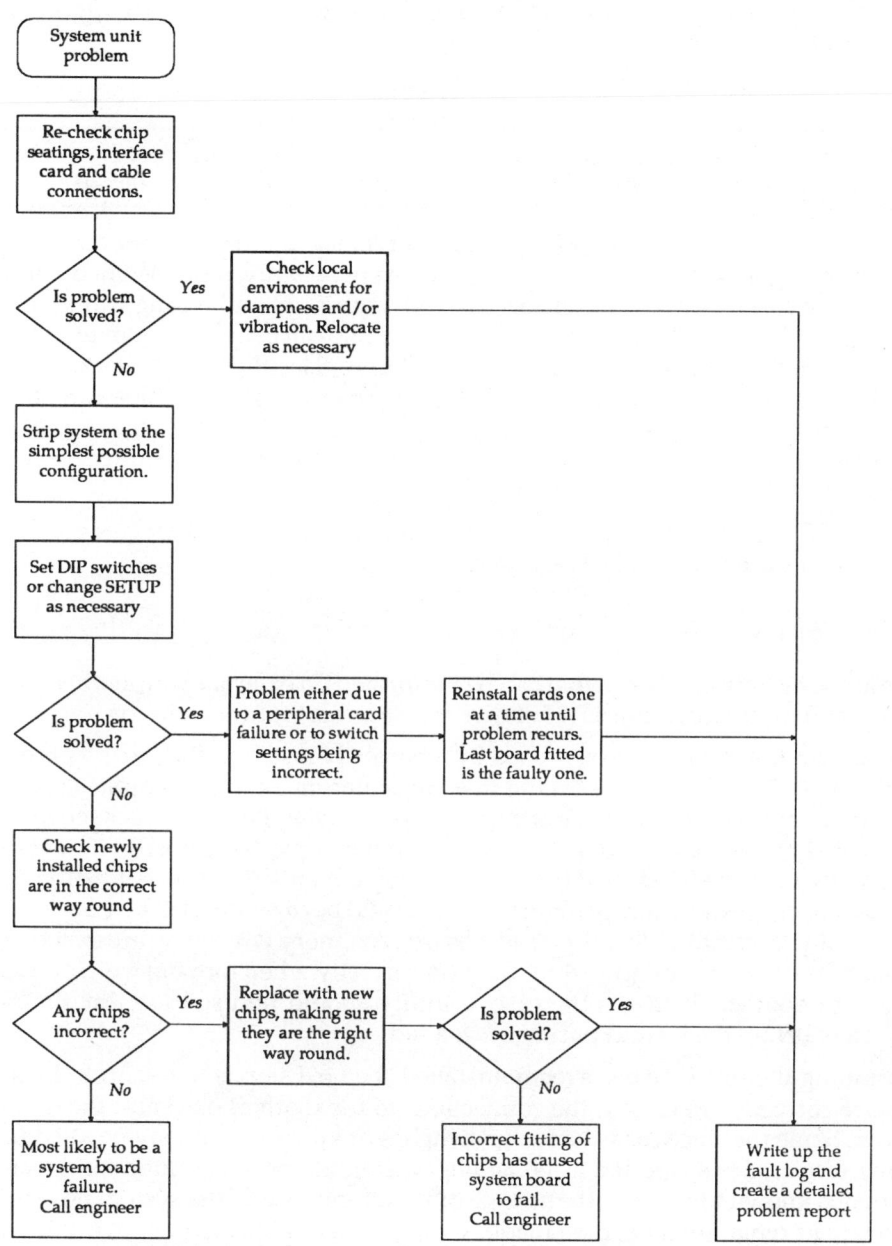

Figure 7.14   Flowchart for diagnosis of system unit

To further isolate the problem, each peripheral card should be re-installed and the system tested after each installation until the problem recurs. This will indicate the board at fault. The board can then be checked for switch setting and chip seatings, but if it still fails it should be replaced.

> BEWARE
>
> *Always write down any changes to system board or option card switches. They may have to be reset at a later stage and serious problems can be caused if they are incorrectly set.*

If the basic configuration still fails their is little else the troubleshooter can do. It is worth checking to see whether any new chips have recently been installed - additional memory or a co-processor for example. Chips have a right and wrong way round in the socket and if they have been incorrectly installed this can cause a system to fail. If this is the case, do not use the existing chip or chips but replace them with working ones and see if the system functions. Unfortunately, incorrectly installed chips can sometimes cause more serious problems on the circuitry of the motherboard and thus even after replacement the system will not function and an engineer is required. The correct installation of new chips is discussed in Chapter 8.

If all the chips appear to be correctly installed, the troubleshooter has gone as far as practical and the engineer must be called.

7.11 DISPLAY UNIT

There are some routine checks that can be performed on external peripherals such as the monitor and keyboard. Figure 7.15 shows the flowchart for the monitor.

Display unit problems can be caused by incorrectly installed software. This may only exhibit when the software is working in a particular mode. For example a spreadsheet can be perfectly well displayed, but a graph drawn using the same package may not be viewed at all if the installation procedure was not completed correctly. If new software has recently been installed, or if the monitor problem only occurs when working with a particular package these compatibility issues should be carefully checked. Some software packages do not entirely clear their settings from memory when they are exited and thus occasionally a monitor might fail to function correctly when moving from one software package to another. If this is the case, a utility should be used to clear the memory completely before the second package is loaded.

Assuming the software is correctly installed the next step is to re-check the interface cards are correctly seated and the connections to the motherboard and the monitor are in order. Some interface cards have dip switches or jumpers that may need adjusting. If the interface card is suspected as being faulty it should be substituted for a compatible card that is known to work with the type of monitor in use. If the system now functions a permanent replacement can be made. If the problem appears to be with the monitor itself it should be substituted or sent to an engineer for repair.

> WARNING
>
> *Never attempt to dismantle a monitor. It contains lethal voltages and should only be handled by a trained technician.*

TROUBLESHOOTING COMPONENT FAULTS 135

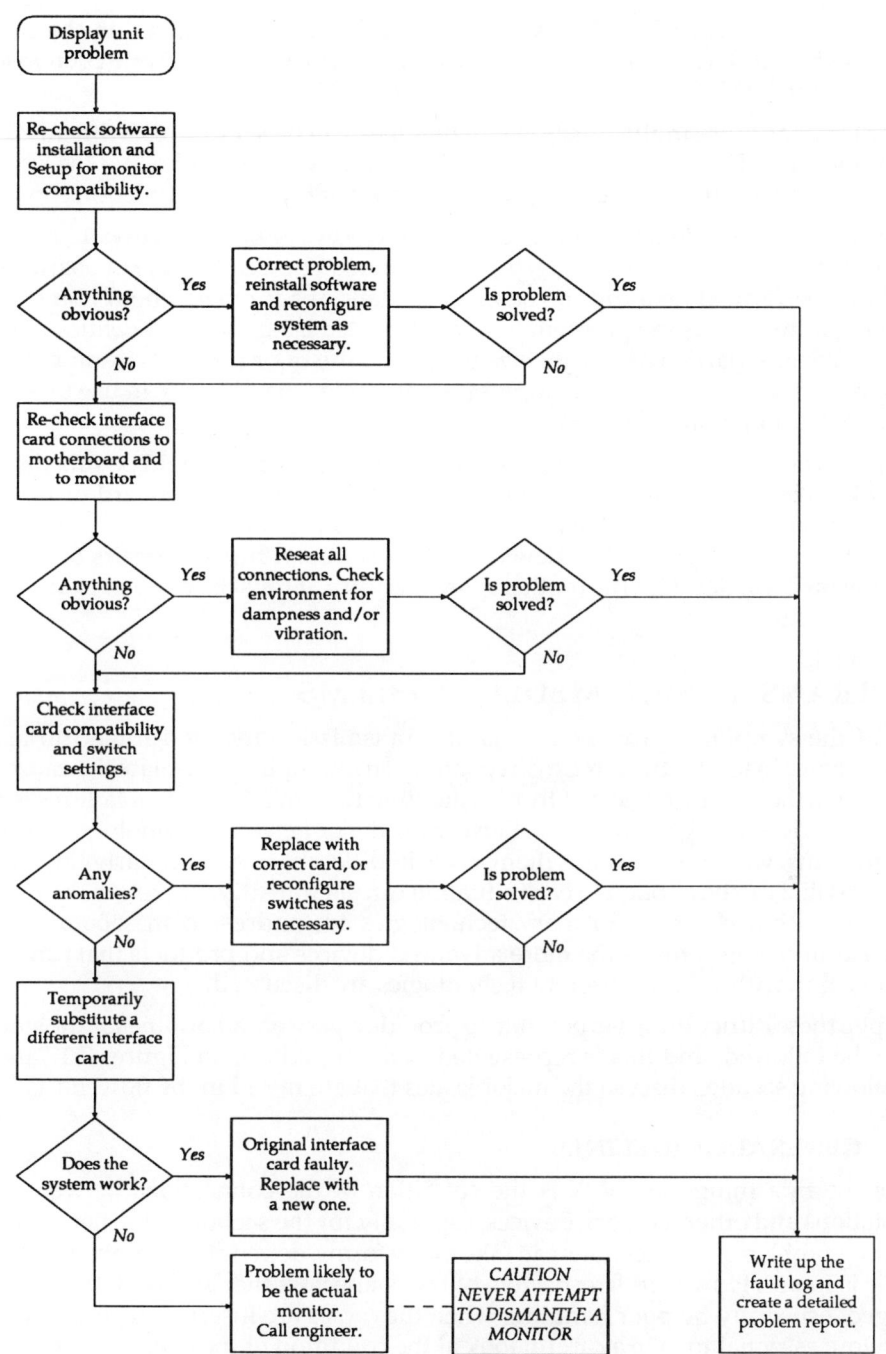

Figure 7.15 Flowchart for diagnosis of display unit

7.12 KEYBOARD

The flowchart in Figure 7.16 shows the routines that can be followed in the case of a suspect keyboard. The first area to check is that the correct drivers have been installed, either through the SETUP screen or in the CONFIG.SYS file.

Some keyboards are multi-functional in that they can be set to work with an XT or an AT type machine. This is usually controlled through a switch on the back of the keyboard. If this switch is incorrectly set the keyboard will invariably cease to function completely.

If the keyboard problem is associated with sticky keys or odd keys that do not always function, it may be that the key contacts need cleaning. The cleaning of keyboards should actually be performed on a routine basis and details of how to go about it are given in Chapter 7. If this solves the problem it is worth considering the practicalities of using a keyboard cover – particularly if the system is in a dusty or dirty environment. In any event a dust cover for the entire computer is advisable when it is not in use to minimise general dust settling on the system.

If these basic routines do not solve the problem the keyboard should be substituted for another known working one. This will prove whether it is the keyboard or the device circuitry on the motherboard that is at fault. If it is the keyboard that is faulty, it is usually more cost effective to purchase a new one than to attempt further repairs on the faulty one. If the problem lies with the motherboard circuitry, it must be handed to an engineer for further tests.

7.13 TRANSMISSION MEDIA PROBLEMS

Many of the symptoms produced by faulty transmission media can tend to lead the troubleshooter in totally the wrong direction when attempting to isolate the cause of the problem. Furthermore, the task of troubleshooting transmission media failures is not an easy one to address in general terms. Each of the major network technologies have their own problems, which will exhibit themselves in different ways. Similarly the tools and techniques that can be applied to each situation can vary greatly. Therefore the problems associated with each of the primary technologies are addressed in separate sections below. Additionally some of the more advanced devices and products that can be used in conjunction with several different technologies are discussed.

Despite these difficulties, it is possible to provide a very broad outline for the steps that need to be followed, and this is represented in the flowcharts in Figures 7.17 and 7.18. The following sections discuss the major issues that are raised in the flowcharts.

7.13.1 GENERAL GUIDELINES

One of the first things to check is the condition of the connections between cables, workstations and other network devices, especially for the section of the network that is exhibiting problems. Connections can take many forms, depending mainly on what type of cable is in use. However, irrespective of the connectors that are used, they can all be damaged, especially by poor handling when the cables are inserted or removed, and it is therefore essential to take a careful look at the condition of the connections.

Unfortunately, in some situations it is very difficult to locate all of the connections, especially between cables, as they may be hidden in ducting. However, such hidden connections rarely give trouble; it is the accessible ones which tend to fail.

TROUBLESHOOTING COMPONENT FAULTS 137

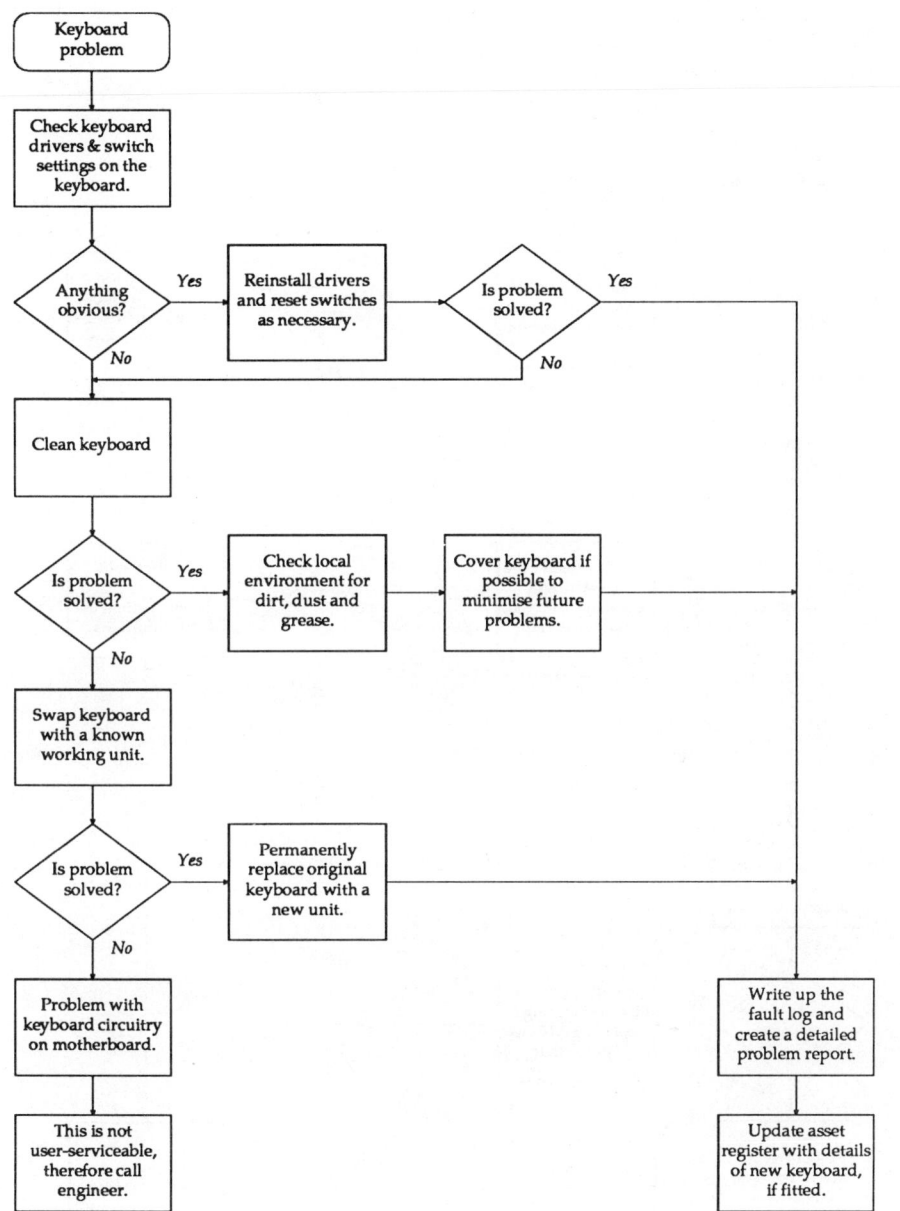

Figure 7.16   Flowchart for diagnosis of keyboard

138 NETWORK MEDIA PROBLEMS

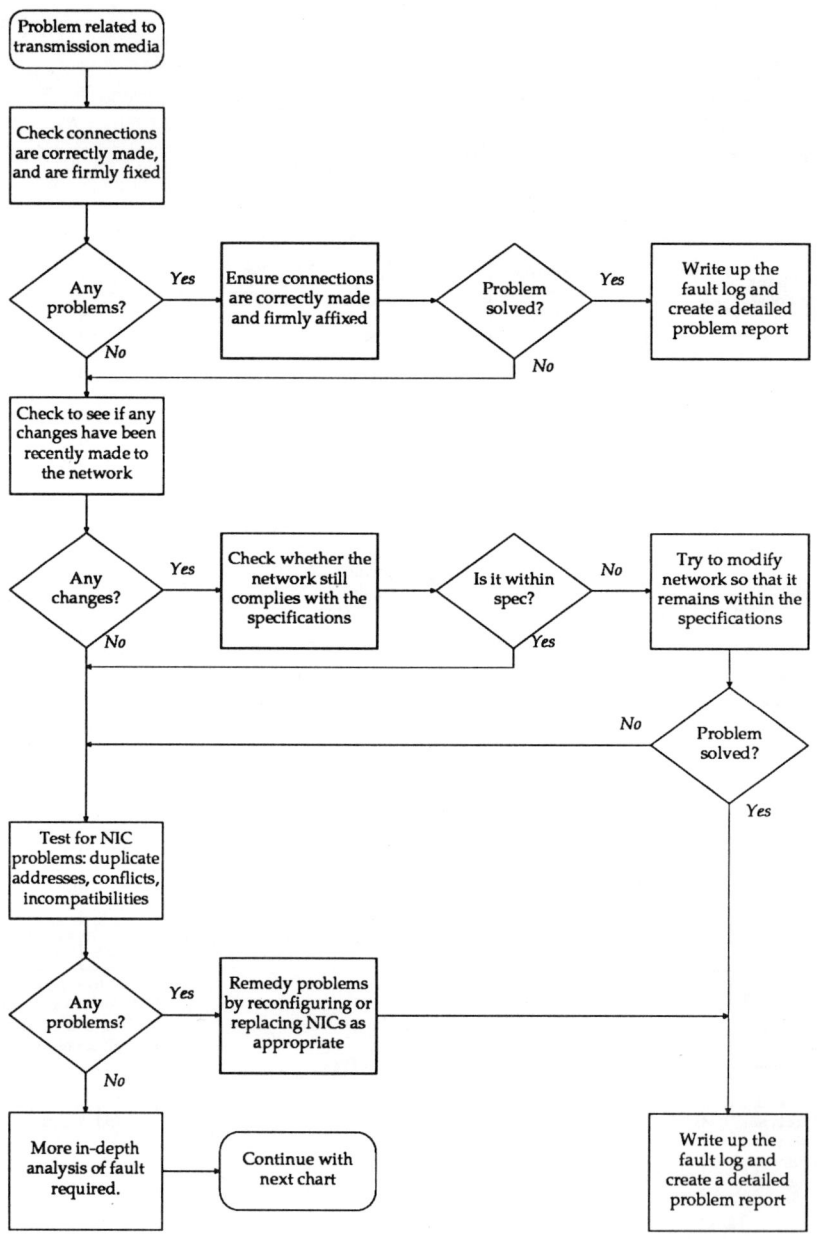

Figure 7.17 Flowchart for diagnosing media problems

TROUBLESHOOTING COMPONENT FAULTS 139

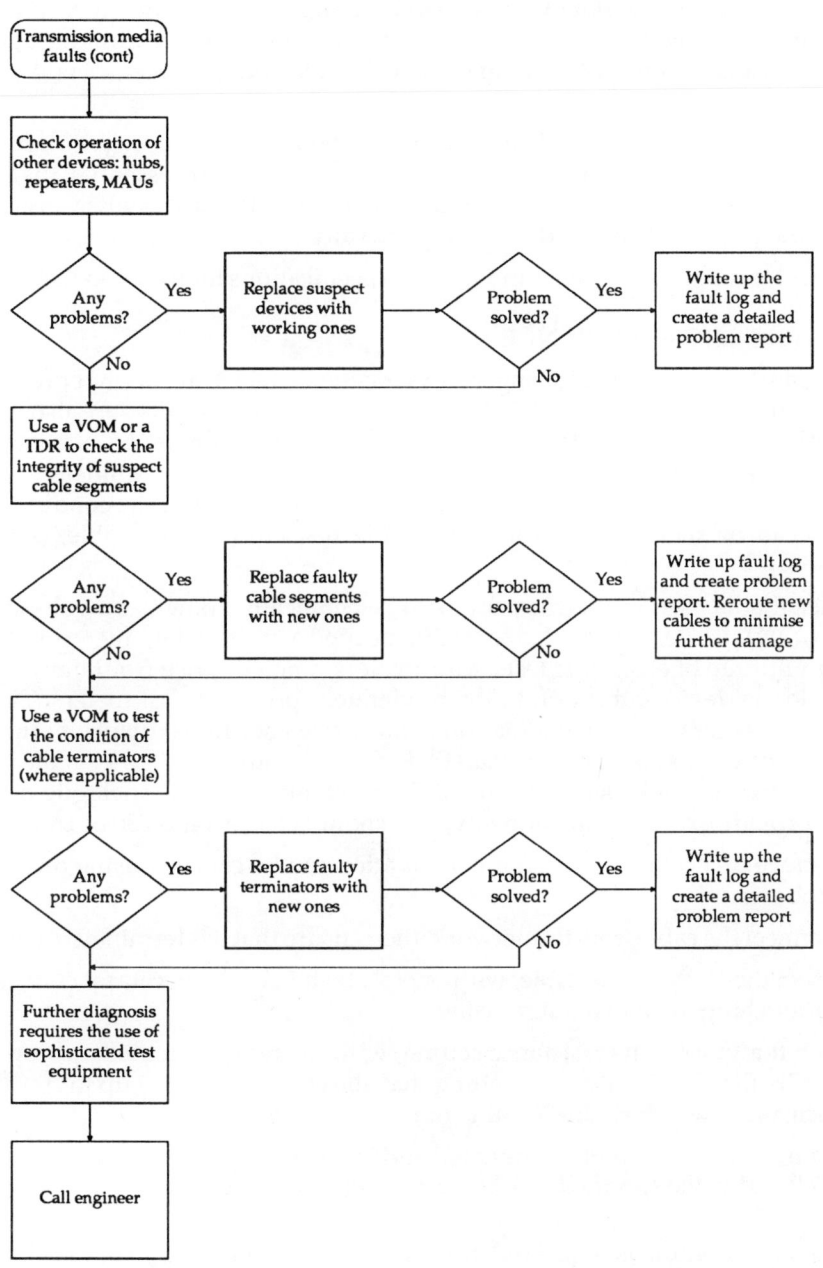

Figure 7.18 Flowchart for diagnosing media problems

7.13.2 NETWORK SPECIFICATIONS

The next thing to check is whether or not the network is within the specifications laid down by the manufacturers. If it exceeds these limitations in any way, the results can be highly unpredictable. Failure to ascertain whether the network is within the specifications will mean that many of the diagnostic techniques outlined below will produce erroneous results.

In many situations it is impossible to determine whether or not the network conforms to the specifications once it has been installed. It is therefore essential that this is confirmed when the network is first installed and configured, and also when any changes are made to the network to expand or modify it in any way.

Sections 7.14 through 7.17 discuss the various specifications for the main technologies.

7.13.3 MEASURING RESISTANCE

LAN cables must generally meet stringent specifications, which are often represented in terms of a technical code, such as RG-58A/U or RG-62/U. Other devices are also required to meet similar specifications, for example cable terminators must be of a particular resistance. When the cable has been assembled with the required terminators, various properties can be measured. One of the most valuable indicators of the condition of the system that can be measured in this way is the resistance of the cable/terminator combination.

The device that is used in this measurement is technically known as a volt-ohm-milliammeter, or VOM. The VOM is also sometimes called a multimeter, due to its ability to perform a multitude of electronic tests. Multimeters range in price from the very inexpensive analogue devices, through to the moderately priced digital meters. The most expensive multimeters offer a combination of analogue and digital displays, and are of much greater accuracy and resilience than their cheaper counterparts. From the point of view of the network troubleshooter, one of the moderately priced analogue or digital meters will provide excellent functionality, and should cost around £30 or so.

The resistance of a cable/terminator combination can be checked using one of these devices as follows:

- Disconnect the cable from the network, then ensure that it is terminated at one end.
- Connect the VOM to the cable, with one probe touching the central core, and the other touching the metal outer casing.
- Switch the VOM to its resistance setting, with the range specified appropriately. Typically the VOM will have a setting that allows resistances of up to 200 ohms to be measured, which is ideal for this purpose.
    - If the cable is properly terminated and is undamaged then the reading should fall within the specified resistance. For example, for Ethernet it should measure between 48 and 52 ohms.
    - If a low reading is registered, for example between 0 and 10 ohms, then there is a short somewhere. This could be in the cable or it could be in the terminator at the other end.
    - If a high reading is shown, usually significantly above 150 ohms, then there is possibly a break in the cable (ie it is open) or the terminator is missing or damaged.

If the condition of the terminator is suspect, then its resistance can be measured in a very similar way, by connecting the probes of the VOM to the central and outer connectors or the terminator plug.

The remedial action that is required is dependent upon the precise nature of the fault:
- If a single cable segment is being tested, and the tests reveal that there is either a short or a break, then the entire cable should be replaced with a new one.
- If multiple segments are being checked together and the above tests reveal an open circuit on the cable then check the connections between separate cable segments first, as it is surprisingly common for one section of the cable to become disconnected from another.
- If multiple segments are being checked and the tests reveal that there is a short circuit, then it will be necessary to determine which of the individual segments or connectors is at fault. This means testing each segment in turn, in isolation from the others.
- Terminators should also be replaced with new ones if they are found to be faulty.

If the tests reveal that there is a problem (either an open or a short) then a time domain reflectometer (TDR) can be used to locate the fault. This device allows cable problems to be located with the cables in place, and work on the principle of radar. TDRs can often be applied to several different technologies, and are discussed in detail below.

7.13.4 FAULT ISOLATION

In many situations it is impossible to isolate the fault to a particular device or component, even using the above guidelines. If this is the case then one of the best approaches is to sequentially change every suspect device for a good one, checking for the problem after each change. Eventually when the faulty component is replaced the problem will no longer exhibit itself.

Whilst this technique is long-winded, it generally produces results. However, it does rely on the fact that there is a sufficient number of spare components available for the changes to be carried out. Many organisations do not have the finances available to allow this to happen, and are therefore forced to call in the maintenance company or engineer.

7.14 NETWORK TECHNOLOGIES

As the specifications differ widely between different technologies, it is impossible to provide a general discussion that will relate to the problems, tools and techniques that apply to the different systems. Therefore, the following sections briefly examine each of the major technologies, outlining the appropriate specifications, problems and products that are particular to each one.

7.15 ARCNET

Whilst ARCnet is considered by many to offer a slightly more robust environment for data transmission, the actual hardware used by the technology generally offers little in the way of built-in diagnostic tools. Therefore, it is necessary to rely on add-on devices and third-party software products when troubleshooting ARCnet LANs.

7.15.1 SPECIFICATIONS AND HARDWARE

There are several different implementations of ARCnet, some of which involve the use of coaxial cable, some allow for twisted pair cable to be used, and some work with fibre-optic cables. However, the original specifications dealt purely with coaxial cable, and it is from this that all others have been developed. Hence this section confines itself to a discussion of the coaxial based ARCnet technology, which is currently the most popular and reliable.

The following hardware is used in ARCnet LANs:

- **Cable**
  RG-62/U 93 ohm coaxial cable.
- **NIC**
  The NIC is installed into every station on the network. It is available in either high impedance or low impedance forms. See below for further details.
- **Passive hub**
  A device that allows a network signal to be relayed. It has four ports to which network cables can be attached. Any unused port MUST be terminated with a 93 ohm resistor.
- **Active hub**
  A device that not only relays a network signals, but conditions and amplifies it as well. Active hubs have eight ports, and whilst it is recommended that unused ports be terminated, it is not strictly necessary.
- **BNC terminators**
  Special 93 ohm terminating plugs are required to ensure that electrical reflections do not interfere with network transmissions.
- **BNC connector plugs**
  Standard BNC connector plugs are used on each end of a cable segment.
- **BNC connector jacks**
  Standard BNC connector jacks are used to allow the cable to be connected.
- **BNC T-connectors**
  BNC T-Connectors are also used to connect stations to the cable.
- **Active links**
  Active links allow two cables to be connected.

7.15.2 LOW AND HIGH IMPEDANCE BOARDS

Whilst ARCnet specifications are relatively straightforward, they do include the provision for flexibility in the overall design of the network. This flexibility is made possible through the use of different NICs, known as either low-impedance or high-impedance boards. Each defines its own specifications in terms of how different devices can be connected, although with suitable planning both high and low impedance boards can be used on the same network.

The majority of commercially available ARCnet NICs can be switched between high and low impedance mode by modifying jumpers or DIP switches on the card. It is therefore essential to ensure that each NIC is correctly set before the workstation is attached to the network.

7.15.2.1 Low impedance

Low impedance boards allow the network to be configured in a star topology. The limitations are as follows:

- Maximum cable distance from one end of the network to the other is 20000 feet.
- Maximum distance between active hubs is 2000 feet.
- Maximum distance between an active hub and a network station is 2000 feet.
- Maximum distance between an active hub and a passive hub is 100 feet.
- Maximum distance between a passive hub and a station is 100 feet.
- Active hubs can be connected to other active hubs, passive hubs and stations.
- Passive hubs can only be used as an intermediate connection between an active hub and a station.
- Workstations, servers and bridges can be connected anywhere in the network.
- Loops should not be created. This may happen when a cable coming from an active or passive hub passes through other hubs and then connects back to the original. Whilst in general this will not produce serious problems, it is possible to damage some of the hardware.
- Unused ports on active hubs should be terminated using a 93 ohm terminator.
- Unused ports on passive hubs MUST be terminated using a 93 ohm terminator.
- If a network station is disconnected from a passive hub, then its cable should be removed and a terminator installed in its place.

7.15.2.2 High impedance

High impedance boards allow the network to be configured in a bus topology. The limitations are as follows:

- Maximum cable distance from one end of the network to the other is 20000 feet.
- Maximum number of high-impedance boards connected in series is 8.
- Minimum distance between T-connectors is 3 feet.
- Maximum length of cable with high impedance boards in series is 1000 feet.
- Maximum distance between two active hubs when no high impedance boards are connected in series is 2000 feet.
- Passive hubs should not be used with high impedance boards. Additional stations can be connected to a bus topology network by linking cables via active links, or by connecting to active hubs.
- Stations should be directly connected to cables with T-connectors.
- Ensure that both ends of each length of cable are terminated with either an active hub or a terminator.
- Loops should not be created.

As can be seen from Figure 7.3, it is very easy to combine the bus topology and the star topology under ARCnet by choosing the appropriate boards and hub configurations.

144 ARCNET

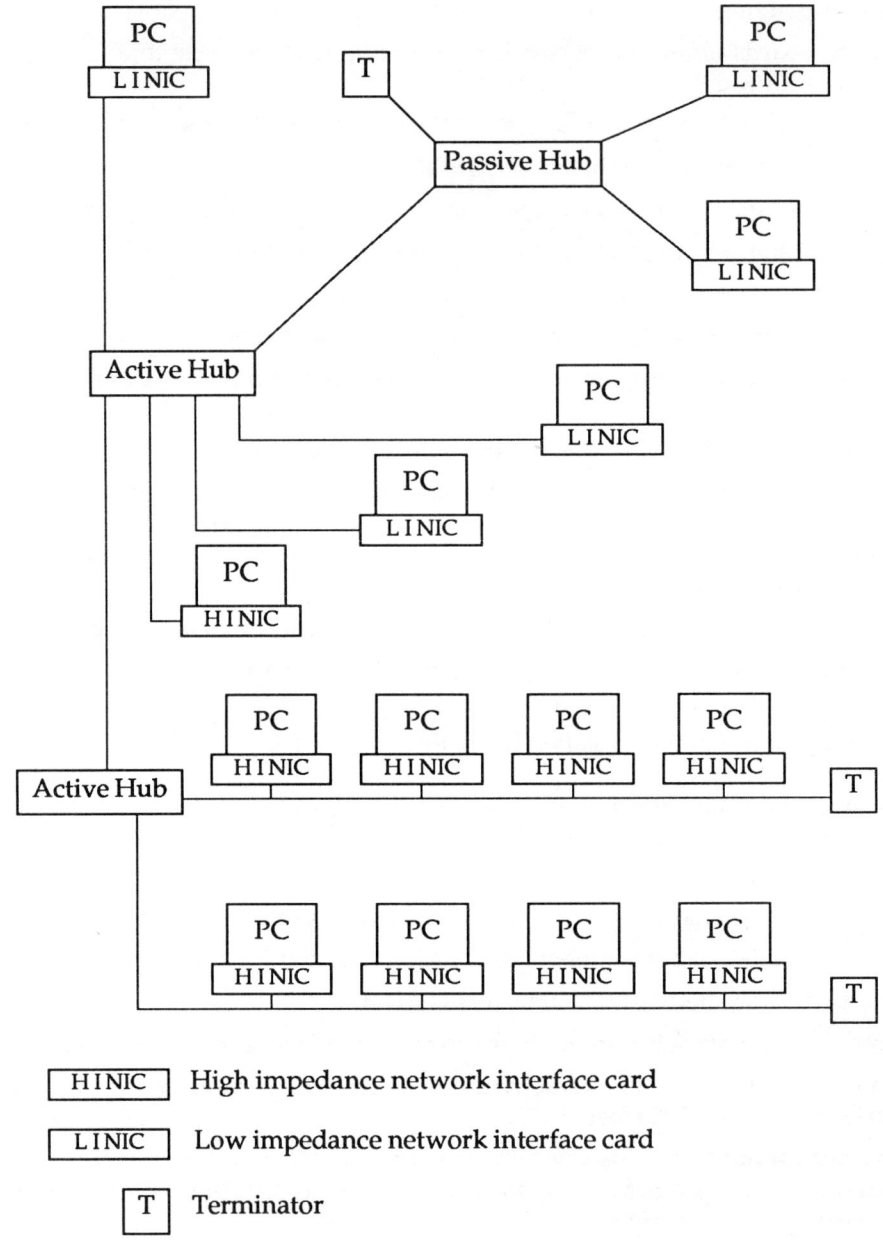

HINIC	High impedance network interface card
LINIC	Low impedance network interface card
T	Terminator

Figure 7.19 A typical ARCnet LAN configuration

7.15.3 TROUBLESHOOTING ARCnet

A wide variety of products are available to help in the diagnosis and identification of ARCnet problems. Some of these are hardware based, whilst others are purely implemented in software.

7.15.3.1 ARCview

A typical example of such a product is *ARCview*, a software tool developed by Standard Microsystems Corporation (SMC), one of the most well known manufacturers of ARCnet interface cards. ARCview will run on any LAN workstation with the exception of the file server, subject to the fact that the workstation contains either an SMC ARCnet board or one that uses exactly the same IPX.COM as an SMC board.

Unlike some other diagnostic tools ARCview is a foreground program, which means that it takes control of the workstation to the exclusion of any other applications. ARCview produces a variety of statistical figures that indicate the usage of the network, including the following:

- The ID of each PC on the LAN
- The time a workstation first spoke
- The time a workstation last spoke
- How many packets were transmitted
- A bar graph showing over a period of time how many packets were transmitted in each 30 second period
- The total number of RECONs that occurred.

A RECON is a reconfiguration operation, something that occurs every time a workstation is added to the LAN. These should generally be fairly irregular, but in the case of a problem the number and regularity of the RECONs can increase dramatically. As the number of RECONs increases the network performance will gradually degrade, finally resulting in entire network failure. Typical problems that will produce extraneous RECONs include:

- Bad drivers
- Shorted cables
- Loose connections
- Failed components
- Exceeding the distance limitations imposed by a passive hub
- Faulty passive hubs.

Whenever a RECON occurs ARCview will log the details to an ASCII file on disk. This data can then be used to help in the diagnostic process.

ARCview offers relatively little in the way of detailed analysis of hardware problems, and offers no diagnostic ability at all. However it does serve as a very efficient and inexpensive early warning system, especially if it is in day to day use for monitoring network performance and utilisation.

7.15.3.2 The Network Tester

Unlike ARCview, *The Network Tester* is purely a hardware device. It is also produced by SMC, and will work with all ARCnet NICs that are available, irrespective of the manufacturer. One end of the device is connected to the NIC connector, and the other end is connected to the LAN cable; thus it is effectively placed in serial with the network connection.

The sole purpose of the Network Tester is to indicate whether a RECON is in progress, or whether there is a more serious problem with the network. It provides this information through a single LED.

- When the light is on continuously then the network is operating normally.
- When the light blinks, a RECON is in progress.
- When the light is extinguished then there is a more serious problem with the network, such as a loose connection to a hub, or possibly a failed hub or other device.

Some ARCnet boards also have small LED indicators on the back, and whilst the facilities provided by these boards are not identical to the Network Tester, they function in a very similar manner.

7.16 ETHERNET

Whilst ARCnet may be thought of as being 'deterministic' in nature due to its token passing protocols, Ethernet may be thought of as 'probabilistic', as it has no hard and fast rules dictating when a station can transmit. This tends to introduce its own problems, both in determining whether the hardware, software or firmware is at fault, and in diagnosing the cause of the problem.

Many of the problems that are encountered are peculiar to the particular transmission media in use, and this in turn affects how the troubleshooter will approach the problem. Similar problems occur when dealing with systems which only partially conform to Ethernet specifications. For these reasons, the following discussion relates to Ethernet networks implemented using coaxial cabling, although many of the techniques are applicable to twisted pair systems as well.

7.16.1 SPECIFICATIONS AND HARDWARE

The specifications for Ethernet follow very closely the guidelines laid down by the IEEE 802 committee. There are however a number of differences between true Ethernet and the original 802 specifications. For example, Ethernet specifies that 50-ohm coaxial cable is used, whereas the 802 specifications allow for a greater variety of transmission media. Generally the specifications relating to Ethernet require closer tolerances than those defined by the IEEE committee. The following list outlines some of the definitions that are encountered, and some of the major specifications that devices must adhere to:

- **Trunk segment**
  Ethernet, as with all other LANs, allows for the interconnection of computing devices. Such devices are attached to one long main cable, known as the Trunk Segment Cable. It is limited in terms of its length and the number of stations that can be connected to it.

- **Repeater**
  To extend the size of the network beyond these limitations a repeater may be used. This relays signals between two trunk segments, amplifying them on the way.

- **Cable**
  Two types of cable are used, known as *thin* and *thick*. The type of cable determines the specifications for the overall LAN.

7.16.2 THIN ETHERNET CABLE

Thin Ethernet cable is 0.2 inch RG-58A/U 50 ohm coaxial. This is generally more restrictive than thick cable (see specifications below), but is generally easier to set up and maintain.

- NIC

  The NIC is housed in the station, and allows for connection to the thin Ethernet cable.

- BNC connectors

  BNC connector plugs and jacks are used throughout the network to connect cables to devices. The plugs are fixed to the cable and the jacks to the hardware.

- BNC barrel connectors

  These are used to join two lengths of thin Ethernet cable.

- BNC T-connectors

  The two opposing jacks of the T-connector act as a barrel connector allowing two lengths of cable to be joined. The remaining plug attaches to the BNC connector jack on a NIC.

- BNC terminator

  A 50 ohm BNC terminator plug is used at certain points of the network to minimise electrical interference. Some BNC terminators have a special grounding lead.

7.16.2.1 Limitations

- Maximum number of trunk segments is 5.
- Maximum trunk segment length is 607 feet.
- Maximum network trunk cable length is 3035 feet.
- Maximum number of stations connected to one trunk segment is 30. (Repeaters count as one station on each trunk segment to which they are attached).
- Minimum distance between T-connectors is 1.5 feet.
- A terminator MUST be attached to each end of every trunk segment.
- One of the terminators must be grounded.
- Barrel connector splices should be kept to a minimum. This will enhance the reliability of the system.

7.16.3 THICK ETHERNET CABLE

Thick Ethernet cable is 0.4 inch diameter 50 ohm coaxial. The following types are permissible:

- Belden 9880, Belden 89889
- Montrose CBL5688, Montrose CBL713
- Malco 250-4315-0004, Malco 250-4314-0003
- Inmac 1784, Inmac 1785

The use of thick cable allows for larger networks, but requires more careful installation and maintenance.

- **NIC**
  The NIC is housed in the station, and allows for connection to the thick Ethernet cable.
- **Transceiver**
  Stations on the network communicate through external transceivers that are attached to the main network cable.
- **Transceiver cable**
  The NIC is connected to the transceiver with a Transceiver Cable.
- **N-Series male connectors**
  N-series male connectors are installed on both ends of each length of thick Ethernet cable.
- **N-Series barrel connectors**
  These are used to join two lengths of thick cable.
- **N-Series terminator**
  An N-series 50 ohm terminator is used at certain points of the network to minimise electrical interference. Some terminators are used to ground the network, and these have a special grounding lead.

7.16.3.1 Limitations

- Maximum number of trunk segments is 5.
- Maximum trunk segment length is 1640 feet.
- Maximum network trunk cable length is 8200 feet.
- Maximum number of stations connected to one trunk segment is 100. (Repeaters count as one station on each trunk segment to which they are attached).
- Minimum distance between transceivers is 8 feet.
- Maximum transceiver cable length is 165 feet.
- A terminator MUST be attached to each end of every trunk segment.
- One of the terminators must be grounded.
- Barrel connector splices should be kept to a minimum. This will enhance the reliability of the system.

7.16.4 COMBINATION THIN/THICK CABLE NETWORKS

Networks consisting of a combination of thin and thick Ethernet cable can be created in two ways:

- Thin-cable trunk segments can be joined to thick cable trunk segments using a repeater. Up to five such segments can be joined in this way.
- Thin and thick cable can be used together to form a single trunk segment through the use of appropriate adapters. Special rules relating to the overall length of each section apply in this case.

Figure 7.4 shows how an Ethernet LAN can be constructed using both thick and thin cable, using a repeater to link the two independent trunk segments.

TROUBLESHOOTING COMPONENT FAULTS 149

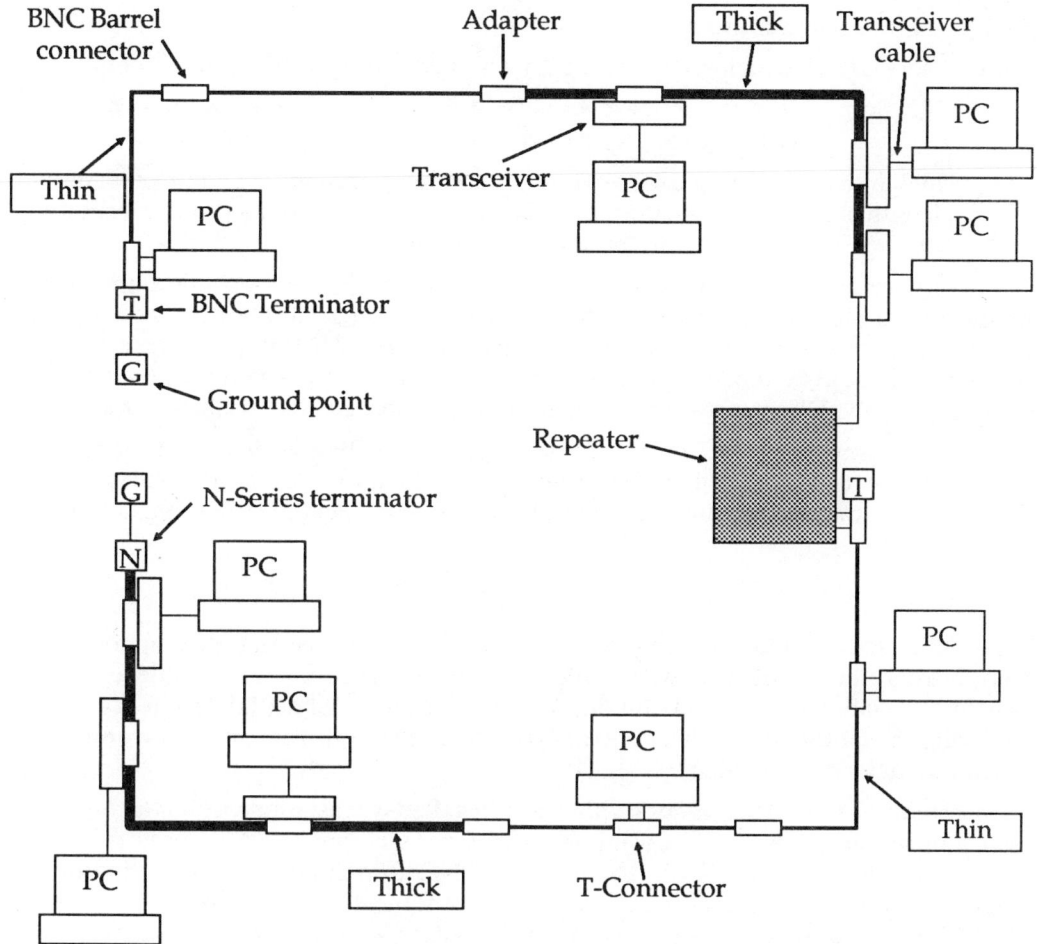

Figure 7.20　A typical Ethernet LAN configuration

7.16.5　TROUBLESHOOTING ETHERNET

Most hardware faults in Ethernet networks fall into three categories:
- Cable failure
- Transceiver failure
- NIC failure.

7.16.5.1　Cable failure

Because Ethernet is primarily a bus topology, any damage to the actual bus cable will generally cause the network to fail, or at best generate large amounts of error conditions. Thus in the event of such a situation occurring the cable provides a logical point to start from in fault diagnosis.

7.16.5.2 Transceiver failure

Transceivers take two forms, depending on whether thick or thin cabling is employed.

- With thin cabling the transceiver is built into the NIC, and failure can only be corrected by replacing the entire card.
- Thick Ethernet cabling uses separate transceivers and NICs, and links them with a length of cabling. The connections between the cable and the transceiver or NIC can cause problems, as can the actual cable itself.

Transceiver problems usually show themselves in the form of a single station being unable to communicate with the rest of the network. In such situations it is often found that the transceiver for that station has failed internally. If this is the case then the transceiver should be replaced to determine if it indeed was the source of the problem. Alternatively the NIC can be disconnected from the transceiver to disable it temporarily.

Some transceivers have LED indicators showing basic diagnostic information, whilst others can be tested with loop-backs to the workstation. Some are provided with diagnostic routines which allow the troubleshooter to isolate the fault with a minimum of effort.

7.16.5.3 NIC failure

Most NICs are supplied with diagnostics routines which will accurately diagnose faulty components either in the host workstation or on the NIC itself. Thus the quickest way to isolate NIC failures is to run the appropriate routines. Remedial action consists of replacing the faulty NIC with a good one, a process that will take only a few minutes if a working device is available.

One common failure that occurs with newly installed workstations relates to the setting of a jumper on the NIC. This jumper determines whether the NIC uses the DB-15 connector (thick Ethernet, or AUI cable), or the BNC (thin Ethernet cable). If this jumper is incorrectly specified then the NIC will not communicate with the rest of the network at all. Therefore double check this setting on the NIC prior to closing the system unit box.

A similar problem relates to the fact that the specification for Ethernet and IEEE 802.3 are slightly different, and in fact use different wiring schemes for connecting the NIC to the transceiver on thick-cable networks. As most NICs and transceivers support both Ethernet and IEEE 802.3 it is essential to check that the appropriate jumpers have been set on these devices. The cables for the two standards are different, and cannot generally be used interchangeably.

7.16.6 TROUBLESHOOTING PRODUCTS

As Ethernet is one of the most popular technologies, there is a wealth of third-party products available for support, maintenance and diagnosis operations. Typical of such products is *Network Inspector*, from Tiara systems.

7.16.6.1 Network Inspector

Whilst this is purely a software product, it must be used in conjunction with an appropriate Ethernet NIC from Tiara Systems, as only these NICs have the special diagnostic chips on them used by the program. Thus it is not an especially cheap tool, as the NIC and software retail for around $2000.

Installation is quick and simple, and the product will work on any workstation on the network that is equipped with a suitable NIC. The program files are copied to the workstation disk, and the special drivers supplied are loaded into the network operating system. The program can then be executed in the same way as any other application.

Network Inspector allows a variety of statistical reports to be produced, and performs a number of detailed diagnostic tests that attempt to identify and locate network based problems. Such reports and tests can either be conducted for the entire network or for individual stations.

For example, selecting the Network Statistics reports displays three horizontal bar graphs. The first depicts the number of frames per second, the second shows the number of stations on the network and the third shows the percentage of network utilisation. The screen also shows the number of CRC errors, elapsed monitoring time, short frames and frame alignment.

Alternatively an individual station's activity can be monitored. Network Inspector prompts for the ID of the station in question, (it offers no help in automatically selecting one, so these IDs must be known prior to running the program), and then again displays three bar graphs, number values and percentage of network utilisation. Information on the packets going to and from the station is also displayed.

In addition to this basic statistical reporting ability, Network Inspector includes a number of diagnostic utilities, for example the time domain reflectometer (TDR) detects breaks in the coaxial cable within a 10 metre range of the host workstation.

The program also contains the facility to automatically identify the type of adapter card in each workstation on the network.

The FrameView option allows frames to be captured from the network according to simple filters. These may be the origination address, destination address and packet type. This data is then displayed in original form, in ASCII and hexadecimal. No interpretation or evaluation is given to the data. These data frames are temporarily stored in the system memory, prior to being displayed. Thus stations with larger memories will be able to handle larger numbers of frames.

Whilst Network Inspector does offer a wealth of analytical information and diagnostic routines, it is not particularly easy to use. Inexperienced users may find the manual difficult to comprehend, and the online help screens offer little assistance. This is the only major drawback though, and once a user is familiar with the system it will in the majority of situations prove invaluable in analysing and diagnosing network based faults.

7.17 TOKEN RING

The specifications for IBM's Token Ring network technology were originally proposed in 1969, and were based directly on the IEEE 802.5 token ring specification. It also conforms quite closely to the OSI reference model. However, until relatively recently there have been problems relating to many of the products supplied for Token Ring systems, and for this reason it is not as popular as it may first appear.

As with most network technologies, there are two different forms that a Token Ring network may take. The most common is known as a *small movable cabling system*, whilst a more flexible form is the *large non-movable cabling system*. However, this latter form is much more difficult to install, and for this reason it tends to be restricted to large systems that have the backup of a full maintenance contract. Therefore, only the small movable cabling system is considered here.

7.17.1 SPECIFICATIONS AND HARDWARE

Token Ring specifications follow very closely the IEEE 802.5 specifications. From a practical point of view, the following are the most important issues:

- **Adapters**
  The term Adapter is used by IBM to refer to the NIC in the stations on the network. Two types of adapter are available:
    - The PC adapter is for standard bus stations such as the PC, XT, AT and PS/2 Model 30.
    - The TRN/A adapter is for Micro Channel Architecture (MCA) stations such as the IBM PS/2 Models 50, 60, 70 and 80.
- **IBM 8228 multistation access units (MAU)**
  This special device is used to connect up to eight stations in a network. It is effectively a repeater.
- **IBM Token Ring PC adapter cables**
  These are made from 8 feet of IBM Type 6 cable. One end connects to the adapter port of a station, and the other end connects to a patch cable or an 8228 unit.
- **Patch cable**
  This cable is also made of IBM Type 6 cable, and may connected to another patch cable, an adapter cable or an 8228 unit.

7.17.1.1 Limitations

- Maximum number of stations is 96.
- Maximum number of 8228 units is 12.
- Maximum patch cable distance between a station and an 8228 unit (excluding the 8 foot adapter cable) is 150 feet.
- Maximum patch cable distance between two 8228 units is 150 feet.
- Maximum patch cable distance connecting all 8228 units is 400 feet.
- Stations are connected to the 8228 units. Stations within 8 feet of an 8228 unit can connected using just the adapter cable, those further away must use a patch cable.
- The 8228 units must be connected in a ring using patch cables. This is formed by connecting the Ring Out (RO) connector of one unit to the Ring In (RI) connector of the next. This is repeated until a patch cable is connected to the RI connector of the first unit.
- Patch cables should not be spliced, although they may be connected using appropriate connectors.
- When installed, they must be protected from sources of electrical and magnetic interference, excessive temperatures, physical damage etc.

Figure 7.5 shows a typical Token Ring LAN.

TROUBLESHOOTING COMPONENT FAULTS 153

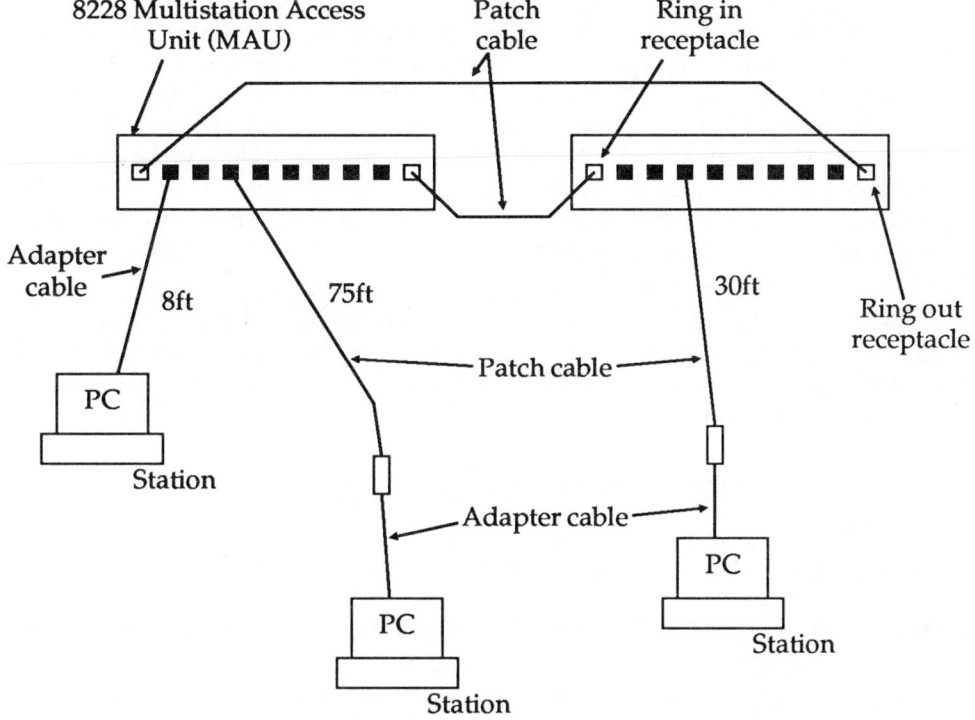

Figure 7.21   A typical Token Ring LAN configuration

7.17.2   TROUBLESHOOTING TOKEN RING

One of the most important features of the Token Ring technology is that until recently all the chips that were used on NICs were produced by Texas Instruments. These chips were available in two forms, either the 4 Mbit/s TMS380 chipset, or the 16 Mbit/s TMS380C16 devices. Both of these chipsets included special diagnostic and error-checking routines which enable the LAN hardware to identify many different problems. These functions comply with the IEEE 802.5 standard, and include the following features:

– Monitoring of hardware and software errors
– Tracking configuration details, such as the current active monitor
– Controlling various parameters, such as token priority and ring number.

In addition to these in-built facilities, there are a small number of diagnostic products available which use the routines provided in the hardware to simplify the process of fault diagnosis and rectification. Examples of such products include *Token VIEW-4* by Protenon Inc, *Sniffer* by Network General Corp, and *Token Ring LAN Manager* by IBM.

The first of these, Token VIEW-4, uses the built in diagnostics to identify problems. Additionally, when used in conjunction with Protenon's own Intelligent MAUs the system can automatically lock out faulty stations from the network, thus ensuring that problems in one station do not affect the overall operation of the system.

154 TECHNOLOGY INDEPENDENT SYSTEMS

Protenon calls the MAUs *Intelligent Wire Centres,* and the software is effectively a sophisticated database that contains records of which ports on each intelligent wire centre are in use, which stations are connected etc. It also provides details on each station's network address and its current status. This information is generated by the program automatically, and is used to form an overall map of the physical topology of the system. In the event of a fault occurring the map is used by the program to automatically lock the problematic station out of the network. Alternatively, if the intelligent MAUs are employed, then entire sections can be removed from the network if necessary, and the system is then automatically reconfigured for the new configuration.

A rather unique feature of the Protenon system is the use of a secondary signal path. This simple four core bus interface is routed from the network manager station to each intelligent wire centre. In the event of a hardware fault occurring that causes the entire network to fail, it is still possible for Token VIEW-4 to attempt to remedy the situation, using this alternate signalling path.

7.18 TECHNOLOGY INDEPENDENT SYSTEMS

Whilst troubleshooting approaches do vary between different technologies, there are a number of systems that can be applied to two or more of these technologies with relative ease. Such devices often work at a hardware level, and in many cases they contain the full functionality of an entire PC, although they are dedicated to the task of monitoring and analysing network activity.

A large number of these devices are *Protocol Analysers,* which give detailed information on exactly what is happening on the network over a period of time. A protocol is just a special standard relating to the way in which information is transmitted during a communication session. It determines the size and format of each data packet or frame, and also how the receiving station should acknowledge reception of the data. Any problems that occur with a network often show themselves in the form of invalid data packets or frames, ie the protocol is not being observed. In such cases the receiving station will not be able to correctly interpret all or some of the data, and will produce an error message.

Unfortunately, ordinary workstations and interface cards are not capable of decoding the information sent in the packet if it is invalid, and this is where the protocol analyser becomes useful. Its prime concern is to monitor every packet or frame that is transmitted, and if required display this information in a readable format, or alternatively record it for later analysis.

The actual packet will contain numeric values, and in some cases the analyser simply displays these on the screen. However it is much more common for the analyser to attempt to interpret the data in some way, for example giving meaningful names to stations rather than just showing their ID. Most analysers also contain a TDR function, allowing shorts and breaks in the cabling to be located.

Protocol analysers are not specific to particular network operating systems, but they are dependent upon the network adapters and cabling system that are in use. The product must also support the protocols in use in the network. For example, with a *NetWare* server the product must support the use of the IPX/SPX decoding. With a *LAN Manager* server it is necessary that the product supports NetBIOS and SMB.

7.18.1 BYPASSING SECURITY

One of the problems involved with these devices is the fact that they access the data at a very low level, without the network operating system being aware of their presence. Thus they can display any data that is transmitted on the network, including confidential data files. It should also be remembered that when a user logs in to the network, they enter their password at the workstation, and this is then transmitted to the file server where it is checked for validity. As the password is transmitted in the same way as ordinary data, it is possible to intercept it with a protocol analyser. Thus the user of the analyser may gain access to user accounts. Some operating systems encrypt the password before it is transmitted, although this is currently the exception rather than the rule.

7.18.2 SNIFFER

One of the most well known protocol analysers, and incidentally one of the best, is Sniffer from Network General Corp. It is also one of the most inflexible products in terms of the hardware that it requires to operate. The basic system consists of a network interface card, expansion unit and software. It must be installed in either a Compaq Portable III or a Toshiba 3200SX computer, which must be supplied with a substantial amount of memory (typically around 6MB). Network General Corp. will actually supply Sniffer ready installed in one of these machines, but of course the price of the entire package is significantly higher than that of the basic kit.

With the system installed in an appropriate computer, Sniffer can be used for basic analysis of network usage. To realise its full functionality it is necessary to purchase extra modules which allow for the protocol used on the network to be interpreted. These add-on modules typically cost between 10–15 percent of the basic kit price. Sniffer is able to interpret around a dozen different protocols, and in this aspect it is one of the most flexible protocol analysers available. The protocols currently supported include:

- DECnet
- ISO
- NCP
- NetBIOS
- SMB
- SNA
- SUN
- TCP/IP
- XNS

If the required protocol is not directly available, the built-in C programming interface can be used to write specialised protocol interpreters as required. In terms of LAN technologies, Sniffer can be used on Ethernet, Token Ring and ARCnet LANs with no modifications required.

7.18.2.1 Features

Sniffer captures and displays transmitted data, based on user-selectable criteria. Two capture modes are offered, to ensure that no data is missed :

- Standard capture mode analyses the data as it arrives, working on a first-come first-served basis.
- High-speed mode is required in situations of heavy network traffic. It captures all the data first, then analyses it afterwards.

Through the use of the sophisticated capture, filter and trigger options it is possible to instruct Sniffer to only display certain data at certain times. Captured data can be saved to disk for later examination which makes analysis somewhat easier.

As with most protocol analysers, Sniffer has a built-in TDR facility. This is more accurate than many of its main competitors, which helps to justify its very high price tag.

7.18.2.2 Disadvantages

Sniffer is not without its own problems though. One of the most fundamental is the inability of the program to see damaged network traffic. For example, if the first part of any package (the *preamble*) is damaged in some way, then Sniffer is unable to interpret that data. This means that in some situations it is relatively useless. Additionally some users find the way in which data is displayed to be difficult to interpret.

The overall advantages of the product far outweigh the problems though. Therefore Sniffer is generally considered to be one of the most functional and effective protocol analysers available. Unfortunately many organisations will not be able to justify the very high price tag associated with the system.

7.18.3 OTHER PRODUCTS

Many other similar products are available, although as noted above most are not as flexible in terms of the different technologies and protocols that they support. When considering these devices the following questions should be borne in mind:

- Does it support the chosen network technologies?
- Does it support the appropriate network protocols?
- Does it offer TDR facilities?
- How flexible is it in recognising non-standard or damaged packets?
- Does it have a suitable, intuitive user interface?
- Does it provide an adequate amount of statistical information in addition to the technical data?

Some organisations do not need many of the more advanced features, and therefore would benefit from the use of a Traffic Monitoring system rather than a protocol analyser. These products are generally less expensive, and offer a less technically orientated user interface. Therefore many LAN managers feel more comfortable working with traffic monitors than with protocol analysers.

7.19 SUMMARY

The topic of troubleshooting hardware faults is a very broad one due to the fact that faults are obviously dependent upon the particular hardware technology that is in use. Fortunately there are a number of guidelines that are common to all installations, and these should lead the network manager towards a solution in the majority of situations.

Problems that relate to a single workstation are generally the easiest to solve, although they may involve considerable cost if a display unit or local hard disk drive fails. This is also the case with the file server, although it is of paramount importance to remedy the problem as quickly as possible in this case, in order that the network can be reinstated into a working condition.

Problems that are due to failures in the transmission media can be much more difficult to deal with. Whilst the majority of media problems tend to be simple, such as cable breaks and poor connections, they do take a considerable amount of time to diagnose and isolate. If there is no simple solution, it will then be necessary to address the task of diagnosing, identifying and remedying the fault. Many products are available to assist in this task, although rarely will the use of such a system on its own be sufficient. It is more likely that the network manager will have to use a number of different hardware or software products, combined with a large amount of common sense if transmission media problems are to be remedied.

8 Optimising Performance

8.1 OPTIMISING SYSTEM RESPONSE TIMES

One of the most frequent complaints raised by users is that the network is simply too slow. This typically occurs with those users involved in disk-intensive tasks, as once loaded, an application tends to execute at the same speed on networked and standalone systems, other than when accessing the disk. Disk intensive tasks include database interrogation and modification, accounts work, stock control, client management etc.

It is also important to remember that certain applications are disk intensive, notably those that make use of a programming technique known as overlays. Overlays are often used for application programs that are too large to fit in memory all at once. The overlay technique allows the system to load only those parts of the software that are immediately required. Therefore, when swapping between the different functions offered by an application, the system may need to load in several different overlays. On a network this can severely impair the performance of the program. Overlay files usually have a file extension of .OVR or .OVL. An overabundance of these files for any given application tends to indicate that it could be highly disk intensive.

8.2 PERFORMANCE LIMITATIONS

There are actually three primary components that may limit the performance of the network by causing bottlenecks:

- File server file caching and CPU saturation
- Efficient use of the communications channel bandwidth
- Disk channel utilisation.

If any one of these components is operating at less than optimum efficiency, then the performance of the whole system will be brought down to that level. For example, if two out of the three components are working at 100 percent efficiency, and the third is only able to operate at 25 percent, then the overall system performance will also drop to 25 percent of its possible maximum. Thus one small problem can drastically affect the entire network.

8.3 BALANCING REQUIREMENTS

Achieving the ultimate solution in terms of LAN performance is usually a case of making a number of trade-offs. For example, performance is normally increased only through extra expenditure, and usually a higher performance network will be more difficult to manage. Therefore, the first step in the optimisation process is to identify and prioritise the criteria that the LAN must conform to. Typical factors to bear in mind include:

- Performance, ie the speed of transfer of data between the file server and the network stations.
- Maximum size of the network, in particular the number of stations it should cater for.
- Expenditure, both for the initial investment, and in terms of the ongoing costs.
- Manageability, ie how easy it should be to monitor and analyse performance, utilisation and individual user's activities.
- Maintenance, including whether or not the LAN should be maintained by in-house staff, or whether maintenance contractors should be used.

The process of identifying and prioritising these requirements will significantly simplify the process of choosing the most suitable configurations and components for the network. It will also provide a set of ground rules which can be used to assess the level of service and performance delivered by the network as it grows and expands.

8.4 IDENTIFYING THE BOTTLENECK

When attempting to remedy performance related problems, it is wise to attempt to rate each component of the network in terms of its efficiency, ie how well it is actually working compared to how well it should be working. The first components that should then be considered for upgrade or replacement are those with the worst efficiency rating, as these will often produce the most dramatic increases in overall productivity and performance.

If problems are not tackled in this way then it will often be found that the obstacle simply moves to the next most inefficient component. For example, a file server's performance rating can theoretically be improved by adding sufficient RAM to raise the cache hit ratio to 90 percent or more, and by adding a second disk drive and adapter to duplex the I/O requests. In practice, the problem will often be found to move to the network adapter or LAN driver, as these components will often be unable to handle the increased volume of data that the file server can now process.

By tackling the least efficient components first, large performance gains can quickly be achieved and the other less critical problems can be tackled when time or money permits.

8.5 PERFORMANCE VARIATIONS

Performance levels exhibited by components may vary greatly according to the current workload. In times of high network utilisation it can be difficult to measure exactly how well a particular section or device is performing, as the workload will fluctuate from minute to minute. For this reason it is recommended that performance measurement be carried out when there is little or no general network traffic, perhaps afterhours or even at weekends.

Utilities can be used to simulate extended periods of low, medium and high network activity in a very controlled manner. Thus the performance of selected components can be monitored and measured in order to determine the efficiency of the various network devices. Additionally this technique allows potential problems to be identified before they occur, as during such a testing session the network will usually be stressed beyond normal everyday limits.

Once the efficiency levels of the prime components have been ascertained, they can be upgraded or replaced as necessary to gain the required level of network performance. In many situations there will be insufficient funding to allow all of the bottlenecks to be removed, and in such cases it will be necessary to reach a compromise between ideal performance levels and expenditure.

8.6 UPGRADING COMPONENTS

Very few organisations have the funding to allow the components of their LANs to be continually upgraded with state-of-the-art devices. Therefore it is necessary to appreciate the issues affecting the performance of various components, and how the efficiency of these components can be improved.

8.6.1 CACHE RAM

File servers are usually supplied with what is known as 0-wait state RAM. This means that the memory chips are quite fast, noticeably more so than 2-wait state RAM for example. In fact recent benchmarks have shown that an 8MHz file server using 0-wait state RAM actually exceeds the throughput figures of a 12MHz server using 2-wait state RAM.

It is vital to bear this fact in mind when considering the addition of extra RAM for file caching. Although the system board may well have 0-wait state RAM, it is quite possible to purchase an add-on memory board that uses 1- or 2-wait state memory. Thus the potential advantage of using the add-on board is severely limited. In some rare cases the addition of a slower memory board can actually degrade overall performance.

8.6.1.1 CACHE CAPACITY

The amount of caching RAM that should be provided is often a subject of contention. The success of the caching is dependent not only upon its physical capacity, but also upon the software that is being used. A well designed database program for example will make much better use of caching facilities than a poorly designed one.

Two approaches can be taken to resolve the issue of cache size. The approach taken depends on many factors, although two of the most important are the capacity of the server disk drives, and the number of different applications that will be used by network users.

With high capacity drives, it is more than likely that there will be five or more different applications in everyday use. In such situations it is best to base the size of the cache on the size of the disk drive. A typical ratio is 4KB or 8KB of cache memory for every 1MB of disk capacity. Thus for a 600MB drive, the cache would be between 2400KB and 4800KB. Many network operating system designers recommend that a minimum of 1 or 2MB cache memory is supplied, irrespective of the size of the disk drive.

In situations where the number of applications used is small, the size of the cache can be based on the amount of memory that would allow a cache hit rate of 90 percent or more to be achieved. Hit rates of less than this value will cause the network performance to be noticeably impaired. In most operating systems, the hit rate is reported in terms of the number of disk requests serviced from the cache compared to the number of disk requests serviced directly by actual disk I/O. The value is often subjective (ie estimated), but should still be in excess of 90 percent if performance is to be maximised.

8.6.2 INDEXED FATS

Novell NetWare allows its users to make use of a facility known as Turbo FATs. A FAT is a file allocation table, a special area of disk used by the operating system to maintain control of the allocation of disk space. The FAT is usually fairly large, and can typically be in excess of 600KB. The Turbo FAT allows these areas to be given special treatment, in order to increase the throughput of data and minimise the retrieval times. It also reduces the loading on the file server CPU, a critical factor in high performance file servers.

8.6.3 BRIDGES AND ROUTERS

Every bridge or routing device introduces a delay into the transmission and communication of data. Therefore an excess of these devices in the data path between the originator and destination will reduce performance levels considerably.

A popular technique for overcoming this problem is to use a backbone and subnetwork configuration. Any station on a subnetwork can access any other station connected into any point on the entire network by going through a maximum of two bridges. This will minimise the handling overhead and considerably reduce the associated delays.

8.6.4 DISK CHANNEL

The issues of mirrored and duplexed disk drive configurations are far from simple, and normally introduce many uncertainties in terms of the relative performance of the system. There is in fact a large amount of variability between the different duplexing and mirroring systems that are available, most notably due to incompatibilities between devices. These incompatibilities can far outweigh the benefits offered by such a configuration. Thus it is essential to ensure that the chosen disk drives and controllers are in fact 100 percent compatible, both with each other and with the overall system.

If it is assumed that the disks and controllers have been correctly chosen and configured, then the performance gains through these systems are surprisingly small. However the losses are more noticeable in certain situations. The following summarises the relative performance levels of single, mirrored and duplexed configurations:

- For write operations, single and duplexed configurations achieve almost equal throughput, whilst mirrored disks will typically achieve about half of that.
- For overlaid disk read operations, all three configurations achieve almost identical results. The reason for this is that it is the cache memory that determines the overall speed in such situations.
- For sequential disk read operations similar figures are again generated, although the performance from the duplexed configuration is marginally better than the others.

Overall figures tend to indicate that in an environment in which read operations dominate, then the increased security and performance offered by a duplexed configuration more than offset the extra investment. Similarly, if a mirrored configuration is currently in use then the cost of upgrading to a duplexed system is negligible when compared with the benefits.

8.7 WORKSTATION MEMORY

The memory of the workstation is used by many different software systems. It must contain not only the workstation operating system, such as DOS, but also the software drivers for any peripherals, the network drivers, and resident utilities that are required as well as the required application program and data. Thus more memory is used by networked systems than by standalone PCs.

Unfortunately when working with DOS there is a limitation of 640KB memory imposed on the system. In many cases this is simply not enough for all the software that is required. Consequently a way must be found to overcome this barrier.

8.7.1 BREAKING CONVENTIONAL MEMORY LIMITATIONS

The restriction on the amount of memory that can be used directly is due to DOS, and the origins of the problem are routed in the late 1970s.

When DOS was first applied to the PC, the onboard memory capacity of the system was a mere 16KB, and even if this was expanded, the motherboard could still only accommodate 64K. The fact that this could be further expanded to 640K through the use of expansion boards was considered by many to be totally irrelevant, as memory chips were prohibitively expensive.

640K was chosen as the limit due to design restrictions on the actual 8088 processor. As it had only 20 address pins, it could access a maximum of 1MB of memory. This was to include BIOS, other ROMs, screen mapping area and any other form of memory fitted to peripherals etc. Therefore a total of 384K was allocated for system use, leaving 640K for the user. This is known as the real or base memory.

Later developments introduced the 80286 processor, which has 24 address pins. Thus it can theoretically access 16MB of memory, although its performance is restricted to maintain compatibility with the 8088 and 8086 chips. Thus even the 80286 will only access 1MB total memory, unless it is specifically informed otherwise. The way in which it can be told to access the remainder of the memory is not straightforward.

At the time the AT was launched, with its 80286 processor, IBM introduced the term *extended memory*. This referred to the memory situated between the 1MB barrier and the 16MB limit. This term is often confused with the other memory related terms, namely real memory, base memory, system memory and expanded memory. Before proceeding further with the discussion of how to overcome the DOS limitations, it is useful to define these terms:

- **Real memory** refers to the 640K of memory that is available for use by applications and data. Unless using DOS version 5, this area must also contain the primary DOS files, any special configuration data, and any TSR programs that are executed. The network software is one such TSR program.
- **Base memory** is exactly the same as real memory, and the terms are often used interchangeably
- **System memory** is sometimes used to refer to the entire memory installed in the

computer. However, it technically refers to the 384K assigned for use by the system, between the 640K assigned as real memory and the 1MB upper limit.
- **Expanded Memory** refers to the use of special techniques that allow the extra memory to be utilised by DOS applications. Expanded memory is discussed in greater detail below.
- **Extended Memory** refers to the area of memory between the 1024K allocated to the real and system areas, and the 16MB upper limit for the 80286 processor.

These different regions are illustrated in Figure 8.1 below.

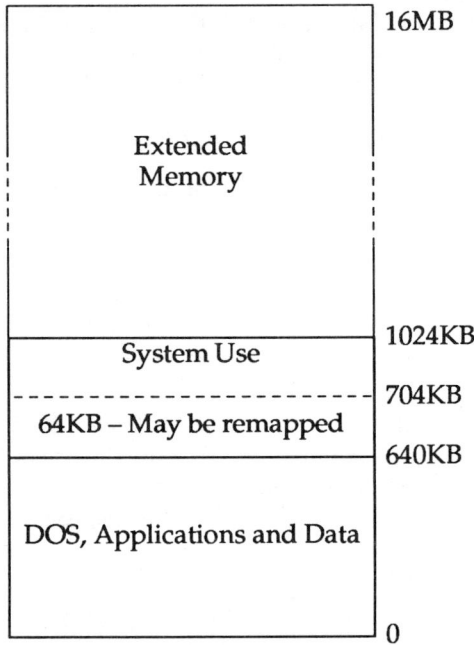

Figure 8.1 Memory usage for an 80286 processor

With these definitions in mind, each of the ways in which the conventional limitations can be overcome will be discussed.

8.7.2 BREAKING THE BARRIER

Current PC configurations usually contain a minimum of 640KB, and are being increasingly supplied with 1, 2 or 4MB as standard. Despite this, DOS still restricts the user to directly accessing only the first 640K, so the remainder has to be accessed through other techniques and methods.

There are three primary ways of doing this:
- Remap a portion of the system area
- Use expanded memory
- Use extended memory directly.

8.7.2.1 Remapping the system area

There are a number of products available that will remap the memory usage so that some of the memory in the system area can be accessed by DOS. This is based on the fact that IBM originally allocated 384K of memory for the system's use, although not all of this is actually required. Therefore, some of the physical RAM can be remapped into the spare spaces to provide an additional 64K of storage. This facility is available to all machines.

Unfortunately, most modern software products already take advantage of this feature in their ever increasing attempts to offer new facilities and abilities. Thus the use of an appropriate remapping package may provide benefits in some situations, but will offer no advantage to users of modern applications.

8.7.2.2 Use expanded memory

During the mid-1980s, many spreadsheet users were discovering that they simply did not have enough physical storage capacity within the DOS 640K limit. Therefore a way of overcoming this barrier had to be found, or users would begin switching to other operating systems and applications that could make better use of the available memory.

The result of this was expanded memory, in the form of a proposed expanded memory specification (EMS). The first EMS was produced in 1985 by the partnership of Lotus Development and Microsoft, but this was soon superseded by the Lotus-Intel-Microsoft EMS which is often referred to as LIM EMS 3.2.

This software facility allowed programs to access up to 8MB of RAM using a technique called bank switching. The principle involves the allocation of 64K of base memory as a page frame, a special area through which memory from beyond the 1MB barrier could be transferred. Using the system, any memory access request that exceeded the standard DOS limit was trapped by the software. The software then automatically fetches the appropriate area from the extended memory, and places it within the 64K page frame. The request is then rerouted to the page frame, and the application accesses the data.

There is obviously a small performance loss due to the extra routine that must be executed. However, for most users the ability to gain an extra 8MB of storage far outweighed this disadvantage. There were in fact other limitations to LIM EMS 3.2, and not surprisingly the software has been upgraded since to improve and enhance it. The latest version is LIM EMS 4.0 which allows up to 32MB of expanded memory to be implemented, and can be used by many different PC products.

8.7.2.3 Use extended memory

More and more modern software products are making direct use of extended memory, thus giving access to the full 16MB on board RAM. The use of this technique means that there is no performance loss, as the extended memory is treated in exactly the same way as the base memory.

Typical examples of such products are Lotus 1-2-3 Release 3, and DataEase, both of which used advanced programming techniques to bypass the need for EMS, and access all extended memory directly. This technique has the additional advantage of being much easier for the user to set up, as they need to have no technical knowledge whatsoever.

8.7.3 THE 80386 AND 80486 PROCESSORS

The advent of the newer Intel processors has removed many of the problems associated with memory management. Systems using these processors will often allow the user to divide the onboard RAM into separate areas to be allocated as expanded and extended. Thus the handling of EMS etc is greatly simplified. However, the fundamental problem of the DOS limitation is still present, and so applications developers are still required to use sophisticated programming techniques to achieve the desired results. The use of these more powerful processors brings its own memory problems though, not least of which is the speed with which memory requests can be serviced. Processor speeds of 25MHz and 33MHz are very common, but memory chips are still relatively slow, and sometimes cannot cater for these high clock rates.

Note that these limitations are inherent in DOS; they do not apply to other operating systems such as OS/2 and Unix. These are not without their own problems, some of which are discussed below. Although the latest version of DOS, DOS 5.0, still retains the basic 640K memory area, the product comes with its own EMS driver and also loads the majority of the DOS shell into high memory. This has the effect of freeing up the majority of the 640K area for applications and data use.

8.7.4 OPTIMISING MEMORY USE WITH WINDOWS

The current version of MicroSoft's Windows operating environment, 3.0, provides three different modes of operation. Not all of these are available on all computer systems though, and hence functionality can be somewhat limited on certain systems:

- Real mode is the simplest of all. Any PC can run Windows in Real mode as long as it has at least 640KB of RAM, although for best performance it is recommended that additional expanded memory is installed. Real mode offers the most limited flexibility, as it does not directly access any extended memory. Real mode provides maximum compatibility with previous versions of Windows applications.

- Standard mode is only available on computer systems with 80286 or greater processors, and is the default mode of operation. Standard mode provides access to extended memory, and allows the user to switch between non-Windows applications. Standard mode requires that the computer system have at least 1MB of memory.

- 386-enhanced mode allows Windows access to the virtual memory capabilities of the 80386 and 80486 processors. This feature allows Windows to use more memory than is actually available by using the disk as temporary storage. It also allows non-Windows applications to be multi-tasked. To use 386 enhanced mode the computer system must be based around an 80386 or 80486 processor, and must have at least 2MB of memory.

Thus programs running under Windows, on an appropriately configured system, may use any combination of conventional, expanded, extended and virtual memory. Furthermore there is no need to reboot the machine or make changes to the configuration data when changing between applications that have different requirements, as Windows handles all the memory management itself.

8.7.5 UTILITIES AND APPLICATIONS

There are many different utilities available which purport to solve all memory problems. However, the exact choice of product is not simple, and depends heavily upon the hardware that is in use at the time. For example, different products are required for 286 and 386 based systems.

To help in making these decisions, the following sections describe how some of the most common utilities can be employed in breaking the DOS memory barrier. Each section describes the way the product works, and the situations in which it offers greatest functionality.

Most of the products work by allowing certain programs to be moved from the base 640K memory to the space between the video RAM and the ROM BIOS at the top of the 1MB address area.

8.7.5.1 Hy-Card

The Hy-Card is applicable for 8088 based systems, and works by adding memory to the computer in the aforementioned area. Software device drivers are then placed in this area by the program that accompanies the card. These drivers include IPX, NETx, NETBIOS and INT2F. The exact amount of memory made available is determined by the exact hardware configuration of the system, and which of the device drivers can be relocated is dependent upon this fact also.

If RAM availability is the primary concern, and purely text based applications are in use, then it may be worth considering down-grading the display adapter, perhaps to an IBM monochrome card. This device requires only 4K of display memory as opposed to the 64K used by the Hercules monochrome for example. This extra 60K can be put to good use in many situations. Similarly a network card can be selected that does not use memory in this region, thus freeing more space.

8.7.5.2 All-Charge-card

The All-Charge-Card works in exactly the same was as the Hy-Card, but is applicable to 80286 based machines. The same issues affecting the performance and operation of the card apply to both systems.

8.7.5.3 QRAM

The QRAM software package must work in conjunction with a rather specific hardware configuration. For the software to function, the system must either be based on the Chips and Technologies 286-based NEAT chip set, or it must be an 8088 or 80286 system containing one of the following LIM 4.0 boards:

- AST
- Everex
- Micron Technology
- Intel.

Some other less well known manufacturer's boards are also supported, and fuller details regarding these are supplied in the manual that accompanies the QRAM product.

QRAM works with the hardware to allow device drivers, TSRs and the network shell to be mapped into high memory. The system includes an analysis routine to determine the most effective method for mapping the different items, in order to make the best use of the available hardware resources.

8.7.5.4 LANSpace

LANSpace is also applicable to 80286 based systems, and allows NETx to be loaded into high memory. It also includes a program to allow NETBIOS to be released from memory, thus liberating a further 21KB, although this is only usable by applications that do not require NETBIOS to be present.

8.7.5.5 QEMM and 386-To-The-Max

These two systems are very similar, and are applicable only to 80386 and 80486 based systems. They are both reasonably priced (under £80), and allow device drivers and portions of the network shell into high memory. Both of these systems are purely software based, and take advantage of the enhanced memory management features available in the newer processors.

8.7.6 COMPARING DIFFERENT PROCESSORS

Generally speaking, 8088, 8086 and 80286 based systems require hardware solutions to memory management problems, as the processors do not have the flexibility to cope with the problems themselves. Thus the products that work for these machines tend to involve a combination of hardware and software, and hence are correspondingly expensive.

80386 and 80486 processors include a great deal of flexible memory management facilities, and hence solutions to memory management problems on such systems are considerably cheaper as they consist purely of software. This applies equally well in most respects to the 80386sx chip as well.

Therefore, if memory management is thought to be a likely problem when considering the purchase of a new system, it may well be cheaper in the long run to purchase an 80386 or similar system rather than one based on the 80286 processor.

One product that works for any system, albeit in a rather primitive way compared to its competitors is TurboPower Software's Marknet and Relnet utilities. These simple programs allow the network shell to be unloaded from memory, thus freeing a significant amount of space. Obviously the user will no longer be able to communicate with the network, but if used in this way the utilities provide a very efficient solution to memory-hungry applications that are executed from a local drive.

8.7.7 FACTORS TO CONSIDER IN ASSESSING MEMORY USAGE

In many cases it is unnecessary to go to the expense and trouble of purchasing and installing a special memory management system such as those described above. Solutions to memory management problems can often be achieved through the examination and modification of a variety of DOS and network related parameters.

The version of DOS that is in use can significantly affect the amount of memory available. DOS 4 requires the greatest space, and noticeable gains can be made by switching to a lower version, such as 3.2, or by upgrading to DOS 5.0. As many installations are still using DOS 3.X it is recommended that an upgrade to DOS 5.0 be made, as it will almost certainly prove advantageous for all network users. A secondary problem associated with DOS 4 is that when it is installed, the system automatically enables almost every feature that is provided. Thus a great deal of space is wasted on facilities that may never be used. Therefore it is suggested that a careful examination of the DOS files is carried out after the operating system has been installed, and any extraneous commands etc are removed. The files that are most affected in this way are CONFIG.SYS and AUTOEXEC.BAT. Savings of over 50K have been made in this way.

In CONFIG.SYS, the BUFFERS=X line determines how much space DOS allocates as temporary storage during disk intensive operations. However, NetWare also uses its own buffers, and so the CONFIG.SYS entry is effectively redundant when using network based applications. Therefore it can be removed to free more memory. If standalone applications are to be used then it may be necessary to reinstate the command and reboot the system, as many applications will refuse to run if there are insufficient buffers allocated.

New NetWare shells have recently been made available that use less memory than their predecessors. Additionally drivers have been made available that allow the shells to be placed either in the real memory area, in expanded memory, or in extended memory. Use of the extended memory technique means that the shell will occupy less than 7K of conventional base memory, the only penalty being a performance loss of between 10–30 percent, due to the need for continued switching.

8.8 WHY OPTIMISE?

Many LAN managers feel that there is no need to optimise the performance of their network if all appears to be going well. Others feel that it is necessary to optimise the performance of the system in order to maximise the effectiveness of the current investments, to provide users with the most productive work environment, or simply to stay up to date with new technology.

Whatever the reason it is essential to approach the subject in a controlled, logical manner. The worst thing of all is to invest large sums in new technology or upgraded devices without first ascertaining the root cause of the problems that are causing poor performance. The end results from such an approach are usually frustrating, especially when the performance is limited by a number of subtle problems, each of which must be solved in order to resolve the overall situation.

8.9 SUMMARY

This chapter has illustrated a number of different areas in which network performance can be enhanced. These range from installing cache memory to improved installation methods and better management.

The most important point to bear in mind when considering optimal performance is that if a balance is not maintained between hardware, software and the operating system, the result can be an overall reduction in performance leading to even more complaints from the users.

9 Security Issues

9.1 WHY IS NETWORK SECURITY IMPORTANT?

Network security performs two major functions:
- It protects the network against unauthorised access and modification
- It protects the users from themselves.

Many organisations take no security steps whatsoever, thus allowing any user to log onto the network as a supervisor, with all of the supervisor's associated powers and abilities. Even networks with no perceived need for security will benefit to some degree by the implementation of such measures, not least because they protect the users from themselves. For example, if you tried to remove all the files from your floppy disk with the ERASE *.* command, but were actually logged onto a network directory as a supervisor then you would delete all the files from the current directory. However, if in the same situation you were logged onto the system as a user with no delete rights, then you would not be able to achieve the same degree of destruction.

Despite the use of the most sophisticated security systems available, a network still has one major weak link in its security: the personnel. No access control routine can prevent an authorised user signing on to the system and then allowing an unauthorised person to gain access to confidential data. Similarly, many users find memorisation of account codes and passwords too much of a chore and so write them on pieces of paper which are then taped to the desk or monitor. Thus any casual passerby would find it very easy to gain access to the system using the account number and password. Therefore it is essential to consider the concepts of user training and education when looking at the overall issues of computer security.

9.2 NETWARE SECURITY

Novell NetWare, like many other network operating systems, provides security enforcement at two levels:
- The Login process
- File and Directory access.

Whilst the discussions in this chapter will be based around those features applicable to NetWare, the same concepts and methods are employed in the majority of other network operating systems as well. In particular user accounts and passwords are employed by almost all network operating systems, and thus the careful use and management of such features is of prime importance in maintaining network security.

9.3 THE LOGIN PROCESS

The first line of defence against unauthorised access is the Login process, as this determines who can actually gain access of any form to the system itself. Novell provides a variety of methods for controlling access, most of which are based around the ideas of account names and user passwords. Other measures use hardware dependent details, such as node addresses. Each of the fundamental techniques are discussed below.

9.3.1 ACCOUNT NAMES

Broadly speaking, Novell users may be divided into two categories:
- Those who modify data on the network
- Those who examine data on the network.

Ideally, any user who may require access to the system for any purpose should be assigned their own unique account name. However, in some circumstances this is impractical and a simpler scheme is employed. As an absolute minimum standard, unique names should be provided for
- Any user who saves or modifies data on the network
- Any user who has access to any expensive IO device, or has access to any peripheral or services that may incur charges.

It will soon be found that for any network serving more than a few users, the task of maintaining user IDs becomes a difficult and extremely time consuming one, even with the utilities provided with NetWare. In such cases it is essential to weight the advantages of security and the ability to analyse system usage for each account against the expenditure requirements in terms of human resources that will be necessary to manage such a system.

Supervisor accounts are a special form of user account. Supervisors are provided with unlimited access to all data, programs, peripherals and services that are available through the system, and as such have almost unlimited powers over the operation of the network. To avoid any unnecessary complications due to accidental commands and operations being performed, it is recommended that any user who is deemed to be a supervisor is assigned two accounts. One of these is a normal account with standard user rights of access for performing everyday tasks, and the other is a special supervisor account that is used exclusively for network management and monitoring activities. The use of two accounts of this form means that network supervisors are less likely to cause damage to essential data, nor are they likely to jeopardise the ongoing operation of the system if they accidentally delete an entire disk, or execute a malfunctioning program.

9.3.2 PASSWORDS

Passwords are the most commonly used tool for validating the identity of a user. Thus it is essential to keep a password absolutely secret, especially if the account name needs to be disclosed to other users for any reason.

The structure of a password determines how successful it will be in deterring unauthorised access. A Novell network allows passwords to be between one and ten characters in length, although the default minimum length is more usually set to five or more characters. The ideal content of a password is a collection of random letters and numbers.

However, people find it very difficult to remember such passwords, and will usually write them down on a piece of paper so as not to forget them. Obviously, this in turn introduces its own problems.

Given free choice, users will usually select an easily remembered password. These should at all times be discouraged, as the use of such passwords makes it much easier for an intruder to gain access to an account. Common choices to beware of include:

- Nicknames
- Spouse's names
- Children's names
- Pet's names
- Words associated with hobbies
- Words associated with business projects
- Words associated with items of interest such as cars, sports etc.

Passwords can be assigned either by the supervisor or by the user themselves. Each has its advantages and disadvantages:

9.3.2.1 Supervisor assigned

The choice of password by the supervisor means that the actual content of the password can be made obscure, although this may introduce the problem of the user writing the password down if it is too obscure.

However, as the supervisor has to generate passwords for all users, this scheme means that it is very easy for the supervisor to gain access to another users account and impersonate them whilst performing any operations. Such accesses may be monitored by a tracking system (see below) and will be assigned to the user's account rather than the supervisor's account. This could in turn lead to expenses being incorrectly charged to the account, or more seriously, security breaches being attributed to the user rather than to the supervisor.

A second problem with this scheme is due to the distribution of passwords. A secure method of distributing passwords to each and every user must be determined. Obviously electronic mail cannot easily be used as any other user may gain access to the confidential password information. Internal paper mail systems are safer, but not totally secure. If every user is required to come and see the supervisor in person, then a list must be drawn up detailing each and every user account with the corresponding password - a security risk in itself. Additionally, such processes may be totally impractical if there are many users.

9.3.2.2 User assigned

If users are allowed to choose their own passwords then the problems associated with a central list of all passwords become irrelevant. However, the problems of users choosing familiar words or phrases becomes dominant. The only cure for this is to institute a training programme that sensitises users to the problems of computer access and security.

One technique that can be successfully employed in such situations is to encourage users to construct a simple, meaningless, sentence. The first (or last) letter of every word can then be extracted to create the password. For example, if the phrase was chosen as "I Have A Small Black Cat" then the password becomes IHASBC taking the first letter of every word, or IEALKT if the last letter of every word is chosen. The use of such a technique means that it becomes much more difficult for an intruder to guess at the password chosen by a user, even if they do know the person well.

9.3.2.3 Forced password changes

One of the NetWare utilities, SYSCON, can be used to force passwords to be changed on a regular basis, a technique which can drastically reduce the number of security breaches. This is due to the fact that many security breaches fall into a distinct pattern, in which a period of time passes between the point at which security is breached and the point at which the intruder actually finds the data that is of interest. This period may be several weeks or months, and so a programme of regular password changes will in many cases cause future unauthorised access attempts to fail.

This scheme will also ensure that users do not use meaningful passwords as it prevents the re-use of previous passwords. Thus users will soon find that they run out of meaningful, everyday words, and will have to resort to the use of less obvious terms and phrases.

9.4 FILE AND DIRECTORY ACCESS

Once the user has gained access to the system, the second line of defence comes into operation. Each file or directory can be assigned any combination of eight trustee rights, which limit how the user may access the data in that file or directory. A new user begins with no rights at all, and hence can access no programs or data at all. The supervisor then adds rights, either individually or as a member of a group.

9.4.1 NOVELL NETWARE ACCESS RIGHTS

The NetWare security rights are very similar in principle to the attributes that are applied to any file by DOS.

9.4.1.1 Read

This permits information to be read from a file. It is usually used in conjunction with the Open and Search rights.

9.4.1.2 Write

This allows information to be written to an existing file. It does not allow a new file to be created, or an old one to be deleted. In practice it will be found necessary to also have Delete, Create and Read rights for any file that is to be written to.

9.4.1.3 Open

This permits you to open an existing file. You must have Open rights before you can either read or write data to a file.

9.4.1.4 Create

This right permits the creation of a new file or subdirectory. It is also necessary to have this right before data is written to a file.

9.4.1.5 Delete

This allows the deletion of an existing file or subdirectory. It is also necessary to have this right before data is written to a file.

9.4.1.6 Search

This right allows you to view a directory. It is also necessary to have this right before you can copy a file or write a file to the directory.

9.4.1.7 Modify

The Modify right allows a file's status flags to be changed.

9.4.1.8 Parental

Parental rights allow you to specify rights to the directory for other users. Parental rights allow you to grant and revoke rights to either individuals or groups.

The use of parental rights is an essential tool for NetWare security management. It is important not to grant parental right to most users as this will minimise the amount of control that can be exercised over the network by the supervisor.

9.4.2 MANAGING ACCESS RIGHTS

One natural division of network responsibilities is to assign one individual to the task of making the network work efficiently, and a separate individual to the task of maintaining applications software. If the applications software is situated in a group of subdirectories from a common \APPS directory, then providing the applications manager with parental rights to the \APPS directory allows the management of software rights to be off-loaded from the primary network manager.

9.4.3 SECURITY EQUIVALENCE

NetWare allows the security and access rights of one user to be made equivalent to those of another. This tool provides a simple and flexible method of maintaining security rights, but introduces its own problems.

Such problems are encountered as the network is expanded and users are assigned new tasks or responsibilities. For example, a department recruits a researcher to help an existing user in the analysis of a variety of statistical data. As the new user is performing exactly the same job as the existing one, a new account is created and provided with security equivalence of the original researcher's account. Thus the two users are able to work on the same data, using the same applications, with a minimum of effort on the part of the supervisor. However, security equivalence continues to track any changes in the privileges of the master account. Thus when the original researcher is assigned to a new project, monitoring fluctuations in particularly confidential data, the second researcher automatically gains the same rights of access.

This illustrates the pitfalls of using only security equivalence to manage network

9.4.4 GROUP SECURITY

Managing network security on an individual basis becomes very tedious, time consuming and error prone when dealing with any but the smallest networks. NetWare provides a simpler method of maintaining adequate security through the use of Group rights. Such group rights are applied to every member of the group, allowing staff with common jobs to easily share data, applications and peripherals.

9.4.5 ADDITIVE SECURITY

The NetWare security system is additive rather than exclusive. Thus starting with the access rights held by an individual, these rights are increased when the user is made a member of a group, and increased again if the member is made a part of another group. If an individual is assigned membership of a group that lacks a privilege that the user has gained from another source then the group membership does not remove that security right for the individual.

9.5 PHYSICAL SECURITY

The most fundamental form of computer security begins with physical security of the actual hardware. For example, if the workstations and servers are held in locked offices, and the cable routed through locked service corridors and wiring closets, then the intruder must first violate and overcome these physical security measures before they can attempt to access the system.

In addition to these basic physical security measures, NetWare provides two of its own forms of physical security measures:

- Node address restrictions
- Time of day restrictions.

9.5.1 NODE ADDRESS

Most network cards, including Token-Ring, EtherNet and PC-Network, are supplied by the manufacturer with a unique network node address or serial number that cannot be changed by the user. Some network cards, such as ArcNet, have switchable node addresses. A few network adapter cards have no provision for unique addresses. LocalTalk is one such card.

Any account or group of accounts can be restricted to the use of one or more node addresses. This is usually achieved through the use of the SYSCON utility, and can be made as stringent as restricting one user to using the network facilities from a single node address, or as general as allowing any user to access network resources from any node address at all. In academic environments this facility may be used to restrict access to particular laboratories or terminal rooms to particular groups of students, researchers or staff. The use of node address restrictions in this way is a useful tool in controlling the allocation of scarce resources.

Where gateways are used to permit access to mainframes, the node address can be used to preserve the confidential nature of sensitive mainframe data. For example, in large organisations the personnel records and accounts information are often held and processed on a mainframe. Access to this data can be restricted to those node addresses within the personnel and accounts departments, which in turn can be made secure with physical locks etc. Thus access to sensitive data can be restricted to only those machines in appropriately secure areas.

Certain printer server and mass storage backup software requires accounts to be created with privileges beyond those normally allocated. If such accounts were accessed by unauthorised personnel then severe damage or disruption could be caused to the system. However, there is no reason why such accounts cannot be restricted to running only from certain nodes. Thus the printer server account can be run from the workstation that is directly attached to the printer, and the backup software can be run from the workstation connected to the backup hardware. By ensuring that these workstations are maintained in a physically secure environment, the possibility of unauthorised access is effectively minimised, with no additional inconvenience experienced by the users.

Node address is an especially restrictive form of security, and will not be required in the majority of situations, especially where effective account code and password measures are implemented.

9.5.2 TIME OF DAY

Any account can be restricted from accessing a server or gateway in terms of the time of day. For example, ordinary users in the accounts department can be restricted to access the appropriate data and applications only during working hours. This restriction is typically activated with the SYSCON utility, and provides an additional degree of security for confidential data. Indeed such time-oriented security measures are considered mandatory by many computer professionals, especially those working with financial data. In academic environments the use of time of day restrictions can help to force load levelling, preventing the system from over-use during peak hours.

The time of day restrictions are also useful when managing a backup system. Often such systems require that all users be logged off the system before the software will execute. This task can be simplified by ensuring that all users are denied access during the scheduled backup times.

9.6 TRANSACTION TRACKING

Whilst NetWare itself provides no transaction tracking capabilities, there are numerous third-party products that can perform this process for NetWare networks. Two of these are LT Audit and LANtrail, both of which provide a full audit trail, outlining which user accessed which data or application and when. Transaction tracking systems tend to consume vast amounts of disk space, as they naturally have to store a lot of data. Thus it is often necessary to compromise and only run the tracking software during certain times. It is preferable to make these times as random and unpredictable as possible in order that intruders do not become used to the tracking routines employed.

As explained above, an audit trail outlines who accessed which data or application, and when they did so. As such, the audit trail can illuminate any abnormalities that may occur. For example, Why is Andy Johnson accessing the system in the middle of the night? Why is Mary White accessing financial accounting data when she is actually assigned to the personnel department? The audit trail does not provide answers to such questions, nor does it prevent unauthorised access, but it does highlight any unusual activity that requires further investigation. It may be that Andy Johnson is just extremely dedicated to his job, and that Mary White has actually been transferred to a different department, but it may be that these accounts are being used by unauthorised personnel.

9.7 INTRUDER TRACKING

Whilst it is not feasible for a manual typist to try and break an unknown password, it is a simple matter for a computer programmer with even the most rudimentary knowledge to create a program that automatically tries every combination of five-, six-, seven- etc letter passwords. Without appropriate defensive measures such an attack will certainly succeed even if it takes a long time. NetWare provides such measures in the form of an intruder tracking facility. After a specified number of unsuccessful Login attempts, NetWare disables the account until the Supervisor resets it.

The limit of unsuccessful attempts is determined by the supervisor, and need not be a particularly small number. In fact, even with a five character password there are over 60 million combinations, so setting the limit to 20 or even 50 unsuccessful attempts will almost certainly thwart any attempt of this nature whilst still remaining transparent to legitimate users.

9.8 THE SECURITY UTILITY PROGRAM

One of the NetWare utilities is called SECURITY, and it is the job of this utility to report on any 'holes' in the security system that it may find. These may include:

- Accounts with supervisor equivalence
- Accounts with other high levels of privilege
- Accounts with directory rights assigned at a volume level
- Accounts with short passwords
- Accounts with missing passwords
- Unlimited retry Logins
- Other password weaknesses
- Users who do not have a Login script.

The use of the Security utility on a regular basis will help in the control and monitoring of the network, and provide the supervisor with a concise summary of any possible weaknesses.

9.9 BIOMETRICS

In highly sensitive situations, especially those in which access to the data could be disastrous for the organisation, the in-built security features of NetWare can be supplemented with biometric security devices. These are external devices which are usually used to protect either a single workstation or a group of workstations, and so are often used in conjunction with network node restrictions.

The term *biometric* implies the measurement and quantification of natural features, and biometric devices tend to measure personal characteristics such as fingerprints, hand geometry, retina patterns, voice patterns and signatures. All of these are difficult to forge, and so provide an excellent basis for a security procedure. Despite the fact that fingerprints have formed the foundation for identification in the criminal justice system for many years, it is only recently that automated authentication of biometric data has become sufficiently accurate. The current state-of-the-art systems provide error rates of less than 1 percent.

Biometric devices can be used to secure either a single workstation, or as an entry control device to a room containing several workstations. Similar strategies involve the use of a biometric device to produce a unique short-term password, which is then entered in addition to the standard user account number and user password.

Of the available biometric technologies, signature analysis is the least expensive, with suitable devices retailing for around £400 upwards. Voice recognition systems are more expensive, and retail for £700 upwards. Fingerprint readers will cost in excess of £1000, whilst a hand geometry scanner will cost over £2000. Most expensive of all is the retina scanner, a device that will cost around £4000.

9.10 SUMMARY

Without doubt every network installation should have some level of security, if only to save the user from making silly mistakes. The more widespread a network becomes, both in terms of the number of workstations and type of applications in use, the more levels of security are required. Despite the size and complexity of an installation, a key point to bear in mind is that the system is supposed to be, above all else, easy to use and useful to the user. Too many levels of security can reduce usage and this can, in extreme cases, reduce the overall productivity of the organisations.

10 Data Protection

10.1 PREVENTING DISASTER

There are many preventative measures that can be taken to protect data from the effects of a system failure. These steps can range from simple, but effective, backup techniques, to the most elaborate duplexing and mirroring schemes.

NetWare provides a certain degree of protection in its SFT forms. SFT stands for System Fault Tolerant, and implies that an SFT operating system is able to continue operating at a satisfactory level even if the system suffers partial failure. The precise way in which a partial failure is handled is determined by the sophistication of the system. NetWare SFT is available in three different levels:

- Level I provides transaction tracking and hot-fix capabilities
- Level II allows disk mirroring and duplexing to be implemented
- Level III provides facilities for mirrored servers

10.2 SFT LEVEL I

Level I provides transaction tracking and hot fix capabilities

10.2.1 TRANSACTION TRACKING

Transaction tracking is a software feature of NetWare SFT that must be used in conjunction with a database management system that is capable of standard transaction tracking (ie the monitoring and recording of file read and write operations etc.).

When a database program updates some of the information that it stores, it is often necessary to perform several individual file operations to complete the single transaction. This is especially true when working with indexed database files. Transaction tracking allows the individual operations to be treated as a single process, thus guaranteeing that either all of the operations are performed or none of them at all. This effectively minimises the chances of data corruption due to system failure in the middle of such a process.

For example, an indexed database file is to be updated. Separate file operations are required for both the database file itself and the index file. If the power was to fail after the database information has been updated, but before the index had been updated, then the entire index file would be incorrect.

With transaction tracking enabled, the system follows a slightly different procedure:

- The system starts by recording the start of an update in a special transaction area.

- Each individual file operation is then performed, and its effects noted in both the database and index files, and the transaction area.
- If the operation completes successfully then the tracking system removes the information from the transaction area.
- If the operation is interrupted for some reason, such as by a power failure, then the transaction area will contain a record of a partially completed update when the system is powered up again. The tracking system then backs out of the entire operation, thus maintaining the integrity of the database.

10.2.2 HOT FIX

Due to their very mechanical nature, it is certain that a hard disk will fail at some time. At this point it is probably unusable, and should be replaced with a new unit. However, even during normal use it can be found that the magnetic surface of the disk degrades, and provides less than satisfactory storage capabilities in some areas. Whilst nothing can be done to prevent the former failure from occurring, it is possible to minimise corruption due to data being stored in these unreliable areas. The scheme employed by NetWare to combat this problem is known as the Hot Fix.

When SFT NetWare is installed, it designates a small portion of the disk to be what is known as the hot-fix table. Thereafter, whenever data is written to the disk, the system automatically reads it back and checks this information against what was written. If there are any differences, then the system writes the data to the hot-fix table instead, and marks the original area as unusable. Thus in this way NetWare can transparently recover and correct a fair number of disk errors which occur due to media deterioration.

10.3 SFT LEVEL II

Level II provides disk mirroring and duplexing capabilities.

10.3.1 DISK MIRRORING

Most disk controllers found in AT and PS/2 type machines are capable of controlling two independent physical hard disks. Disk Mirroring uses this facility by requiring that a matched pair of disks be installed in the server. Each of these disks is a perpetual backup of the other, ie they contain precisely the same data. Thus placing two 330MB disks in a server will still only provide a total of 330MB of storage.

Every write operation is performed on both drives, and so the information is guaranteed to be the same. If either disk fails for any reason, then the system can continue to operate with no data loss at all, using the remaining disk drive. The failed component can then be replaced in an orderly manner, rather than having to do it in a state of panic in order to minimise the downtime.

Disk mirroring incurs a small performance penalty when performing write operations. Because the disk controller can only perform one operation at a time, twice as much time is required to write data to a pair of mirrored drives than is required with a single drive. In practice the use of additional cache memory will minimise this deterioration as the writes can be cached.

Mirrored disks can provide a small performance gain in some situations when performing read operations. For any read operation NetWare only accesses one of the drives

DATA PROTECTION

(unless an error is detected). It determines which drive to access according to the position of the read heads at the time the request is received, and it will always direct the read operation to the disk in which the heads are closest to the required disk track.

10.3.2 DISK DUPLEXING

Duplexed disks require not only duplicate disk drives, but also duplicate disk controllers. Due to the fact that an AT or PS/2 can only handle a single MFM or ESDI disk controller, it is necessary to use a specialised device. Novell manufactures a special card known as a *disk co-processor board*. This is a high performance disk controller card that replaces the standard AT disk controller. Core International offer a similar device that works as a high performance ESDI bus controller for IBM MCA systems.

To duplex disks two of these controllers are placed in the server, each of which is attached to either one or two physical disk drives. As these controllers can operate at the same time, there is no performance loss for duplexed write operations. When reading data, the performance gain is quite significant, even over that offered by mirrored disks.

In addition to these performance gains the system is much more tolerant of faults, as it can not only cater for the failure of a disk drive unit, but also for the failure of one of the disk controller cards.

10.4 SFT LEVEL III

Level III provides server mirroring.

Server mirroring requires that the system is provided with two servers, each of which contain precisely the same information. The system is then unaffected by failure of any part of the server, whether it is the disk unit, the controller, or even the circuitry in the server's system unit itself.

As the server is normally the most expensive component of a network system, there is a natural reluctance to purchase two of them, especially if no gain in storage will be achieved. However, server mirroring is an ideal feature for mission-critical systems, where interruption of network services would cause serious disruption and financial loss to the organisation.

However, mirrored servers do provide quite significant performance gains, especially in networks that require a high throughput. For example, if two read requests occur at the same time, one server will implement each one. When a read and a write request occur at the same time, one server performs the physical write immediately, whilst the other first caches the write operation, services the read request, and only then performs the write. Thus performance can be noticeably improved in situations with such clashes.

10.4.1 APPLICATION THEFT

One threat faced by all networks is that of application theft by users. The reason for this is that all users require read, open and search access to directories containing applications in order to run them. Any user with these rights can also copy the files to a local directory and thus obtain an illegal copy. Fortunately there are several possible courses of action to counteract this problem.

10.4.1.1 Hiding files

Files can be hidden from the user using the DOS hidden-file attribute. This ensures that the files are not displayed when the directory is listed, nor can they be copied. The NetWare HIDEFILE utility can be used to achieve this effect. However, this strategy is only partially successful as most users are aware of how to reverse the change, and thus unhide the files so that they can be copied.

10.4.1.2 Scattering

Search mappings can be used to allow the different parts of a program to be stored in different directories. If the user attempts to copy only those files from the most obvious directory, they will not be able to run the program as certain sections will be missing. This strategy is effective in many situations, although any user who has a good knowledge of the application will realise that a part or the program is missing and go looking for it.

10.4.1.3 Make software less appealing

Software can be made less desirable by only storing those parts of the package on the network that are required for day-to-day use. Thus all unused device drivers, installation programs, overlays etc can be erased from the application directory, or moved to a secure area. Using this technique means that software will only be useful to anyone who will actually be running the application on an identically configured hardware system. This approach can have the added benefit of sometimes releasing substantial amounts of space.

10.4.1.4 Execute protection

The most effective approach of all is to make use of the NetWare execute-only attribute. This attribute can only be set by the supervisor, and is only applicable to files with a .COM or a .EXE extension, and prevents users from either copying or listing the contents of the file. The attribute is set through the FILER utility, by choosing the File Information option. Note that the use of this attribute means that the file cannot be copied to any other location, whether it is a server directory or a local disk unit, thus preventing illegal copying.

Unfortunately it is not possible for anyone, even the supervisor, to reset the attribute, although the file can be deleted by the supervisor. Similarly, as the file cannot be copied, it is not possible to back it up to tape either. Thus to prevent any possible problems it is essential to copy the file (before it is flagged as execute only) to a secure directory accessible only by the supervisor. Also in this area should be a log detailing where each program normally resides. This allows the program to be backed up, and also allows remedies to be made for any other problems that develop with the application.

Another problem experienced in conjunction with the execute protect attribute is the fact that some applications will not run properly when flagged in this way. In some cases it is possible to patch the program to overcome the problem, although this will usually void any warranty, and will often break the licence agreement. Thus it is important to contact the application developer before embarking on this course of action.

10.5 VIRUSES AND INOCULATION

Most computer users, and certainly all network managers and supervisors, have by now heard of the computer virus. Indeed many users have actually had first hand experience of the computer virus in one form or another, and have learnt to their cost the problems that the virus brings.

10.5.1 VIRUS INFECTION

In terms of standalone systems, the virus is a problem that is coming under control. Many packages are available for limiting the spread of the virus, as well as reversing their effects if they do attack a system. Most of these systems use sophisticated programming techniques to ensure that the program remains in the computer's memory whilst the user is working on other applications, and thus monitors all appropriate operations and commands that are issued. Any attempt by a virus to attack either the system memory or one of the disks is immediately noticed and thwarted.

Similarly, due to the fact that most viruses are spread through the use of floppy disks, packages offer scanning facilities that allow suspect disks to be checked for the presence of any viruses. These packages can often recognise hundreds of different types of virus, and normally offer remedies to the majority of them.

10.5.2 VIRUSES IN THE NETWORK ENVIRONMENT

In the network environment viruses pose a different problem. Due to the fact that many viruses are executed when a system is booted from a floppy disk, it is quite rare to find a network system infected in this way as they usually boot from a hard disk. However, booting a workstation from an infected floppy may well infect the network, as will using an infected application on such a system. The effects of infection will initially be noticed on the host workstation, although the virus could soon spread throughout the network if it has been so designed.

Viruses are TSR programs, and as such attempt to remain in memory whilst the user completes other tasks. Network software is also TSR in orientation, and this fact can introduce conflicts between the valid network software and the virus. In many cases it will be found that this conflict results in the workstation crashing, effectively locking the user out of the system. Whilst this is inconvenient for the user, it usually signifies that the virus has also crashed and has not been able to infect other workstations or parts of the network.

If a virus does manage to infect the network it will soon spread to the file server. If it is a boot sector type virus, it will usually attempt to write its code directly to the disk, in the area that DOS usually assigns as the partition record, boot sector or FAT. In this way it will be executed again when the system is next powered up. In NetWare, as well as many other network systems, the layout of the server's disk is vastly different to that used by DOS, as the operating system uses its own unique format. Thus when the virus attempts to write to the disk it actually overwrites the wrong area, and creates its code in an unusable format. The next time the network operating system attempts to access data from the corrupt area the system will crash. Similarly, if the system is switched off, and then powered up again, the operating system will attempt to read data from the corrupt area and again crash. Thus the network becomes unusable, and total network failure occurs. Due to the non-standard nature of the disk format used by network operating systems it is almost impossible to reverse the situation. Often the only solution is to reformat the entire disk, and re-install the most recent backup.

It should be noted that there are some viruses designed to take advantage of the network environment. Rather than conflict with the operating system, these viruses use the facilities that it provides to spread quickly through the network, infecting as many different applications etc as possible. These viruses are often malicious, destroying users data after a set period of time. They will often try to access other networks through the use of gateways and modems, thus spreading even further. The solution to this form of virus involves the system being powered down and the virus being removed carefully from every infected area.

One famous 'virus' to hit a network was the Christmas virus. This was a simple Christmas greeting program produced by a student in one of the USA universities, and was not really a virus at all. The simple executable program was sent by the author to all users on his mailing list. On executing the program a picture of a Christmas tree was displayed together with a message conveying season's greetings. At the same time the program sent copies of itself to all the users on the current person's mailing list. As mailing lists often consist of 20 or more other users, the program soon began to spread far and wide. The university network was connected to one of IBM's proprietary mainframe networks, which in turn was connected to most other universities, and a large number of corporations, including the majority of America's Fortune 500 companies. Many users that received the program executed it, and the subsequent loading caused the entire network system to seize. The total cost to IBM, the universities, and the corporations linked to the network is thought to be in excess of $2 billion in lost revenue and disruption.

10.5.3 PREVENTING VIRUS INFECTION

The problems associated with computer viruses can quickly become very serious in the network environment. For example, there are numerous documented cases of a virus infecting an entire network within minutes of first being introduced. Once this happens, the network managers will often find themselves working 24 hours a day in an effort to reverse the damage.

As in most situations, prevention is better than cure. When dealing with computer viruses, preventative measures take many different forms. The following list outlines the most common steps that can be taken to reduce the likelihood of virus infection:

- Always write-protect original applications and operating system disks. It is impossible for the data on a disk to be altered if it is write-protected, and thus it cannot be infected.

- Always boot from a hard disk, and only use the original write-protected operating system disk when recovering from a virus or a system crash. On floppy disk systems, ensure that the boot floppy is write-protected. Distinctive looking floppies, for example coloured ones, can be used to denote these write-protected disks.

- Remove all extra COMMAND.COM files from networked hard disks. This file is a prime target for viruses, and the existence of several copies will just increase the risk of this happening.

- Never use the original disks for an application as the day-to-day work disks.

Copies should be made and the originals kept in a safe place. Copy protected software introduces its own problems, and the vendor should be contacted in order to obtain a security backup in these cases.
- Set the read-only attribute for all application and system program files. This prevents a virus from being able to corrupt a program.
- Restrict user access as much as possible. This is not because the user cannot be trusted, but because the virus cannot be trusted. If a user inadvertently loads a virus, then that virus is restricted to accessing those sections of the network to which the user has rights. It cannot normally exceed these limitations.
- Keep several generations of good backups so that data can be restored after a virus attack. Applications should be restored from the original diskettes (which should not be infected) rather than from the backup media (which may be).
- Institute a user awareness programme which highlights the possible dangers associated with viruses, and shows how viruses typically infect systems. The programme should emphasise that users must not pirate software, and must never load such software onto the network.
- Produce rules that make it an offence for a user to load a piece of software onto the network unless it has been checked for viruses first. Use a proprietary checking system for this, and ensure that it does actually work. There have been cases of virus detection software being marketed which was unable to detect any viruses at all.
- Provide all network users with a set of anti-virus guidelines. This should not only set down the preventative procedures that should be used, but it should also provide a contact name and telephone number in case of emergency.

10.5.4 CURING VIRUS INFECTION

Once the system has been infected, it will be necessary to remove all traces of the virus as quickly as possible. One of the first steps to take is to shut down the network. This may not be popular, but it is the only guaranteed way to ensure that the virus does not continue to spread.

Secondly, proprietary virus detection systems should be used to attempt to identify, analyse and locate any infected files or areas of the disk. In many situations it will be necessary to use several different systems in order to ensure that all occurrences of the virus have been detected.

Once the virus is located, it can be destroyed or inoculated using a similar program. An alternative method, and one which is inherently safer, is to reformat the entire disk, and reinstall applications from original disks and data from the most recent backup. However this takes a very long time indeed, so is impractical in many cases.

It is also very important to check all local disks on workstations to determine whether they have been infected or not. On a LAN with over 100 stations this is also very time consuming, but must be done in order to prevent the chance of the network being reinfected when it is operational again.

The final step, and one of the most difficult, is to contact all users who have used floppy disks in networked stations, and check their disks for viral infection. If no formalised disk checking procedures were in use beforehand then now is the time to start introducing them. If even a single disk is omitted from this checking process then it is quite possible for all of the remedial work to have been in vain, as the virus can quickly reinstate itself.

In many cases it is difficult to determine if the system is indeed infected with a virus. If the manager is unsure, then there are a number of tests that can be performed to clarify the situation. Viruses usually work on a special trigger, and until the trigger occurs they lie dormant in the computer, seemingly inactive. Common triggers include the following:

- System times such as 9.00 am, noon or 5.00 pm
- System dates such as Friday the 13th, April 1st, the 13th of any month, special date sequences such as 9th September 1990 (9/9/90)
- Profanities
- Politicians Names
- Little used DOS commands.

By applying these triggers, the LAN manager may well activate the virus. If it is done in a controlled manner then the amount of damage that the virus does can be limited. This is much safer than waiting for the virus to trigger in an everyday situation, where the damage could be very costly and wide-ranging.

10.6 DISASTER RECOVERY

Every computer environment contains elements of risk. Some of the risk is handled through appropriate security measures, whilst the other portion concerns the environment and the measures that are taken in order to prevent disasters from occurring, and to handle problems if they do occur.

Previous sections have covered the issues of security and the preventative measures offered by the various levels of SFT NetWare. However, the overall concerns of disaster planning have not yet been discussed, and these are some of the most important decisions that must be taken in the management of the network.

10.6.1 DISASTER RECOVERY PLANNING

Disaster recovery planning is the process of formalising arrangements for the procedures that will be put into operation in the event of partial or total system failure occurring. It is important to attempt to address all possible risks within the context of disasters, and as such the following issues may be considered appropriate:

- Unauthorised access, either in the form of disclosure of data, or possibly the problems of malicious damage.
- Theft of systems, both hardware and software.
- Failure of hardware devices, including workstation and server system units, local drives on workstations, centralised hard drives in servers, power supplies etc.
- Failure of software systems, including those faults due to overuse of the network.
- Problems due to the power supply, either in the form of total failure (blackout), partial failure (brownout), or other miscellaneous faults such as spikes, glitches and surges.

- Natural disasters, such as floods, storm damage, fire.

The remedies to these problems take various forms, the effectiveness of which are dependent upon how well the measures are implemented.

The problems of unauthorised disclosure of data, malicious damage to network data, and theft of systems have been covered in previous sections and can be counteracted through the use of appropriate physical, hardware and software security measures.

10.6.2 HOT SPARES

Hardware failure will happen, irrespective of the precautions that are taken. Backups and fault tolerant systems will help to minimise the loss and disruption, but the actual process of replacing the failed component can be time consuming and does include a number of pitfalls. For example, if the main drive unit on a server fails, then it is necessary to replace it with a new one. However, before the backup data can be restored to the new unit, the disk must be analysed and formatted with the COMPSURF process. In some situations this can take a full day or more.

It is important to many organisations to minimise downtime due to such situations, and one way of achieving this is to keep an inventory of hot spares. These are components such as:

- Ready COMPSURFed disk drives
- LAN adapter cards
- Server memory boards with RAM already installed
- Cabling
- Connectors
- Active components such as Token-Ring media access units and Ethernet concentrators
- Hard and floppy disk drives for workstations
- Power supply units
- RAM chips or SIMMs

Ideally these components should be preconfigured, so that they can be ready for use with as little delay as possible when a failure occurs.

In some situations it may not be possible to immediately diagnose a fault, especially where servers are concerned. The downtime can be minimised if this happens by maintaining an entire server as a hot spare, so that if the primary server fails the secondary is immediately swapped in, and the most recent backup restored. The fault that caused the primary server to fail can then be diagnosed carefully and accurately, without having to worry about rushing to re-enable the system.

Obviously, small organisations are at a significant disadvantage in terms of maintaining an inventory of hot spares. In an organisation with 20 or 30 servers, the cost of a backup server is minimal in comparison to the overall cost of the network. However, a company using a single high-performance server will find it much more difficult to justify the cost of a spare. In many cases the best solution is a maintenance contract, in which the dealer, manufacturer or maintenance organisation guarantee to supply backup hardware within a specified time frame. Care must of course be taken in selecting an appropriate organisation, as there are still many unreliable firms offering such services.

10.7 BACKUPS

The loss of data from a network is usually much more devastating than the loss of data from a standalone computer. This is because the network is usually used by many different users, some of which share or create common data. Thus the recreation of such data is an immense task, and is often simply not feasible. Additionally, the details connected with the network administration are also sizeable, involving data such as user accounts, security methods and structures, privileges etc. Thus it will also be time consuming to recreate this information.

10.7.1 BACKUP MEDIA

The only acceptable solution to the problem of possible data loss is to ensure that adequate backup measures are taken. Thus if the system does fail and data is lost, then at least partially up-to-date information can be restored. The choice of how and when to backup is not a simple one, and there are many different strategies that address these issues. However, the secondary choice of what media to use for the backup is also very important, although it has become almost standardised for the majority of firms.

There are three fundamental choices:
- Floppy disk
- High capacity demountable disk (Bernoulli, DataPac, WORM)
- Tape.

10.7.1.1 Floppy disk

Floppy disk backups are simply not realistic. To back up even 100MB of data from a server will require nearly 300 standard 5 ¼" floppies. The time and effort required to actually perform the backup process are immense, and in the long term it will prove to be financially disastrous.

10.7.1.2 High capacity demountable disk

Recent technology improvements have meant that high-capacity removable disks are becoming more and more common. Typical examples include the Bernoulli drive, the Tandon DataPac, and the CD-ROM (otherwise known as a WORM). These devices offer very large storage capacities in a relatively small physical size. The problem with them is that they are still quite expensive, both in terms of the initial hardware costs for the drive, and in terms of the ongoing costs that are required for the media.

10.7.1.3 Tape

Magnetic tape is by far the most popular backup media, due to its ease of use, competitive pricing and reliability. The most common form is QIC (Quarter Inch Cartridge), although half inch tape is also available. Such devices are provided in many capacities, ranging from 20MB or so to over 600MB on a single tape.

10.7.2 STRATEGIES FOR BACKING UP

There are a number of different strategies that can be applied to the process of backing up. The appropriate strategy that should be applied to a particular situation depends upon the size of the network file system, the capacity of the backup device, and also the volatility of the networked data.

In the following discussions it is assumed that the backup device is a standard QIC drive. The strategies also apply to systems employing other devices, although device dependent details may change.

10.7.3 PLACEMENT OF THE BACKUP DEVICE

NetWare allows the tape drive to be connected either directly to the file server (a local device), or to a workstation on the same network as the file server (an external device).

If a local device is used then the server must be taken off-line in order to perform the backup, which is frequently not a viable option. The use of an external device means that the data from the server can be backed up whilst the network is still up and running, indeed it is essential for the network to be operational if the backup is to be successful.

10.7.4 SCOPE OF THE BACKUP

The backup need not involve all of the data stored on the server. Indeed in many situations this is not possible. Therefore the scope of the backup may be one of the following:

- Complete backups
- Directory-based backups
- Change-based backups.

10.7.4.1 Complete backups

This may be the best strategy if the capacity of the backup system either meets or exceeds the capacity of the file server, although it can be time consuming. This is the simplest form of backup to restore, and is generally considered to be the safest form of all.

10.7.4.2 Directory-based backups

If the server is structured such that data is stored in directories that are separate from the applications then a directory-based backup strategy may be better. As applications tend to remain fairly stable, it is only necessary to backup those areas of disk containing data, and to only backup the applications when they change. This strategy can make the backup process significantly faster and easier, especially when the file server capacity exceeds that of the backup device.

10.7.4.3 Change-based backups

Most backup systems allow only files that have changed to be backed up. Thus a complete backup can be carried out every Friday afternoon, and then change-based backups carried out at the end of every other day. In the event of a failure the most recent complete backup is restored first, followed by the individual change-based backups in the order in which they were made.

10.7.5 FILE VS IMAGE BACKUPS

Most backup systems allow the user to choose between making an image or a file backup. An image backup records all the data on the entire disk and stores it in a special format detailing where each piece of data was taken from. A file backup records only the data files stored on the disk, and stores them in a more flexible manner.

An image backup must be restored onto a disk of exactly the same geometry (number of cylinders, heads and sectors) as the one it was taken from. Thus if an 80MB disk fails, it will be necessary to restore the backup onto another 80MB drive, even though there may be a 330MB unit on the shelf that was about to be used to upgrade the server.

A file backup can be restored onto any disk (as long as it has sufficient capacity for the data that is to be restored). The file based backup also allows the restoration of single files or groups of files that may have been accidentally corrupted or destroyed.

10.7.6 MULTIPLE BACKUP STRATEGIES

It may be appropriate in some organisations to use several different strategies for backing up. For example, if an organisation has several departments, each may be made responsible for backing up their own data. The centralised network manager may also make complete backups of all file servers connected to the internet. The regularity with which each of these types of backups is made can be balanced in order to minimise costs whilst still maintaining a satisfactory level of protection.

10.7.7 ROTATION SYSTEMS

Ideally, backup tapes that contain data should never be reused. Thus there will be many security copies of the data in the event of a failure. However, there are very few situations where this is economically viable, so a rotation system is usually employed. Such a system requires that tapes are reused after a given period. The length of this period determines how many tapes are required, as well as how safe the data is.

The worst case scenario is one in which a single backup tape is used, and is overwritten every day with current data. If the system were to fail in the middle of a backup operation then there would be no security backup copy of previous data. Therefore, a minimum of two tapes should be used in rotation. When rotating tapes, the oldest data should be overwritten first. Thus the tapes will be as up-to-date as possible.

Some organisations use a combination of rotation and permanent storage:

- Once every week a complete backup is made. The tape used for this is rotated after a set period.
- Every day a change-based backup is made. The tape used for this is also rotated after a set period.
- Once every two or four weeks a complete backup is made, and the tape is stored permanently.

Assuming 15 tapes are used in the rotation sequence, then it is unlikely that any serious data loss will occur as there will normally be at least two complete backups, plus two weeks of change based backups to restore from. The overhead of using 12 or 24 tapes every year will normally be acceptable to most organisations in the interests of safeguarding their data.

10.7.8 STORAGE OF BACKUP MEDIA

Storing backup tapes in the same building as the server does little to protect the organisation if the building is flooded out or burned down. The only satisfactory solution is to keep at least one backup in off-site storage, so that in the event of such a disaster all is not lost.

This point was brought home to the Open University in Milton Keynes, Great Britain, when their computer centre went up in smoke. It was noted at the time that the fire was particularly fierce, and it took a while for the Fire Brigade to gain control. The reason for this was that every one of their mainframe backup tapes was stored in the room next to the actual computer; magnetic tape is highly inflammable, and once alight is very difficult to extinguish.

There are some companies around who will take care of secure storage of backup media, and will usually take care of arrangements for rotation of tapes etc.

10.8 POWER

Computer systems are dependent upon power, and this is usually supplied by a third party power company. The quality of service delivered by the power company is sometimes less than satisfactory, with problems including partial or total power loss, as well as spikes, transients and surges.

All computer systems are affected by such problems, and they will indeed prove inconvenient for people working with single user machines. However, networks are often used by many hundreds of people, and such problems will then affect everything at once.

10.8.1 CAUSES OR PROBLEMS

Identification of power supply problems can be difficult, time consuming and expensive. It is often found that problems are due to poor wiring or connections within the building, and if this is the case there is no remedy except to call in the contractors. Other power supply problems can be due to the location of large pieces of equipment such as lifts, air conditioning units, heating systems, and even smaller items such as microwaves, coffee machines, photocopiers and telephones.

10.8.2 REMEDIAL EQUIPMENT

There are many remedies to these problems which fall into four broad categories:

- Surge suppressors
- Power line conditioners
- Standby power supplies
- Uninterruptable power supplies.

10.8.2.1 Surge suppressors

A surge (otherwise known as a transient or spike) is a burst of power, beyond that usually provided by the power line. Surges are normally of very short duration, but in some cases have been known to last for up to a second. The magnitude of the surge can be anything from a few volts to several thousand volts, and they come from a number of sources. Lightning, changes at the power station, and electrical equipment are all culprits, and they are all factors that are beyond the control of the computer user. Surges can be very dangerous, as they can destroy computer equipment instantly. They can also cause injury to users in some very rare circumstances.

To counteract the threat, a number of surge suppression devices are available. These range in price from a few dollars to several hundred dollars, and unlike most other computer devices, you get exactly what you pay for. The cheapest devices can cope only with smaller surges, and will be destroyed by larger ones. However, there is normally no indicator to say that the device is functioning, and as the power is still supplied the user remains unaware that the power supply is unprotected. More costly devices offer greater protection, and tend to be more robust. They also offer indicators to show that everything is working properly.

10.8.2.2 Power line conditioners

The voltage supplied on the power line may vary, sometimes quite significantly. The most common occurrence is when the voltage drops for an extended period, a situation known as a brownout. However it is also possible for the voltage to rise for an extended period, possibly placing undue strain on the power supply of the computer.

This condition can be counteracted with a power line conditioner, a special device which regulates the level of power supplied to the computer. Prices start in the region of £150, with more expensive devices offering better regulation and more features, often including surge suppression as well.

10.8.2.3 Standby power supplies

The two previous devices protect the system from short term variations, but are of no use if there is a power cut. If this occurs, the computer will simply stop working, with a great deal of consequential data loss and corruption.

To prevent this from happening a standby power supply can be used. This is a special device consisting of a battery, charger and a special switch. Whilst power is supplied normally the battery is topped up by the charger, and the system is supplied with power in the normal way. As soon as a power cut occurs the switch transfers the power line so that the system is supplied from the battery, thus maintaining power at all times. There is a short time delay whilst the switch operates, and it is important to ensure that this delay is less than the maximum acceptable time that the power supply to the system can be interrupted.

10.8.2.4 Uninterruptable power supplies

The uninterruptable power supplies (UPS) also caters for brownouts, but does so without the need for a switch. Again it consists of a battery and charger, but the system is always supplied from the battery, never directly from the main power line. When the power line is functioning normally, the charger keeps the battery topped up. However if a blackout occurs the system continues to operate from the battery with no interruption at all.

The UPS offers the best protection of all, and usually functions as a surge suppressor and power line conditioner at the same time.

10.8.3 SIZING A POWER SUPPLY

Power supplies are rated in terms of either VA or Watts. These terms are equivalent, and indicate the capacity of the battery in the device. The minimum configurations that are available will typically power the system for between five to ten minutes in the event of a power failure, and this length of time increases as the VA rating is increased. In general it is wise to purchase a device with as large a VA rating as possible (all other things being equal), as this gives the greatest length of time for continued operation.

10.8.4 AUTOMATIC DOWNING

UPSs are available that can be connected to NetWare cards so that in the event of a power failure the system automatically begins to shut down. This ensures that there will be no data loss due to the battery power fading whilst the supervisor attempts to finish just one more task. Software required to implement this feature is packaged with NetWare, and will automatically broadcast a message to all users informing them that the system is about to shut down. This means that all users can leave applications etc in an orderly manner, saving data etc before they quit.

10.9 TESTING THE DISASTER PLAN

A disaster plan will usually involve several different stages, with several different personnel performing key tasks. Do not wait for the inevitable to happen before determining whether or not the plan is effective, test it at regular intervals. If it appears that there are loopholes or flaws in the arrangements then take steps to correct them.

Similarly, care should be taken to ensure that backup devices etc are functioning correctly, including any hot spares that are kept in stock, UPSs and standby power supplies, as well as automated routines for automatic shutdown etc.

Remember that failures usually occur at the moment of most inconvenience. Therefore ensure that the plan is still operational if the supervisor is at a conference in the USA, or if their assistant is on vacation. A written record should be kept of the plan, detailing all measures that are required together with the personnel responsible.

10.10 SUMMARY

As more and more organisations are using their networks for mission-critical work, the importance of maintaining a comprehensive system of preventative actions and backups is ever increasing. The threats to the system are numerous and varied, including user errors, accidental damage and malicious attacks, any one of which may result in considerable loss to the firm.

Preventative measures must be taken on all installations, whether they take the form of utilising the built-in SFT levels provided by NetWare or their equivalents in other network systems, or by using third party products and utilities to achieve the same results. However, regardless of what measures are taken to prevent the likelihood of loss of data or system functionality, it is of the utmost importance that a full, up-to-date set of backups are maintained at all times.

11 Measuring User Satisfaction

11.1 A HOLISTIC APPROACH TO MEASUREMENT

There is currently much research being performed into ways of measuring the success and effectiveness of information systems. Much of this research is concluding that there is no simple way to measure the success of an information system, and that in order to quantify its performance in some way a broad range of techniques must be used. Some of these techniques are inherently qualitative, relying on the opinions of experts to deduce some value for the systems. Other techniques are quantitative, allowing a more methodical approach to be taken to the topic. Many of these techniques are discussed in *A Guide to Measuring and Managing IT Benefits* (Remenyi, Money & Twite, 1991), and readers are directed towards this publication for further details.

However, there is one technique that can be performed by all network managers, and will provide a good indication of how well the users perceive the network to be operating. This technique measures user satisfaction through the use of a survey, and has proven to be one of the more effective, and less expensive, ways of measuring the success of any information system.

11.2 USER INFORMATION SATISFACTION

The degree to which users are satisfied with an information system can be measured by comparing their expectations (or needs) of what the system should achieve, with their perceptions of what the system is actually achieving. This comparison can be performed for many different facets of the system and thus an overall picture of how the users view the network can be produced.

- If the users' expectations are greater than their perceptions of the performance of the system, they are obviously not satisfied with the particular aspect in question.
- If the user's perceptions of system performance exceed their expectations then the system is over-performing, and it is quite likely that time and money is being wasted on issues that the users do not believe to be relevant.

By obtaining many such indications it is possible to direct network development and investment into those areas that are believed to be the most important, or into those areas which do not currently meet the user's needs. Through the use of this technique the overall efficiency and effectiveness of the network can often be significantly enhanced.

11.3 USING A QUESTIONNAIRE TO MEASURE THE SUCCESS OF AN OFFICE AUTOMATION NETWORK

The effectiveness of the computer network employed in a large manufacturing organisation is to be investigated. The network was primarily implemented to improve the efficiency of routine tasks such as order processing, stock control and client management. However, more recently it has expanded to cater for a wider variety of software applications, providing facilities way beyond the original specification. Due to this extensive growth, it has been decided that the overall success of the network should be measured. Once this has been achieved, funds can be more easily directed to those areas that are viewed as the most important.

11.3.1 CREATING THE QUESTIONNAIRE

A questionnaire is created that will be presented to each of the users of the network. The main body of the questionnaire consists of 30 questions, each of which concentrates on a particular aspect of the network. It is important in the design of questionnaires to ensure that the questions are unambiguous and easy to interpret and answer, and every attempt to abide by these guidelines has been made in the design of this document.

Each of the questions is answered twice:

- First, the users are asked to state their opinion of the importance of the specified attribute in ensuring the effectiveness of the system.
- Secondly, the users are asked to state their opinion of the performance of the information system in terms of the same attributes.

The final section of the questionnaire requests the user to rate the overall performance of the system, and provides an open-ended question that allows any other comments or suggestions to be made.

All of the questions are answered on a four point scale. For the expectation questions, the respondent can rate their opinion as one of the following:

- Critical
- Important
- Not Important
- Irrelevant.

For the questions relating to the user's perceptions of the actual performance of the system, the options are as follows:

- Excellent
- Good
- Poor
- Very poor.

Note that these responses are equally weighted and have no middle-of-the-road value. Therefore respondents are forced to make a conscious decision with regard to their opinions.

Figure 11.1 shows the questionnaire that was used in the survey.

The Measurement of IS Effectiveness

The following questionnaire has been designed to help assess the effectiveness of the computer network system used to support white collar and knowledge workers in an office environment. It is now used extensively in businesses in Europe as well as other parts of the world. This is part of a measuring instrument developed at Henley - The Management College, where a number of staff work in the area of measuring and managing IT benefits.

The questionnaire has been divided into four parts. Part A relates to demographic details about your position in the firm. Parts B and C use the same set of 30 questions. Part D contains one specific question as well as an opportunity for you to provide open ended comment on the systems.

Your answers to the questions in Part B refer to the system's attributes which you believe are important to the effectiveness of the network system. Your answers to the second set of 30 questions in Part C refer to how the Information Systems Department of the firm performs in terms of these systems attributes.

Finally, in Part D we would welcome any comments that you would like to make concerning your own experience with the computer network and/or with the Information Systems Department in respect of its effectiveness.

The questionnaire uses a four point scale.

First set of 30 questions:	Second set of 30 questions:
Critical	Excellent
Important	Good
Not important	Poor
Irrelevant	Very poor

For example, you might think that ease of access to computer facilities is critical, and therefore your rating in the first set of questions will be:

Irrelevant	Not Important	Important	Critical

If you feel that the performance of the Information Systems Department in providing these facilities is good, this will mean your rating in the second set of questions will be:

Very Poor	Poor	Good	Excellent

The questionnaire should not take more than 15 minutes to complete. All information supplied by respondents will be treated with the utmost confidence.

Thank you very much for your assistance in this research. Please return your completed questionnaire to the survey administrator.

Dr. Dan Remenyi
IT Effectiveness Assessment Services

PART A

Please supply the following information about your position:

Are you a manager, accountant, knowledge worker*, clerk, personal assistant, secretary, typist or other?

Manager	Accountant	Knowledge Worker	Clerk	Personal Assistant	Secretary	Typist	Other

If other, then please specify _____

How many years have you been working in the organisation?

How many years experience have you had working with a PC?

How many years experience have you had working with a PC network?

How many hours per week do you use a PC or a PC network?

* This category includes positions such as lawyer, programmer, doctor etc.

COPYRIGHT TECHTRANS 1991

Figure 11.1 User satisfaction questionnaire - Page 1

200 USER SATISFACTION QUESTIONNAIRE

PART B

Answer the first set of questions by ticking the box which corresponds to your opinion of the importance of the following 30 attributes in ensuring the effectiveness of your system.

1. Ease of access for users to computing facilities.

Irrelevant	Not Important	Important	Critical

2. Up-to-dateness of hardware.

Irrelevant	Not Important	Important	Critical

3. Up-to-dateness of software.

Irrelevant	Not Important	Important	Critical

4. Access to external databases through the system.

Irrelevant	Not Important	Important	Critical

5. A low percentage of hardware and software downtime.

Irrelevant	Not Important	Important	Critical

6. A high degree of technical competence in systems support staff.

Irrelevant	Not Important	Important	Critical

7. User confidence in systems.

Irrelevant	Not Important	Important	Critical

8. The degree of personal control users have over their systems.

Irrelevant	Not Important	Important	Critical

9. Systems responsiveness to changing user needs.

Irrelevant	Not Important	Important	Critical

10. Confidentiality of user's own data.

Irrelevant	Not Important	Important	Critical

11. Provision for disaster recovery.

Irrelevant	Not Important	Important	Critical

12. Piracy avoidance procedures.

Irrelevant	Not Important	Important	Critical

13. System's response time.

Irrelevant	Not Important	Important	Critical

14. Extent of user training.

Irrelevant	Not Important	Important	Critical

COPYRIGHTTECHTRANS1991

Figure 11.1   User satisfaction questionnaire - Page 2

15. Fast response time from systems support staff to remedy problems.

Irrelevant	Not Important	Important	Critical

16. Participation in planning of the systems requirements.

Irrelevant	Not Important	Important	Critical

17. Flexibility of the system to produce professional reports, e.g. graphics and desktop publishing.

Irrelevant	Not Important	Important	Critical

18. Positive attitude of information systems staff to users.

Irrelevant	Not Important	Important	Critical

19. Users understanding of the system.

Irrelevant	Not Important	Important	Critical

20. Overall cost-effectiveness of information systems.

Irrelevant	Not Important	Important	Critical

21. Ability of the system to improve personal productivity.

Irrelevant	Not Important	Important	Critical

22. Ability of the system to enrich the working experience of the staff.

Irrelevant	Not Important	Important	Critical

23. Standardisation of hardware.

Irrelevant	Not Important	Important	Critical

24. Documentation to support training.

Irrelevant	Not Important	Important	Critical

25. Help with database or model development.

Irrelevant	Not Important	Important	Critical

26. Ability to conduct computer conferencing with colleagues.

Irrelevant	Not Important	Important	Critical

27. Users willingness to find time to learn the system.

Irrelevant	Not Important	Important	Critical

28. The use of a service level agreement.

Irrelevant	Not Important	Important	Critical

29. The monitoring of the ISD's performance in delivering services to users.

Irrelevant	Not Important	Important	Critical

30. The use of GUI software.

Irrelevant	Not Important	Important	Critical

COPYRIGHTTECHTRANS1991

Figure 11.1   User satisfaction questionnaire - Page 3

202 USER SATISFACTION QUESTIONNAIRE

PART C

Answer this set of questions by ticking the box which corresponds to your opinion of the performance of the Information Systems Department in terms of the following 30 attributes.

1. Ease of access for users to computing facilities.

Very poor	Poor	Good	Excellent

2. Up-to-dateness of hardware.

Very poor	Poor	Good	Excellent

3. Up-to-dateness of software.

Very poor	Poor	Good	Excellent

4. Access to external databases through the system.

Very poor	Poor	Good	Excellent

5. A low percentage of hardware and software downtime.

Very poor	Poor	Good	Excellent

6. A high degree of technical competence in systems support staff.

Very poor	Poor	Good	Excellent

7. User confidence in systems.

Very poor	Poor	Good	Excellent

8. The degree of personal control users have over their systems.

Very poor	Poor	Good	Excellent

9. Systems responsiveness to changing user needs.

Very poor	Poor	Good	Excellent

10. Confidentiality of user's own data.

Very poor	Poor	Good	Excellent

11. Provision for disaster recovery.

Very poor	Poor	Good	Excellent

12. Piracy avoidance procedures.

Very poor	Poor	Good	Excellent

13. System's response time.

Very poor	Poor	Good	Excellent

14. Extent of user training.

Very poor	Poor	Good	Excellent

COPYRIGHTTECHTRANS1991

Figure 11.1 User satisfaction questionnaire - Page 4

15. Fast response time from systems support staff to remedy problems.

Very poor	Poor	Good	Excellent

16. Participation in planning of the systems requirements.

Very poor	Poor	Good	Excellent

17. Flexibility of the system to produce professional reports, e.g. graphics and desktop publishing.

Very poor	Poor	Good	Excellent

18. Positive attitude of information systems staff to users.

Very poor	Poor	Good	Excellent

19. Users understanding of the system.

Very poor	Poor	Good	Excellent

20. Overall cost-effectiveness of information systems.

Very poor	Poor	Good	Excellent

21. Ability of the system to improve personal productivity.

Very poor	Poor	Good	Excellent

22. Ability of the system to enrich the working experience of the staff.

Very poor	Poor	Good	Excellent

23. Standardisation of hardware.

Very poor	Poor	Good	Excellent

24. Documentation to support training.

Very poor	Poor	Good	Excellent

25. Help with database or model development.

Very poor	Poor	Good	Excellent

26. Ability to conduct computer conferencing with colleagues.

Very poor	Poor	Good	Excellent

27. Users willingness to find time to learn the system.

Very poor	Poor	Good	Excellent

28. The use of a service level agreement.

Very poor	Poor	Good	Excellent

29. The monitoring of the ISD's performance in delivering services to users.

Very poor	Poor	Good	Excellent

30. The use of GUI software.

Very poor	Poor	Good	Excellent

COPYRIGHTTECHTRANS1991

Figure 11.1 User satisfaction questionnaire - Page 5

PART D

Please rate your overall opinion of the computer network system.

Very poor	Poor	Good	Excellent

Please supply any further comments you wish concerning the effectiveness of your computer network system.

_____
_____
_____
_____
_____
_____
_____
_____
_____
_____
_____
_____
_____

Optional

If you are prepared to discuss your comments with the researchers, please write your name below.

_____
_____
_____
_____
_____
_____

COPYRIGHTTECHTRANS1991

Figure 11.1   User satisfaction questionnaire - Page 6

11.3.2 PROCESSING THE RESULTS

Over 400 questionnaires were issued to various members of staff who at one time or other had used the network. Of these 196 were completed and returned. Whilst this response rate may at first seem to be very low, in actual fact it is relatively high due to various incentives that were offered to respondents. In such surveys it is not uncommon to find response rates of 20 percent or less!

The results of the questionnaires were converted into numeric values and entered into a Lotus 1-2-3 spreadsheet. The answers to part A were entered exactly as they were reported on the questionnaire, with the exception of the job categorisation which was translated into a numeric value of between 1 and 8. The answers to parts B and C were converted to numeric values as follows:

Value	Part B	Part C
1	Irrelevant	Very poor
2	Not Important	Poor
3	Important	Good
4	Critical	Excellent

Once entered into the worksheet the figures could be processed with a minimum of effort.

11.3.3 INTERPRETING THE RESULTS

A variety of different calculations and comparisons were performed, both for the figures as a whole, and for the different categories such as by job, length of service, amount of PC experience etc. In each of these comparisons the mean average figures were used.

11.3.3.1 Measuring the gap

First, the user's expectations and perceptions were compared, by plotting each of the figures on a line graph. To simplify the comparison, the difference between the expectation and perceived performance was also plotted; this latter measurement is referred to as the *Gap*, and is the prime indicator for facets of the system that should be enhanced. Figure 11.2 shows the graph produced in this way.

It can be seen from this graph that certain key points were deemed to be very unsatisfactory (a large negative gap), whilst others were thought to be over performing. In particular, it can be seen that positive gaps were obtained for four questions:

    2 – Up-to-dateness of hardware

    8 – The degree of personal control that users have over their systems

    12 – Piracy avoidance procedures

    23 – Standardisation of hardware.

These four facets are viewed as relatively unimportant, with expectation scores of under two in every case. Thus it is most likely that effort spent on these issues could be better used elsewhere. Of course there may be mitigating circumstances which explain these results. For example, very few users would think that piracy avoidance procedures were important; however, the company has a legal responsibility to ensure that software or data is not used by unauthorised personnel or transferred to other systems, and hence the network manager must ensure that safeguards are put in place.

206 INTERPRETING THE RESULTS

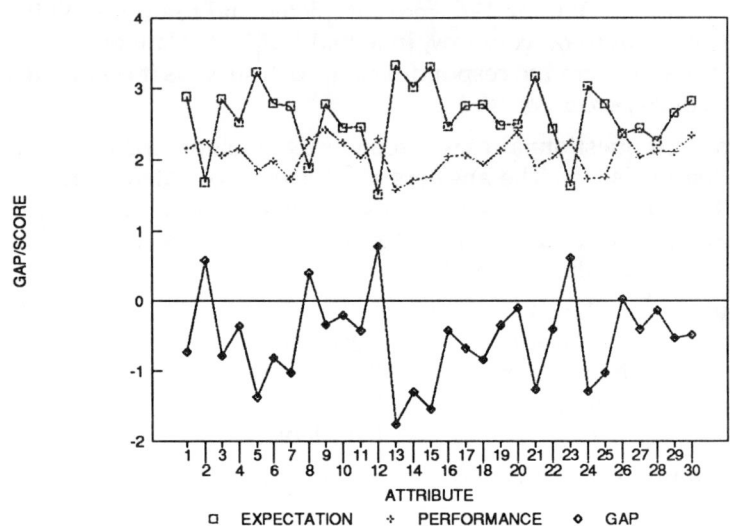

Figure 11.2   Snake diagram showing gaps

The graph also highlights certain facets that are believed by users to be unsatisfactory. There are a number of questions with large negative gaps, although six are particularly noticeable:

  5 – Percentage of hardware/software downtime

  13 – The system's response time

  14 – Extent of user training

  15 – Fast response time from ISD staff to remedy problems

  21 – Ability of the system to improve personal productivity

  24 – Documentation to support training.

These are classic issues that are viewed by most users as being unsatisfactory, as there is always a demand for more and more computing power and investment in training for new products. Despite this, these results should not just be passed off as something to be expected; they are serious issues and are viewed by users as adversely affecting their use of the network.

Various other measurements of the expectation/performance gap can be made and plotted in a similar way. However, they generally reinforce the results presented above and therefore have not been reproduced.

11.3.3.2 Performance measurement

In addition to measuring user satisfaction, it is also useful to measure how different categories of respondents view the performance of the network. This gives further indicators to those issues that require improvement.

The first performance measurement is performed for all users. The performance averages for each of the 30 attributes are again plotted on a line graph, but two other lines are additionally produced:

- The first is the arithmetic average of all performance scores for all attributes. This is known as the *all data average,* and provides a means by which above-average and below-average facets of the system may be identified.
- The second line shows the average response to the last question in the questionnaire, that of the user's overall opinion of the effectiveness of the information system.

Figure 11.3 shows the graph produced with these values.

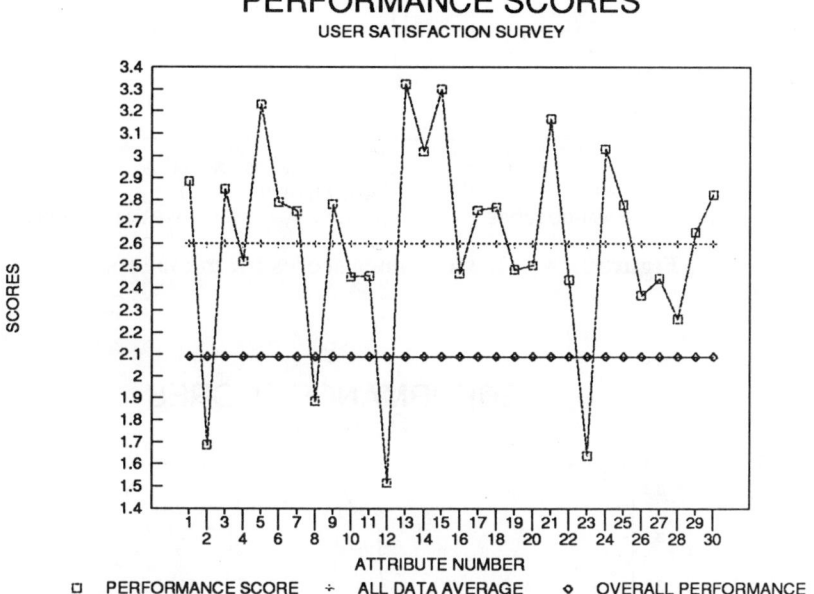

Figure 11.3   Performance scores for all respondents

Note that while the average performance score is around 2.6, the users' overall reaction to the network (the last question) is only rated at 2.1. Obviously there is a certain amount of dissatisfaction with the network as it stands.

The performance graphs were reproduced for different categories of user. This allows the network manager to see what types of users are satisfied with the network, and which think that it is performing badly.

11.3.3.3   Performance measurement by job type

The first categorisation is by job title. Figures 11.4 through 11.11 show the graphs produced for managers, accountants, knowledge workers, clerks, personal assistants, secretaries, typists and other staff respectively.

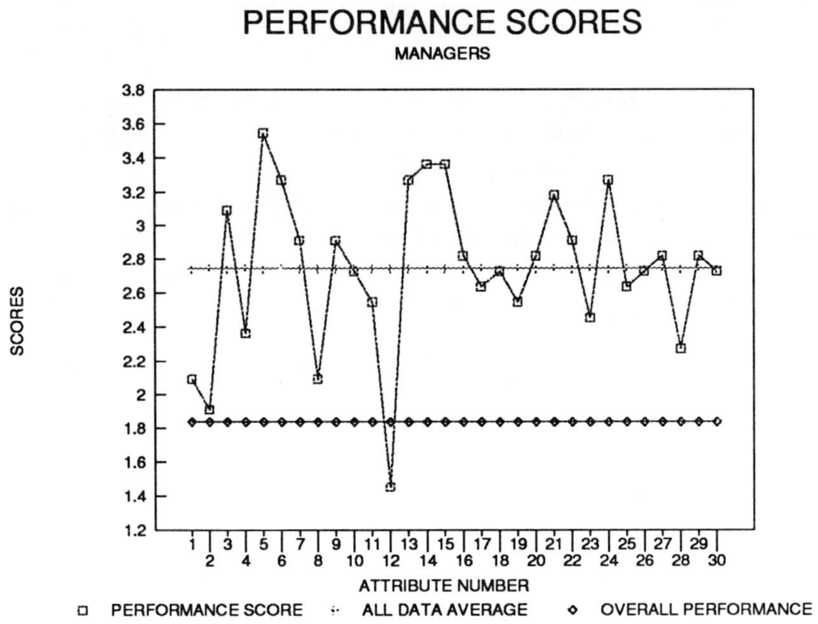

208 PERFORMANCE SCORES

Figure 11.4 Performance scores for managers

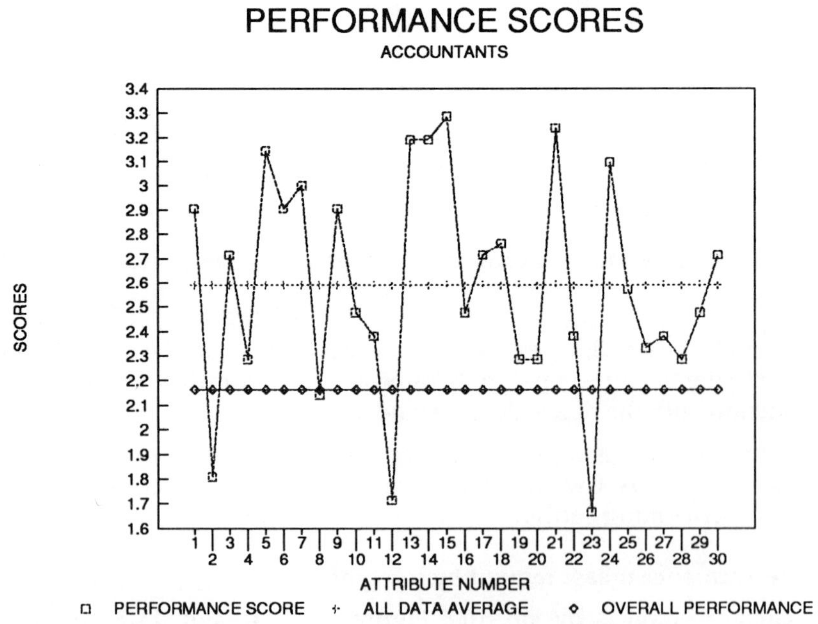

Figure 11.5 Performance scores for accountants

MEASURING USER SATISFACTION 209

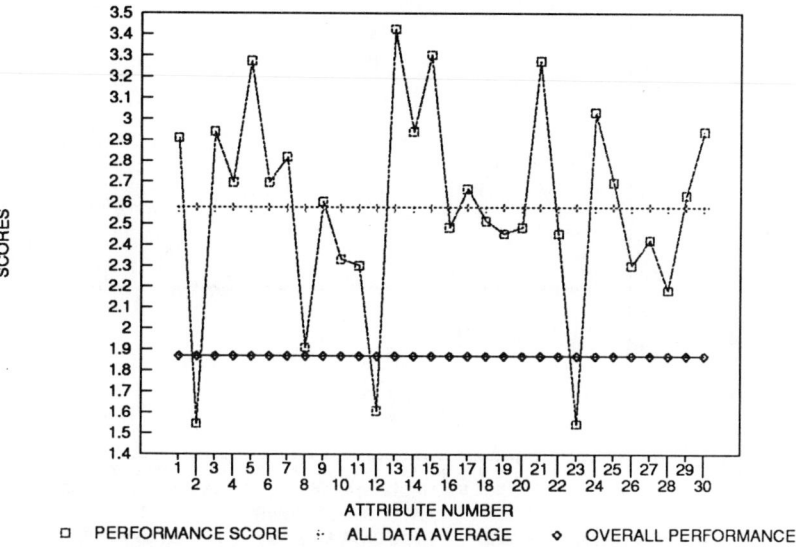

Figure 11.6   Performance scores for knowledge workers

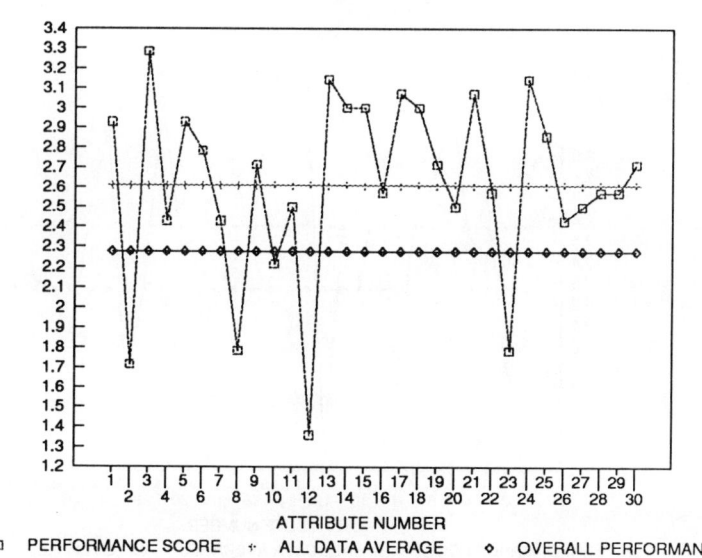

Figure 11.7   Performance scores for clerks

210 PERFORMANCE SCORES

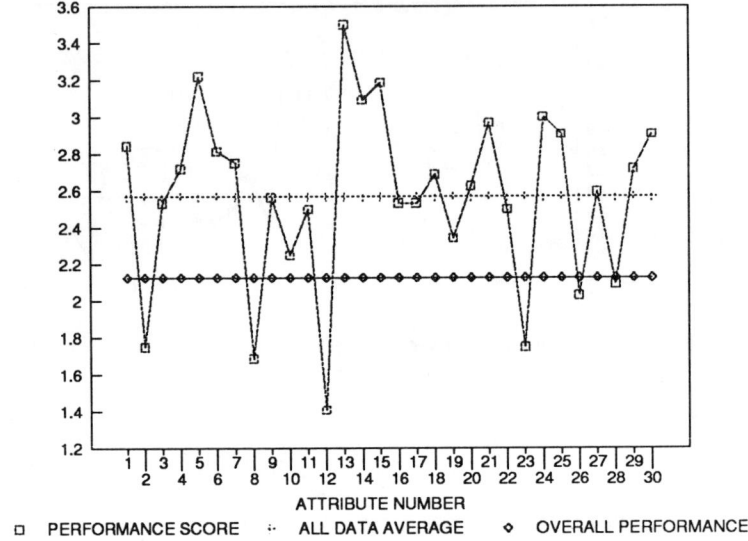

Figure 11.8   Performance scores for personal assistants

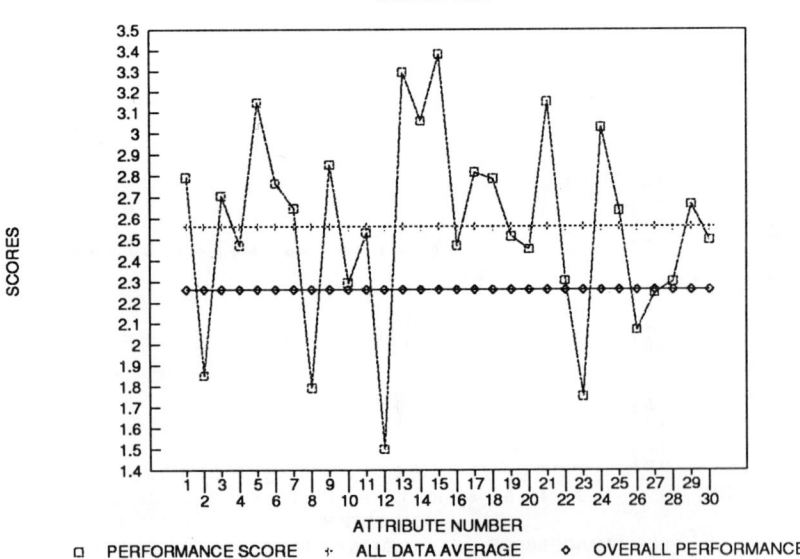

Figure 11.9   Performance scores for secretaries

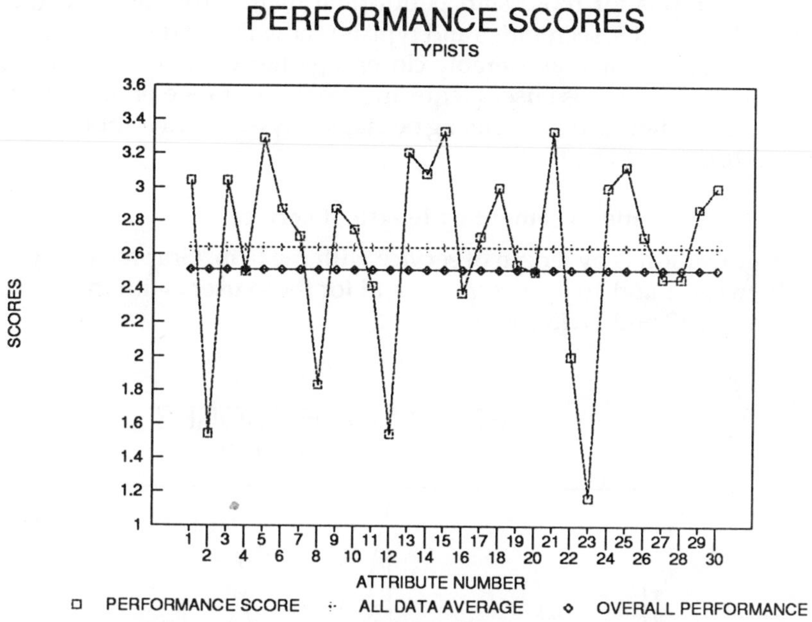

MEASURING USER SATISFACTION

PERFORMANCE SCORES
TYPISTS

Figure 11.10 Performance scores for typists

PERFORMANCE SCORES
OTHER STAFF

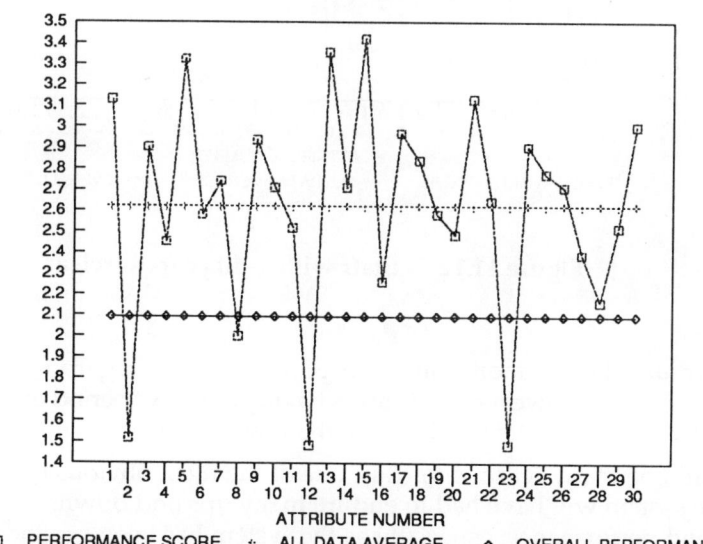

Figure 11.11 Performance scores for other staff

Note that the graphs for those staff performing mainly routine tasks (accountants, clerks, personal assistants, secretaries and typists) show the all data average and overall performance lines as being considerably closer together than on the other plots. From this it would appear that those users requiring a broader range of network facilities or software are less satisfied than those using perhaps only one or two applications. As ever, it is the power users that want more.

11.3.3.4 Performance measurement by length of service

The next categorisation is by length of service with the firm. Graphs were produced for users with between 1 and 10 years service, and for those users with more than 10 years service. Figures 11.12 and 11.13 show the plots.

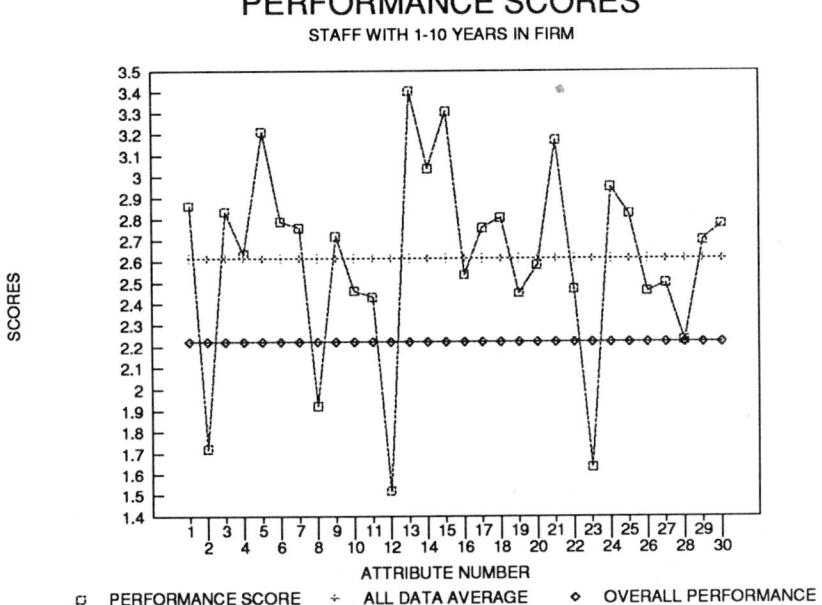

Figure 11.12   Staff with 1–10 years service

In these results there is more consensus of opinion with regard to the overall performance of the system. However, those users having a shorter period of service have rated the performance of the system higher than those who have been with the firm for longer.

There could be many reasons for this, one of the most obvious being that long-time users of the system will have had to endure many ups and downs in terms of network reliability and performance, especially as the system has been expanded so far beyond its original specification. This will inevitably lead to a tarnished view of how the network is currently operating.

MEASURING USER SATISFACTION 213

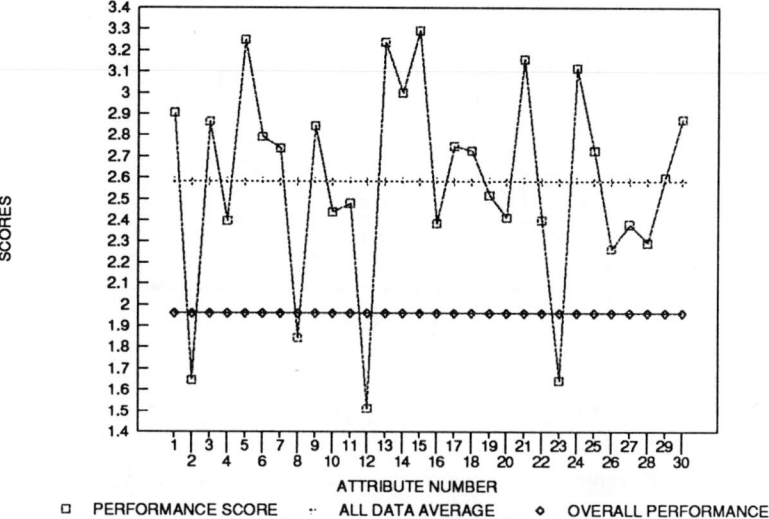

Figure 11.13   Staff with more than 10 years service

11.3.3.5   Performance measurement by amount of PC experience

The graphs shown in Figures 11.14 and 11.15 were produced by categorising the respondents according to the amount of experience they have with PCs.

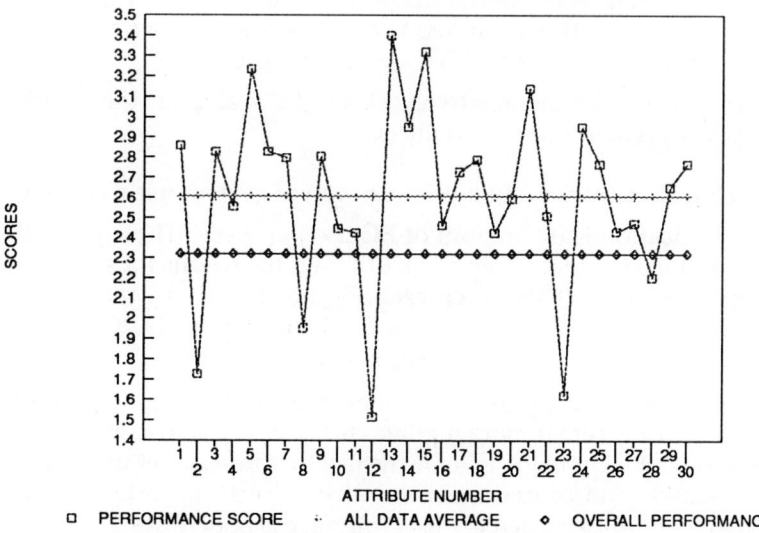

Figure 11.14   Staff with 1–5 years PC experience

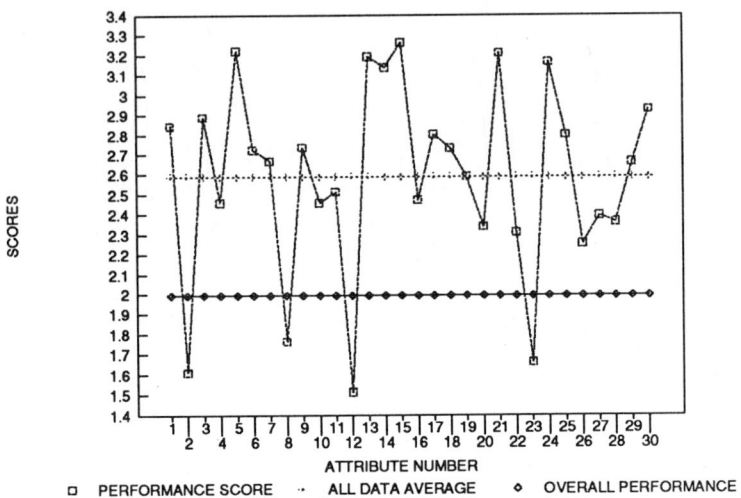

Figure 11.15   Staff with more than 5 years experience

Users with relatively little experience rated the system more highly than those with greater experience. Perhaps the most likely reason for this is that experienced PC users will almost certainly have been using standalone systems for a number of years, and therefore inherently measure the performance of the network against the performance of similar, standalone systems.

11.3.3.6 Performance measurement by amount of network experience

The next categorisation is by amount of network experience. Figure 11.16 shows the results for those users with five or less years network experience, whilst Figure 11.17 shows the results for those users with six years or more.

In this case the results are relatively close, the scales on the graphs making the difference appear greater than it actually is.

11.3.3.7 Performance measurement by amount of system use per week

The final categorisation is by amount of PC use per week. Three groups were defined and a graph produced for each. Figure 11.18 shows the results for staff making use of the system for between 1 and 10 hours per week. Figure 11.19 shows the results for staff using the network between 11 and 20 hours per week and Figure 11.20 shows the results for staff using the network for 21 or more hours per week.

The general trend that is apparent from these graphs is that as respondents make more use of the system, they rate it more highly. This could be due to any one of a number of reasons. However, it is quite likely to be the fact that infrequent users will be unfamiliar with the commands and procedures necessary to perform certain routine operations. This is often a clear indicator that the user interface is poorly designed. Perhaps redesigning the network and application access procedures by following the guidelines laid down in Chapters 3 and 4 could help to reduce this dissatisfaction.

MEASURING USER SATISFACTION 215

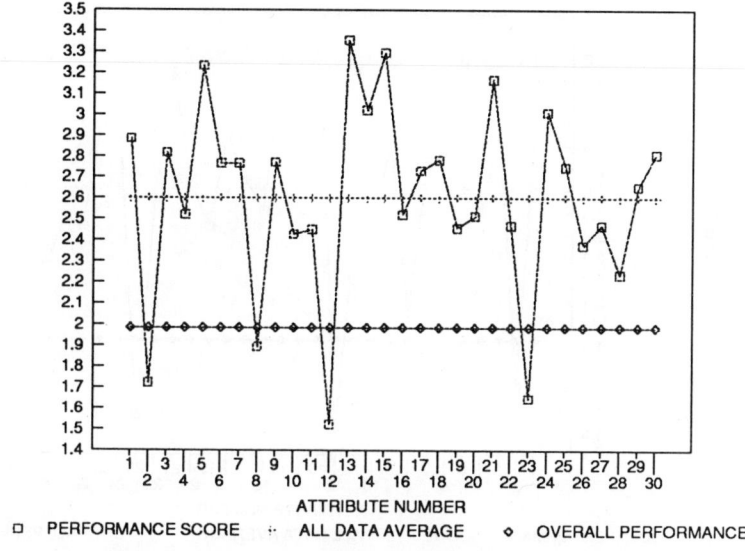

Figure 11.16 Staff with 1-5 years network experience

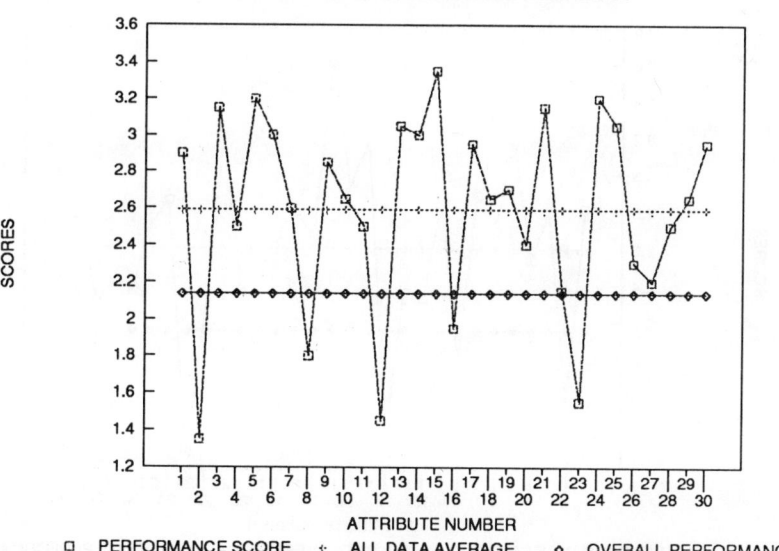

Figure 11.17 Staff with more than 5 years experience

216 PERFORMANCE MEASUREMENT

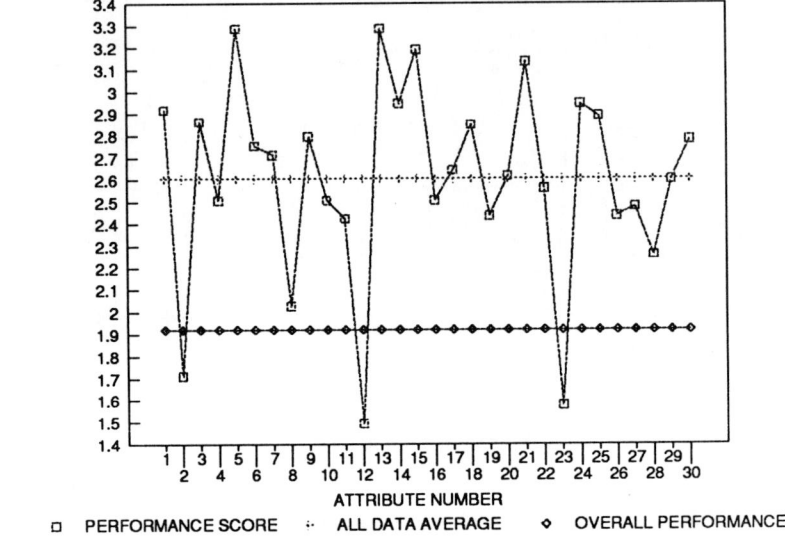

Figure 11.18   Staff using the system for 1–10 hours per week

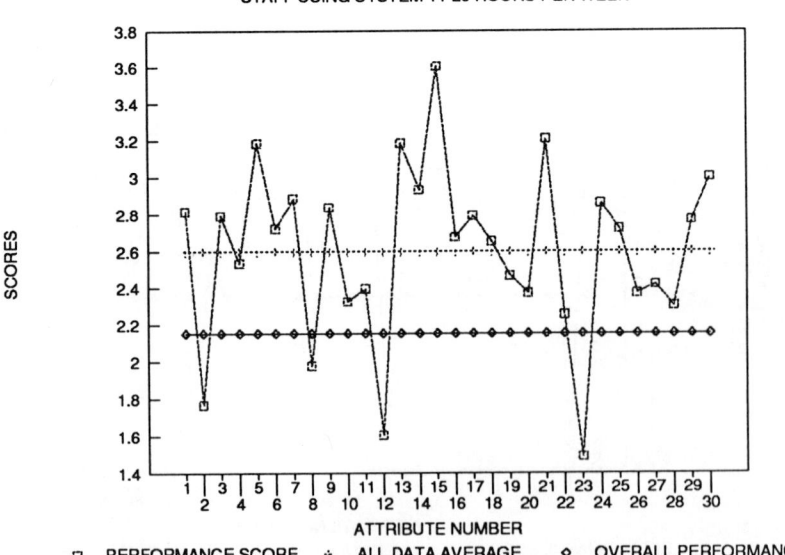

Figure 11.18   Staff using the system for 11–20 hours per week

MEASURING USER SATISFACTION   217

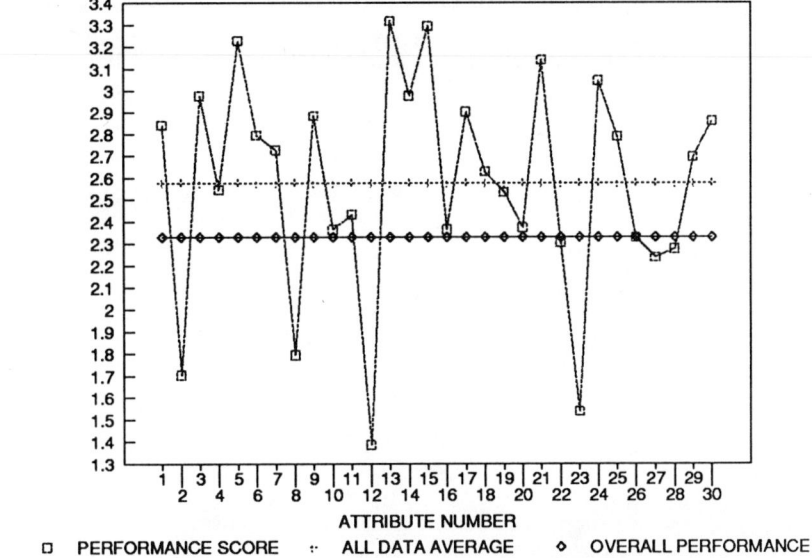

Figure 11.18   Staff using the system for 21 or more hours per week

11.4   REPEAT SURVEYS

The results produced by a questionnaire based survey can be used to redirect the effort of the ISD to those areas perceived by the users to be of most importance. It should always be remembered that needs are constantly changing, and it is therefore important that the survey be repeated at regular intervals, perhaps every six months or annually.

This will have two benefits:
- An ongoing picture can be built up that shows the changing needs and opinions of the users. This allows problems to be addressed quickly and easily.
- Users will feel that they are playing a greater part in determining how they work. For many this will make them more confident in using the network, as they know the reasons that certain changes are being made.

Thus the repeat survey is essential and may be performed with the same or a slightly modified questionnaire.

11.5   SUMMARY

The measurement of user satisfaction and the benefits produced by information systems is a topic of great interest to many organisations. The various techniques that are employed can quantify the effectiveness and efficiency of information systems, allowing firms to see exactly what they are getting in return for the vast sums that are being constantly invested.

SUMMARY

Most well established networks with more in excess of ten users will benefit from such measurement, and the simplest way to perform such quantification is through a user survey. The results of this survey must be carefully analysed, although no special software or knowledge is required. The overall results will allow the ISD to direct their efforts and investments to those issues that are perceived to be the most important, thereby improving the overall efficiency and effectiveness of the network.

12 Conclusion

12.1 FUTURE DEVELOPMENTS

The rapid spread of Local Area Networks has been remarkable to say the least, especially when it is remembered that the first personal computer was introduced a mere ten years ago. But where to from here?

Technology has evolved at such a pace that the standardising authorities must be spending many a sleepless night trying to keep up with the new developments. Just as we have the problem of trying to direct and control the growth of our Networks, they have the job of directing and controlling the growth of the entire industry. No one really knows where the silicon chip will take us over the next ten years, but if it is anything like the last ten we are going to be in for a very interesting ride.

Already the specifications for the 80786 microprocessor have been announced by Intel, and although they will not guarantee the final product will match these specifications, they are looking at moving away from the restrictions of keyboard-entry computers and into the realm of voice-entry. At a possible clock-speed of 200 MHz and containing a mere 20 million transistors on the chip we could at last find a machine capable of running Windows at a respectable speed.

As far as Networks are concerned, the vision of the future can be summed up as simply more of the same. They already allow us to attach our Personal Computers to each other and to machines on various other platforms, such as IBM mainframes, UNIX servers, and Apple microcomputers. Over the next few years we will see products released by most of the major vendors that extend this ability to tie different computers together in increasingly transparent ways.

Both NetWare and LAN Manager already have products available to developers of non-PC platforms, that will enhance the 'Portable' nature of network operating systems. Novell has recently announced products that will provide connectivity to IBM System/370, AS/400, and PS/2 computers. They enable NetWare users to access the applications running on these machines. Interestingly enough, this is also the first product from Novell that sports a graphical user-interface and a centralised management facility that allows the administrator to configure, manage and monitor communication services from a single point. But for most users these products are still just a dream, as the constrictive budgets imposed on many ISDs mean that such technology will remain unavilable for several years. So for now we will struggle along with systems that require a lot of foot-work and patience to manage and maintain.

Appendix 1
Glossary

Access Protocol	The rules for data transmission that LAN workstations must abide by in order to avoid data collisions when sending signals over shared media. Two examples are Carrier Sense Multiple Access (CSMA) as employed by Ethernet, and token passing as employed by Token Ring and ARCnet.
Adapter	A printed-circuit board used to connect peripheral equipment such as disk drives and display monitors to PC.
Address	A unique identifier for a memory location, a workstation node etc.
Address Bus	The collection of tracks on the motherboard that carry the address information between the CPU and memory or external storage devices. On the original IBM PC there were 20 individual tracks, whilst the AT has 24. Systems based on the 80386 and 80486 processors have 32. The number of tracks is often referred to as the bit rating of the bus, thus it may be a 20-bit, 24-bit or 32-bit address bus.
Address	A value representing a unique location in IBM PC memory.
Analogue	Refers to transmission methods that represent a signal in the form of a continuous voltage. Contrasts with digital.
ANSI **American National Standards Institute**	An organisation that sets standards on a wide range of issues from cable specifications to screen customisations. DOS offers the ANSI.SYS device driver to makes the screen and keyboard compatible with the standards established for terminals by the ANSI.
API **Application Program Interface**	The API provides a channel or linkage point between an application and the underlying software which might be an operating system or communications software. Standards organisations are currently promoting APIs as the most strategic route to portability and compatibility.

Architecture	The architecture of the system describes its overall design philosophy. PCs are often described as having an 8-bit, 16-bit or 32-bit architecture, which relates to the size of the data bus on the motherboard.
ARCnet **Attached Resources** **Computing network**	A networking technology promoted by many manufacturers. It uses a token passing bus topology, usually on coaxial cable.
ASCII **American Standard Code** **For Information** **Interchange**	A code representing the 128 different character symbols that can be generated from a 7-bit value, although not all of these characters are printable. The ASCII character set has been expanded to 256 characters for use in the IBM PC, and is now standard for all PC compatibles. Thus 1 byte can represents any single ASCII character.
Asynchronous	A transmission method in which characters can be sent at irregular intervals. Coordination is achieved through the use of a number of start and stop bits.
AT **Advanced Technology**	First 80286 personal computer from IBM
Bandwidth	The range of frequencies that can be passed along a conductor. Analogue circuits are often limited to the frequencies used by the human voice (about 300Hz to 3kHz). Digital circuits generally require greater bandwidths, due to the square wave signals that are used. As transmission rate increases, so must the bandwidth; fibre optic and coaxial cables have excellent bandwidths.
Baseband	A network that transmits signals as a direct current pulse rather than as variations in a high frequency signal. Implies that only one signal can use the communications media at a time.
Baud	A unit of measurement for the speed of digital communications; for practical purposes 1 baud equates approximately to 1 bit per second.
BBS **Bulletin Board System**	An electronic message system.
Bindery	A database used by Novell NetWare to maintain information on users, servers and other network elements.
BIOS **Basic Input/Output** **System**	A collection of special routines that are stored in a special ROM chip in the IBM PC and compatibles. These routines control all standard input and output functions involving the keyboard, display unit, disk drives and interface ports, and start the computer up when it is switched on or reset.

GLOSSARY

BIT
BInary digiT
A bit is the smallest unit of information storage, and can have a value of 0 or 1. Bits are grouped into larger units called Bytes and Words.

BNC Connector
A small connecting device used on coaxial cables. They are locked together with a twisting action.

Boot
A term applied to the process of loading and starting an operating system. The boot process is initiated by the BIOS of the computer system. The terms was used in the early days of computing to describe the startup process for mainframe computers, which were said to pull themselves up by their 'bootstrap.'

Boot ROM
A ROM chip fitted to a NIC that allows the workstation to communicate with a server, and read all the necessary boot code from that server. Thus diskless workstations can be used on the network.

bps
Bits Per Second
A measurement of speed, most often used to quantify the rate of data transfer between two devices such as the microprocessor and the disk drive logic. Should always be represented in lower case.

Bridge
A device that provides for the interconnection of two LANs using similar or dissimilar technologies. Thus bridges can link Ethernet, Token Ring, X.25 etc.

Broadband
A network that transmits information in the form of small variations in a high frequency signal. The high frequency signal is known as the carrier. This technique provides greater performance, but is more complex, than baseband. Implies that several signals can be transmitted over the same medium concurrently.

Broadcast
To send a message to all workstations on the network.

Buffer
A storage location in an electronic chip that is used to temporarily hold data during electronic communication between two devices that are operating at different speeds. Buffers exist in the PC for communicating with the keyboard, the disks and the interface ports.

Bus
A communication circuit in a computer. The IBM PC has a data bus, a control bus and an address bus. Other systems may have additional buses for other purposes. The bus allows multiple BITs of information to be communicated simultaneously, thus enhancing the speed of the system.

Bus Topology
A network architecture using a broadcast technique, in which all workstations receive the same message through the media at the same time.

Byte	A byte is a group of 8 bits, and is the standard unit of storage in a computer system. A byte can represent any decimal value between 0 and 255, or any ASCII character.
Cache	An area of RAM set aside to hold data from the disk that is expected to be accessed again. Further accesses to this data will be very fast, as the information is now already in memory.
CGA **Colour Graphics Adapter**	Usually in the form of a peripheral card, produces a screen resolution of 320 x 200 pixels in four colours or 640 x 200 pixels in two colours selected from a palette of 16 colours.
Channel	A path between two locations (origination and destination) that carries a single stream of information. A two way path is a circuit.
Chip	A slang term for an integrated circuit. Derived from *Silicon Chip*, which describes the material from which such devices are constructed.
Clock	In computer terminology the term clock refers to two things: first, a circuit that sends a consistent, periodic signal that is used to step logic information through a computer circuit, and secondly the logic in the computer that keeps track of the current date and time.
Coaxial Cable	A type of network medium, consisting of a solid copper inner conductor, surrounded by insulation and then a braided copper or foil shield.
Cold Boot	The process of switching the machine on, and starting operations by initialising the start-up conditions. The cold boot process assumes no previous activity in the computer and sets all the registers in the machine accordingly.
Collision	An attempt by two stations on a network to transmit simultaneously over a single channel.
Control Bus	The circuit along which control signals are transmitted. The control bus passes through the major integrated circuits that are installed on the motherboard.
cps **Cycles Per Second** **or Characters Per Second**	Measurements of speeds. Cycles per second is the same as frequency, thus 10cps = 10Hz. Characters per second is a measure of printer speed, often used with dot matrix printers which may have speeds of 25cps, 100cps or greater. Should always be represented in lower case.
CPU **Central Processing Unit**	Refers to the microprocessor, which is the heart of the computer, and its immediate supporting circuitry. This device fetches, decodes, and executes instructions and controls the overall activity of the computer.

CRC **Cyclic Redundancy Check**	A numeric checksum used to determine the validity of data that is transmitted in some way.
CRT **Cathode Ray Tube**	The display screen used in computer systems for viewing data and graphics. CRT displays are available in many different standards.
CSMA **Carrier Sense Multiple Access**	A media sharing scheme that allows workstations to monitor transmissions on the network media. If the channel is not in use then they may be permitted to transmit.
Data Bus	The collection of tracks on the motherboard that carry the data between the CPU and memory or other devices. On the original IBM PC there were 8 individual tracks, whilst the AT has 16. Systems based on the 80386 and 80486 processors have 32. The number of tracks is often referred to as the bit rating of the bus, thus it may be an 8-bit, 16-bit or 32-bit data bus. The size of the data bus determines the *architecture* of the system.
DB-25	A standard set of connectors and plugs that are used in RS-2362C wiring schemes. Each has 25 connectors in two rows; one row has 13 pins, the other has 12.
Diagnostic	An action or program that detects and isolates malfunctions or failures in computer hardware or software.
Digital	Refers to transmission methods that represent a signal in the form of discrete voltage levels. Usually a signal can be either on or off. For example, TTL states that an 'on' signal is represented by a 5V voltage level, whilst an 'off' signal is represented by 0V. Contrasts with analogue.
DIL **Dual In-Line**	Term to describe any device with two rows of connecting pins. Often used interchangeably with DIP.
DIN **Deutsche Industrie Norm**	A German standards organisation. The term is most often encountered in the form of DIN plugs, which are used to connect the keyboard to the system unit.
DIP **Dual Inline Package**	Small semiconductor or switch set formed from a plastic package having two parallel rows of pins for connection to the motherboard.
DIP Switches	Sets of on/off switches used to establish specific device configurations within the system. Each bank of DIP switches usually has eight individual switches.
Disk	A magnetic device for the storage of computer data. PC Disks may be classed as either hard disks or floppy disks, and whilst in principle they are similar, the performance differs greatly between the two.

Disk Duplexing	A technique for fault-tolerant systems in which all information is written to two separate disks, using two separate controllers.
Disk Mirroring	A technique for fault-tolerant systems in which all information is written to two separate disks by the same controller.
Display	The device on which visual information is displayed on a screen. Sometimes referred to as the screen, CRT or VDU.
DMA **Direct Memory Access**	A method for transferring data between the disk drive unit and main memory, by-passing the CPU. This significantly enhances the speed of access to disk data, as the CPU is not tied-down to trivial data transfer operations.
DOS **Disk Operating System**	An operating system for the manipulation of disk based information. The most popular form of operating system is MS-DOS from Microsoft. This was produced for the original IBM PC, and is still by far the most used. MS-DOS may also be encountered under other names, such as PC-DOS as it was licenced to several different manufacturers, including IBM, Compaq, Toshiba etc.
DPI **Dots Per Inch**	Number of dots generated by printers or computer software for every linear inch of paper..
DRAM **Dynamic Random Access Memory**	Most of the RAM that is used by the system is dynamic which means it has to be continually refreshed in order to retain information.
Driver	A short routine or program that controls the I/O interaction between two devices (eg between the disk drives and the computer's CPU). The driver is specific to one particular device.
EBCDIC **Extended Binary Coded Decimal Interchange Code**	IBM code format used to transfer information, particularly on mainframe and mini computers. It is sometimes necessary to use an EBCDIC to ASCII converter in order to read information from a mainframe into a PC.
EGA **Enhanced Graphics Adapter**	Usually in the form of a peripheral card, produces a screen resolution of 640 x 200 pixels or 640 x 350 pixels in 16 colours from a palette of up to 64 colours, depending on the particular card and/or configuration.
EISA **Expanded Industry Standard Architecture**	Standard for computer bus architecture developed to compete with and succeed the AT bus. EISA is a 32-bit bus with 32 address lines. Popular with 386 and 486 systems.
EOF **End Of File**	Term used by many programming languages to indicate the end of a file.

GLOSSARY

EPROM
Erasable Programmable Read-Only Memory
A type of ROM that can be reused. It is programmed with a special device called an *EPROM Blower* that applies a specified voltage to a certain pin on the chip when data is written to it. The contents of the chip can be erased by exposing the device to very intense ultra-violet light for 15-20 minutes

ESDI
Enhanced Small Device Interface
Type of disk drive technology that has become popular recently. Competes with SCSI and is especially popular with high capacity drives.

Ethernet
A network technology originally proposed by Xerox, although now marketed by many vendors including Digital Equipment Corp. and 3Com.

Fault Tolerance
A method of ensuring continued system operation by duplication and diversity. It works on the principle of multiple components performing the same task; when one fails, the others still continue.

Fibre Optic
A transmission technology that represents data in the form of pulses of light, which are sent over glass cables.

File Server
A type of server that holds files and data in private and public directories.

Firmware
Programs and data that are stored in ROMs, PROMs and EPROMs. The BIOS of the computer system is an example of firmware.

Flip-flop
An electronic device that maintains a value of 1 or 0 until acted on by a signal on a certain input pin. Flip-flops form the basis of all electronic memory, and most computer logic circuitry.

Gateway
A device that allows a LAN to be linked to a larger system such as a mainframe computer or a packet-switched information network.

Ground
An electronically neutral connection point. A common contact.

GUI
Graphical User Interface
Interface using Windows, Icons, Menus and Pull-down Screens (WIMPS). Usually operated partly or entirely through the use of a mouse.

Handshaking
The exchange of control codes or specific characters to coordinate data transmission.

Hardware
The physical components of a computer system, including the system unit, the disk drives, the keyboard, the printer, the monitor and all associated devices and option cards.

Head	The electro-magnetic device that transfers data to and from the disks.
Hz Hertz	A unit of frequency, used interchangeably with cycles per second. Thus 1cps = 1Hz.
Hexadecimal	The numbering system using base 16, in which the values above 9 become A, B, C, D, E, and F. Each hexadecimal number can be represented as a 4-bit code, and thus two hexadecimal digits can represent any byte value.
Hot Fix	A Novell NetWare feature that provides fault-tolerant disk usage.
IC Integrated Circuit	An electronic device created on a small silicon flake. It consists of a large number of logic gates and the paths connecting them, formed by very thin films of metal acting as wires. Each IC can perform one or more predefined operations. Integrated circuits are used extensively in all personal computers.
IEEE Institute of Electrical and Electronic Engineers	Long established institute whose members are drawn from industry and who attempt to establish industry standards. The IEEE 802 committee has published many definitive documents on local area networks.
Impedance	An electrical property of a cable that combines capacitance, inductance and resistance. Impedance is measured in Ohms.
Initialise	To set a storage location, counter, or variable to a starting value.
Interface	A boundary shared by two or more devices.
Interface Port	A term used as an overall descriptor for the serial and parallel ports. Whilst these components are used in a different way, they are very similar in design.
IRQ Interrupt Request	Technical term to describe the signal a device sends when it wants attention. Works in conjunction with the interrupt controller on the motherboard.
ISA Industry Standard Architecture	Term used to describe the original 16 bit AT bus.
ISO International Standards Organisation	An American based organisation which produces international specifications. Communications has always been an important area for the organisation and they developed a model to define a conceptual architecture of communications systems called the OSI Reference Model.
I/O Input/output	The process of entering information into the computer or transferring data from the computer to the outside world;

	for example, disk drives, keyboards, and display units are input/output devices.
Jumper	An electrical contact that slides over two connections on a printed circuit board. Often encountered in similar situations to DIP switches.
K	Stands for Kilo, and in computer jargon is equal to 1024. Thus 1KB (Kilobyte) is 1024 bytes, which is a standard unit of measure when describing the capacity of memory and storage devices.
Kb Kilobit	1Kb represents 1024 bits, where 1 bit is a 1 or 0 – the fundamental unit of digital data. Note the use of an uppercase K and lowercase b.
KB Kilobyte	1KB represents 1024 bytes, where one byte is equal to eight bits and is generally referred to as being equal to a character. Note the use of uppercase K and uppercase B.
Kernel	The heart of an operating system. The kernel contains the code to perform scheduling and interrupt handling, but no high level services such as file control.
KHz Kilohertz	One thousand hertz, where hertz is a measure of frequency and 1 hertz is one cycle every second.
LAN Local Area Network	A communications network in which all the nodes are in close proximity to each other, usually in the same building or group of buildings.
LCD Liquid Crystal Display	Type of display popular with laptop computers. Works on the principle of small reflective particles suspended in liquid crystal.
LED Light Emitting Diode	Semiconductor that emits light when electricity is passed through. Common technology for small indicator lights.
Location	A place in memory where information may be stored.
Logic Bomb	A virus which remains inactive until a certain condition is satisfied, such as 90 percent of the memory being used by the operator.
Main Storage	The storage located in the computer for the operating system, programs, and data while they are executing. The main storage in the PC is the RAM memory.
MAN Metropolitan Area Network	Term used to describe a communications network that is geographically too big to be a LAN. Usually implies computers in different buildings in the same town or district.
Mb Megabit	One million bits. Note the use of uppercase M and lowercase b.

MB
Megabyte

One million bytes. Note the use of uppercase M and uppercase B.

MCA
Micro Channel Architecture

A design concept for computers which allows the number of interconnections between components to be restricted and controlled. The IBM PS/2 range are based on the MCA concept, as is the Olivetti P500.

MCGA
Multi-Colour Graphics Adapter

Graphics adapter found on the IBM PS/2 series of computers. Produces a screen resolution of 320 x 200, 640 x 200 or 640 x 480 pixels with up to four colours from a total palette of 16.

Media

Plural of medium. Refers to the cable or wiring system that is used to carry network signals. Examples are twisted pair, coaxial and fibre optic.

Memory

The hardware in or on which programs are stored. There are many different types of memory devices, including RAM and ROM chips, magnetic disks, magnetic tape, bubble memory and optical devices such as WORMS.

MFM
Modified Frequency Modulation

Type of disk drive interface technology. Competes with RLL.

MHz
Megahertz

A frequency of one million hertz.

Microprocessor

An integrated circuit device that executes coded instructions that are entered, integrated, or stored within the device.

Modem
MOdulator/DEModulator

A device that converts digital information into tones so it can be transmitted and received over communications lines such as telephone lines.

Monitor

A high-resolution display unit used for displaying computer data. Monitors often produce sharper images than a standard television display.

Motherboard

The large printed-circuit board (system board) in the computer on which most of the electronic devices are mounted. The motherboard is the primary or main board in the computer. All other interfaces receive control signals or information from the motherboard. Sometimes referred to as the system board.

MS-DOS
MicroSoft Disk Operating System

Most popular personal computer operating system. MicroSoft is the name of the software house that wrote the operating system.

MTBF Mean Time Between Failure	Average period of time between the failure of a component. The term was more prevalent in the days of mini and mainframe computers which could have a MTBF of as little as 30 minutes.
NetBIOS Network Basic Input/Output System	A software system that seeks to link a network operating system with specific hardware.
NetWare	A series of network products developed and marketed by Novell.
Node	A node is the term applied to any device that is connected to a network and that is capable of transmitting or receiving in its own right. Nodes may be personal computers, mini or mainframe computers, printers, terminals, gateways etc.
Noise	The electrical interference that distorts the transmission of data and results in errors in the data. Noise can be caused by the presence of an electrical field such as that generated by electric motors, heaters or TV/Radio in the vicinity of electrical signals.
ns Nanosecond	One billionth of a second. Note the use of lowercase n and lowercase s.
Open Architecture	In the context of this book, a term used to refer to the fact that the IBM-PCs technical specification is known to the general public and that the IBM-PC is mostly composed of standard integrated circuits. This approach allows the PC to be expanded and enhanced in many different ways.
Operating System	A collection of system programs that control the operation of a computer system. It also handles the interaction between parts of the computer system.
OS/2 Operating System/w	An operating system developed by IBM and Microsoft for use with ATs and compatibles. OS/2 is a multitasking operating system.
OSI Open Systems Interconnection	The ISO's OSI model is a set of guidelines for network design, divided into seven layers (physical, data link, network, transport, session, presentation, application).
Parallel Port	The interface used to transmit data from the computer to a remote device, typically a printer. It is also sometimes referred to as a Centronics Interface.
Parity	A numeric check that is performed on data that is transmitted over a channel. The result of the check will be a bit value of 0 or 1.

Peripheral	A device, often sold as a part of the computer, that is connected to the computer to enhance its operation. Examples of peripherals include disk drives, printers, and modems.
Pin	Any of the leads on a device, such as a chip or a SIMM, that plug into a socket and connect it to a system.
Pixel	A picture element. The smallest unit in a display. Usually, this is a dot on the screen.
PM Presentation Manager	Version of the operating system OS/2 which uses a graphical user interface and controls other GUI software such as Lotus 1-2-3/G.
Port	A connection between the CPU and another device, such as an I/O device, which allows data to enter or leave the computer.
POST Power On Self Test	A diagnostic program on the BIOS chip which tests the system on start-up.
Power Supply	A component of the PC which acts both as a transformer and as a switching device supplying a variety of suitable voltages to the computer hardware.
Print Server	A workstation that allows one or more attached printers to be used by other workstations.
PROM Programmable Read Only Memory	A type of ROM that does not have to have its contents defined when it is first manufactured. PROMs can be programmed in the same way as EPROMs, but they cannot be erased or overwritten. Most chips in PCs that are described as ROMs are actually PROMs and EPROMs.
PS/2 Personal System 2	Recent family of personal computers from IBM, successor to the PC.
RAM Random Access Memory	Memory that can be directly read from, or written to, by the CPU. The contents of this memory is lost once the computer is turned off.
Repeater	A device that amplifies and regenerates signals so that they can travel on further cable systems.
Resolution	The measure of sharpness of a display image. Resolution may be described as high or low, or may be quantified in terms of the number of pixels on the screen.
Ring Topology	A network connection technique in which stations are connected in a continuous ring, either directly, or more usually through the use of repeaters. Most ring networks use a token passing scheme.

GLOSSARY

RLL
Run Length Limited
Type of disk drive interface technology. Competes with MFM.

ROM
Read-Only Memory
A type of memory chip that can be read from but cannot be written to or altered. ROM provides permanent storage for program instructions.

Router
A device for linking LANs, similar to a bridge, but works in a fundamentally different way.

SAA
Systems Application Architecture
An IBM defined set of standard interfaces and protocols that IBM intend to implement across their product line, thus providing compatibility and connectivity among IBM products.

SCSI
Small Computer Systems Interface
Recent type of disk drive interface technology that became an official ANSI standard in 1986. Competes with ESDI for the control of high-performance hard disk drives.

Serial Port
An interface which transmits data on a 1 bit at a time basis. It may also be referred to as an RS232 Interface. It is normally used for communications purposes, although some printers must be connected using the serial interface.

Server
A computer on a network that provides file, printer or communications services for other workstation users.

Shadow Ram
An area of RAM set aside for use by the system. Sections of ROM dealing with basic operations are copied into this area to allow the routines to be executed more quickly, due to the fact that the time taken to access the RAM is significantly less than that taken to access the ROM.

SIMM
Single Inline Memory Module
Replacement technology for traditional memory chips. A circuit board with a single line of connecting pins plugs into the motherboard. Surface mount chips make up the memory modules. Differs from traditional memory in that it is a pre-defined assembly.

Software
The programs that determine or control the actions of the computer. Software may be orientated towards providing system control, utilities or applications.

Spike
A short, powerful burst of electrical energy that, if not by-passed (or shorted) to ground, can cause damage to electronic components.

SRAM
Static Random Access Memory
A form of RAM that although still volatile, does not require to be continually refreshed in the same way as dynamic RAM.

Star Topology
A network connection method in which all nodes are linked to a central point.

Surge	A temporary increase in electrical voltage lasting long enough for its effect to be noticed on a meter.
System Board	The main printed circuit board in the systems box containing the microprocessor and other control chips, as well as the ROM and the RAM. Sometimes referred to as the Motherboard.
TDR Time Domain Reflectometry	A technique based on radar principles that allows cable damage to be located with great ease, without having to dismantle the media.
Time Bomb	A virus which remains inactive until a certain time, such as a specific date and time on the system clock.
TPI Tracks Per Inch	The surface of a disk is divided into concentric tracks and TPI defines the tracks per inch radius.
Transient	Brief fluctuations in voltage. Transients can be quite sizeable in some situations, and can destroy equipment if no preventative measures are taken.
Tree Topology	A network connection method in which nodes are connected to a common branch or data bus.
Trojan Horse	A virus which is disguised to be a useful program, often a utility.
Troubleshoot	To systematically locate a computer hardware failure. Software failures are found by systematic debugging.
TSR Terminate and Stay Resident	A terminate and stay resident program is a special form of program which does not remove itself from memory once it has been executed. It simply remains in the background of the computer, ready to be activated by some special event. It is only removed when the computer is switched off or reset.
TTL Transistor-Transistor Logic	A standard which is met by many electronics devices and integrated circuits.
Twisted Pair	Cable comprised of two wires twisted together at six turns per inch. This twisting provides some resistance to electrical interference.
UPS Uninterruptable Power Supply	Power supply with a built-in battery that continues to provide power to equipment after mains power has failed.
VGA Variable Graphics Array	Usually in the form of a peripheral card. Can produce a screen resolution of 640 x 200, 640 x 350 or 640 x 480 pixels in 64 colours from a palette of 256, depending on the particular card and/or configuration.

VINES
VIrtual NEtworking System

A Unix-based network operating system produced by Banyan Systems.

Virus

A special form of computer program, normally created and executed without the operator's knowledge. A virus may be malignant, in which case it intentionally causes damage, or benign, in which case it usually just displays a message. A virus is able to replicate itself and spread to other uninfected systems, often through networks, or the unauthorised transfer of programs or data.

VLSI
Very Large-Scale Integration

Term to describe the complexity of an integrated circuit. Normally implies the device consists of over one million transistors.

WAN
Wide Area Network

A communications network in which the nodes are spread over a wide area. Often WANs have nodes in different cities or even different countries.

Warm Boot

The process of restarting the computer without performing the POST. The warm boot is often initiated through software, or by the user pressing a Reset button.

Word

A group of 2 bytes. A word comprises 16 bits, and can store any decimal value between 0 and 65535. Many of the operations performed by the microprocessor can work with words as well as bytes, thus speeding up performance.

WORM
Write Once Read Many times

Term used to describe laser or optical disks, the data on which cannot be erased, as it can on traditional magnetic disks.

Worm

A rogue piece of software which digs its way into one or more programs, often overwriting data as it goes. Worms are not true viruses as they do not replicate.

Appendix 2
Bibliography and Reading List

Angermeyer J, Fahringer R, Jaeger K, Shafer D, *The Waite Group's Tricks of the MS-DOS Masters*, Howard W Sams, 1988

Beechhold H F, *The Brady Guide to Microcomputer Troubleshooting & Maintenance*, Prentice Hall Press, 1987

Berliner D, with DeVoney C, *Managing Your Hard Disk*, Que, 1986

Brenner R C, *IBM-PC Troubleshooting and Repair Guide*, Howard W Sams, 1988

Brenner R C, *IBM-PC Advanced Troubleshooting & Repair*, Howard W Sams, 1988

Derfler F, *PC Magazine Guide to Connectivity*, Ziff-Davis Press, 1991

Durr M, Gibbs M, *Networking Personal Computers, 3rd Edition*, Que Corporation, 1989

Foster D L, *The Practical Guide to the IBM-PC AT*, Addison-Wesley, 1985

Harris S, Nugus S, *PC Data Recovery and Disaster Prevention*, NCC Blackwell, 1992

Hordeski M, *The Illustrated Dictionary of Microcomputers, 3rd Edition*, TAB Books, 1990

IBM DOS Manual, IBM

IBM Technical Manual, IBM

IBM User's Manual, IBM

Kamin J, *Expert Advisor DOS, Up to and Including DOS 4.0*, Addison-Wesley, 1989

Norton P, *Inside the IBM-PC*, Prentice Hall Press, 1987

Norton P, *The Peter Norton Programmers Guide to the IBM PC*, MicroSoft Press, 1985

Nugus S, Harris S, *Troubleshooting, Maintaining and Upgrading PCs*, NCC Blackwell, 1992

Nunemacher G, *LAN Primer*, Prentice Hall, 1990

Penfold R A, *How to Expand, Modernise and Repair PCs and Compatibles*, Bernard Babani, April 1990

Remenyi D, Money A, Twite A, *A Guide to Measuring and Managing IT Benefits*, NCC Blackwell, 1991

Sheperd S, Digging Deep into Disks!, *.EXE Magazine*, Process Communications, June 1991

Simrin S, *The Waite Group's MS-DOS Bible*, Howard W Sams, 1989

238 BIBLIOGRAPHY AND READING LIST

Somerson P, *PC Magazine DOS Power Tools, 2nd Edition*, Bantam Books, 1990

Stallings W, *Handbook of Computer Communications Standards, Vol 2, Second Edition, Local Area Network Standards*, Howard W Sams, 1990

Stephenson J G, Cahill B, *Microcomputer Troubleshooting and Repair*, Howard W Sams, 1988

Wolverton V, *Running MS-DOS*, MicroSoft Press, 1986

Wolverton V, *Supercharging MS-DOS*, MicroSoft Press, 1986.

Index

80286	25, 29
80386sx	25, 29
80386	25, 29, 54, 166
80486sx	29
80486	25, 29, 166
8086	25, 29
8088	25, 29
access rights	174–176
active hub	142
applications	34–37, 44, 49, 52, 183
architecture	30
ARCnet	12, 22–23, 27, 48, 141–146
AUTOEXEC.BAT	58, 65–66, 68, 77–95, 119, 169
backup	50, 51, 54, 190
media	190
Banyan Vines	57
baseband	17
batch files	72–74, 77, 85–94
bindery	51
BINDFIX	51
biometrics	178–179
black-boxing	63, 78
BNC connectors	142, 147
booting	31
bottleneck	160
bridge	162
broadband	17, 19

BUFFERS	64, 169
bus topology	14–16
cabling	16–19, 42, 52, 113, 136–157, 189
cache	67, 159, 161–162
case studies	47–54
coaxial	17–18, 48
comments	63
communications	10
compatibility	32, 42, 44, 97–101
component	4, 41–43, 111–157
configuration	
hardware	3, 56, 98
software	3, 4, 56, 57, 99–104
CONFIG.SYS	58, 63–65, 68, 119, 136, 169
conflict	3, 44, 97–101
contracts	3
dBase IV	104, 106
demountable disk	190
developments	9
disaster	181–195
planning	188
recovery	188
disk drive	24, 26–27, 28, 31–32, 42, 113, 161, 189
problems	122, 124–131, 132
disk duplexing	162, 183
disk mirroring	162, 182
display cards	113
display unit problems	122, 134–135
DOS	32–33, 44, 59, 64, 168, 185
drive mappings	58–61
environment space	64
EPROM	31
equivalences	48, 175–176
error messages	114
Ethernet	14, 22, 27, 28, 48, 146–151
expanded memory	164, 165

extended memory	164, 165
fault diagnosis systems	107–108
fault log	116–117
fibre-optic	18–19, 49
file allocation table (FAT)	162
file server	11, 24–28, 42, 183
FILES	63
finger trouble	3
floppy disks	31, 53, 113, 124–131, 189, 190
flowchart	112, 120, 121, 123, 125, 126, 129, 130, 132, 133, 135, 137, 138, 139
Gem	33–34
groups	61–62, 176
hard disk drive	24, 26–27, 31, 42, 113, 131, 189
hardware	11, 42–43, 111–157
Harvard Graphics	103
heat	122
hot fix	182
hot spares	189
hybrid	15
IBM	25, 32
IDE	131
IEEE	19–22, 153
impedance	142–144
infection	186–188
injection laser diode (ILD)	18
interface cards	113, 131, 134
interference	16, 18, 19
interrupt	28, 100–101
intruder tracking	178
ISO	19–22
key disk	98, 102
keyboard	113, 122, 136, 137
LAN Manager	57, 219

LAN   10
    technology   9–39
LANtastic   11
legal issues   98
light emitting diode (LED)   18, 146
login   60–61, 66, 172
    script   58, 68–72
Lotus 1-2-3   102–103

Macintosh   33, 44
MAP   58, 59, 69–71
    DELETE   61
    INSERT   60–61
memory   24–26, 28, 32, 52, 100, 102, 113, 161, 163–169, 189

menu   49, 58, 74, 77–90
microprocessor   24–25, 28, 29, 168
minicomputers   9
modularity   63
moisture   122
monitor problems   122, 134–135
monitoring systems   106–107
multistation access units (MAU)   152–153
multi-media   11

Netware   25, 27, 57–75, 77–95, 171
network
    access procedure   57–75
    interface card   19, 24, 27–28, 30, 42, 113, 150
    management   9, 37–39, 46–47, 54–55, 57–75, 105–109, 219

    operating system   4, 25–27, 34–37
    standards   19–24
    technology   9–39
node address   176–177
NWHAT   62, 72

operating environment   32–34, 44, 58
operating system   4, 25–27, 34–37, 44

optical fibre	18–19
optimising performance	159–169
OSI	20–21, 23
OS/2	33, 44
passive hub	142
passwords	172–174
PATH	59–60
PC	9-10, 28
peer-to-peer	15
performance	16, 41, 54, 159–169
phantom machines	113
physical security	176
planning	45, 47, 55
power	51, 193
supplies	113, 189, 122–124
printing	49, 93–94, 99–100
problem categories	3, 41–47
problem report	116, 118
protocol analyser	154–156
questionnaire	198–204
RAM	24–26, 161, 189
RECON	145
reliability	48, 54
repeater	12, 15, 146
resistance	140
ring topology	12–14
router	162
search drives	59
security	19, 48, 51, 155, 171–179
SHELL.CFG	58, 66–68
shielding	18
signal balancing	16
simple drive mapping	59
software	43–44
spare parts	111, 113

spindle speed | 127
stack space | 65
standards | 11, 19–24, 140–154
star topology | 12
surge suppressor | 193
system login script | 68–72
system unit | 122, 131, 133–134
systems fault tolerant (SFT) | 181–183

tape streamer | 50, 190
terminator | 140
time domain reflectometer (TDR) | 53
Token-Ring | 13, 22, 23–24, 151–154
topology | 9, 11–16
transaction tracking | 177–178, 181
transceiver | 19, 148–150
transmission media | 11, 16–19, 136–157
tree topology | 13, 14
troubleshooting | 4, 41, 111–157
trustee rights | 58, 61–62
twisted-pair | 18

uninterruptable power supply (UPS) | 52, 193–195
Unix | 44
upgrading | 161–163
users | 45, 57
    assistance systems | 108–109
    login script | 68
    satisfaction | 197–218
utilities | 105, 160, 178

vibration | 122
virus | 53, 97, 185–188
voice mail | 11

Windows | 33, 68, 166
workstation | 11, 26, 28–32, 42, 163–169

Xenix | 44